Scripture: A Very Theolc

# Scripture: A Very Theological Proposal

Angus Paddison

t&t clark

**Published by T&T Clark International**
*A Continuum Imprint*
The Tower Building, 11 York Road, London SE1 7NX
80 Maiden Lane, Suite 704, New York, NY 10038

www.continuumbooks.com

**British Library Cataloguing-in-Publication Data**
A catalogue record for this book is available from the British Library

ISBN-13:   978-0-567-03423-6 (Hardback)
           978-0-567-03424-3 (Paperback)

Typeset by Newgen Imaging Systems Pvt Ltd, Chennai, India
Printed and bound in Great Britain by CPI Antony Rowe, Chippenham, Wiltshire

To the people of Gloucester United Reformed Church

# CONTENTS

ACKNOWLEDGEMENTS

I am grateful to the following publishers for permission to republish parts of articles that have previously appeared in the following journals. All have been revised for publication in this book.

'P. T. Forsyth, Scripture, and the Crisis of the Gospel', *Journal of Theological Interpretation* 1 (2007), pp. 129–45. Published by Eisenbrauns.

'Theological Exegesis and John Howard Yoder', *Princeton Theological Review* XIV (2008), pp. 27–40. Published by Princeton Theological Seminary.

'Engaging Scripture: Incarnation and the Gospel of John', *Scottish Journal of Theology* 60 (2007), pp. 144–60. Published by Cambridge University Press.

'The Nature of Preaching and the Gospel of John', *Expository Times* 118 (2007), pp. 267–72. Published by SAGE.

Much of this book was written while I was employed as a Research Assistant at the University of Gloucestershire and then a Research Fellow at the University of Nottingham. I should like to record my thanks for the intellectual support both institutions offered and to the students who have asked me – what does theology have to do with Scripture?

# ABBREVIATIONS

| | |
|---|---|
| *Comm. Jn.* | John Calvin, *The Gospel According to St John 1-10* and *The Gospel According to St John 11-21 and the First Epistle of John* (trans. T. H. L. Parker; Calvin's Commentaries Series; Edinburgh: Oliver and Boyd, 1961). |
| *IJST* | *International Journal of Systematic Theology* |
| *JSNT* | *Journal for the Study of the New Testament* |
| LNTS | Library of New Testament Studies |
| *SCE* | *Studies in Christian Ethics* |
| *SJT* | *Scottish Journal of Theology* |

# INTRODUCTION

*Scripture: A Very Theological Proposal* is a contribution to the burgeoning interest in theological (re)engagement with Scripture.[1] The very theological proposal developed in this book takes its rise from a series of convictions in relation to Scripture's status, location and life in the church. In summary form, these convictions can be set out thus. *To attest the texts of the Old and New Testaments as 'Scripture' is to make specific claims about this text: that it is drawn into the activity of the triune God of Israel, that its ultimate destination is the worshiping church and that it has a ministry in shaping Christian thinking and acting. Scripture is not first a source for historical inquiry, nor a text that delights our literary sensitivities; calling these collected texts 'Scripture' points to its commissioned role in the saving purposes of God.*

The particularity of these claims invites us to undertake the exhilarating task of showing how one theological 'claim illuminates another'.[2] An account of what Scripture 'is' is inseparable from the series of divine and human actions in which it is a participant. Scripture is not a text in pursuit of a location – it is *already* located within the reconciling action of God and the practices of the church. The determinedly local hermeneutical stance developed in this book therefore finds itself somewhat underfed by those modes of reading in which the conditions and anxieties of modernity are viewed as 'basic to a description of the context of scriptural interpretation'.[3] Attempts to displace attention to

---

1.   The literature is extensive and much of it will be cited throughout this book. The recent launch of the *Journal of Theological Interpretation* as well as the Brazos/SCM Theological Commentary on the Bible series are just two pieces of evidence for the growing interest in engaging with Scripture theologically.

2.   Stanley Hauerwas, *The Peaceable Kingdom: A Primer in Christian Ethics* (London: SCM, 2nd edn, 2003), p. 62.

3.   Donald Wood, *Barth's Theology of Interpretation* (Barth Series; Aldershot: Ashgate, 2007), p. 98. Two recent books identify some of the theological missteps that modernity made in reading Scripture. Matthew Levering's stimulating *Participatory Biblical Exegesis: A Theology of Biblical Interpretation* (Notre Dame: University of Notre Dame Press, 2008) charts how when history came to be understood as metaphysically non-participatory then theological realities became extrinsic to a 'historical' reading of Scripture. Once this happened, several things happened: there was no obvious way to speak of the continuity between a Pauline community and the contemporary church, 'linear' understandings of history subsumed any talk of the participatory reality of God's

doctrine and the church in favour of a general hermeneutics have blurred theological focus on Scripture. Walter Moberly, a key contributor to the theological
interpretation of Scripture, writes accurately that

> [t]o be Christian means, at least in part, the acceptance and appropriation of certain
> theological doctrines and patterns of living. Yet the task of reading the Bible 'critically'
> has regularly been defined precisely in terms of the exclusion of these doctrines and
> patterns of living from the interpretative process.[4]

More urgent than the hermeneutical anxieties of modernity is that we make
visible the implications of the church's faith and so learn to *see* what Scripture
is, and where it is most fittingly located. To presume that the Bible is intelligible 'apart from specific theological convictions and practices' is to fall prey to
what Richard Topping aptly calls an 'optical illusion'.[5] We do not by nature
always see what Scripture is – which is why we first need to have our eyes
prised open by the Holy Spirit and then have our sight corrected by the church.
A proper emphasis on the office of the Spirit needs therefore to be placed
alongside the awareness that 'one cannot see just by looking. Transformation
is required if one is to see realistically'.[6] If nothing else I hope to encourage
you, the reader, to look again at Scripture, to read it with imaginative awareness of the regions in which it is most properly fixed and located.

Seeing Scripture is an exercise in seeing the actions in which it is a participant, and so we should properly speak of not just seeing Scripture but also of
seeing *beyond* Scripture. Karl Barth's category of Scripture as a 'witness' is
helpful here in reinforcing the kind of vision required. To have one's attention
grabbed by a witness is to look away from her and towards that to which she
witnesses. The aim of reading a text written by a biblical author like Paul is
not to seek out the putative historical circumstances *behind* this or that

---

history and 'historical' exegesis was seen as distinct from 'mystical' or 'spiritual' exegesis. When
the understanding of history and time that comes through faith is ruled out of court, pre-packaged
debates such as those framed around the 'Jesus of history' and 'Christ of faith' begin to become
intelligible. Levering's book could be helpfully read alongside Peter M. Candler, Jr, *Theology,
Rhetoric, Manuduction or Reading Scripture Together on the Path to God* (Radical Traditions;
London: SCM, 2006). Candler traces how, after the Reformation, Scripture became identifiable as
a 'thing' detachable from its native habitat in the church's communal practices of reading and
liturgical worship. When people began to *see* Scripture as a 'physical object . . . as opposed to an
ongoing story continually performed and re-narrated in the liturgy' (18) a host of hermeneutical
problems, framed apart from attention to the church, emerged.

    4.   R. W. L. Moberly, *The Bible, Theology, and Faith: A Study of Abraham and Jesus*
(Cambridge Studies in Christian Doctrine, 5; Cambridge: Cambridge University Press, 2000), p. 5.

    5.   Richard R. Topping, *Revelation, Scripture and Church: Theological Hermeneutic Thought
of James Barr, Paul Ricoeur and Hans Frei* (Ashgate New Critical Thinking in Religion, Theology
and Biblical Studies; Aldershot: Ashgate, 2007), p. 160.

    6.   Emmanuel Katangole, *Beyond Universal Reason: The Relation between Religion and
Ethics in the Work of Stanley Hauerwas* (Notre Dame: Notre Dame University Press, 2000), p. 100.

pronouncement, but to look towards the reality which so radically reorientated Paul's life. Just as when we look out of a window at people staring upwards and yet cannot see the plane they are doubtless staring at, so too Paul 'sees and hears something which is above everything, which is absolutely beyond the range of my observation and the measure of my thought'.[7] Reading Paul as a *witness* upturned by grace, rather than prioritizing his status as author, is to follow the direction of his gaze, daring to see that which he points us towards. Good witnesses urge us to look not at them but at that which they indicate to us – a 'successful' witness is one who recedes as his object of attention begins to absorb our attention.[8] Scripture is then not the end point of our vision, but is rather an invitation to see in what kind of contexts it is intelligible *as Scripture*.

The plan of this book can now be set out.

Chapter 1 explores Scripture's location in the purposes of God and the life of the church with a determination not to see the two in competition with each other. If we think that we face a dilemma whether to speak of Scripture either out of attention to God or attention to the church, we have made a misstep.[9] We can only see Scripture from within a series of interlocked and overlapping claims and so by following the logic of the truism that '[e]very Christian doctrine seems to require every other for its clear presentation'.[10] Key aids to seeing Scripture in this chapter are P. T. Forsyth, John Webster and Stanley Hauerwas.

Chapter 2 turns to Scripture's role in Christian ethics. Echoing Stephen Fowl and L. Gregory Jones, I advance that Scripture is not a resource waiting to be 'used' in our ethical performance. We need rather to reason with Scripture, and in John Howard Yoder we find just such a scriptural reasoner who wills to participate in the reality Scripture makes known. Finally, we explore how the virtue of patience can help sustain the sheer difficulty of reading Scripture.

Chapter 3 invites us to consider how Scripture and doctrine relate to one another. Scripture and doctrine are not, of course, to be merged into one another, but neither should they be isolated from one another. After offering some criticisms of recent works in Christology, I turn to a reading of the witness that is John's Gospel, seeing what he sees with the help of a host of theological voices. As far as is possible, I seek to make a very theological proposal in relation to Scripture in which scriptural reading itself plays a part.

---

7. Karl Barth, *The Word of God and the Word of Man* (trans. Douglas Horton; New York: Harper & Row, 1957), pp. 62–63.

8. For more on this theme of witness in Barth's thought, see Richard E. Burnett, *Karl Barth's Theological Exegesis: The Hermeneutical Principles of the Römerbrief Period* (Grand Rapids: Eerdmans, 2004), pp. 221–30.

9. Cf. Hauerwas, *Peaceable Kingdom*, p. 62.

10. James Wm. McClendon Jr, *Systematic Theology*, vol. 2 (3 vols; Nashville: Abingdon, rev. edn, 1994), p. 123.

Chapter 4 seeks to embed Scripture *within* theological thinking by inquiring into the nature of preaching in company with John's Gospel. It is necessary to turn to preaching if, as I maintain throughout this book, Scripture as the church's book is unintelligible apart from its liturgical environment. How preaching 'works' is a question that we can answer by attending to the actions and lives of which it is part. Removed from these contexts we will lack a properly *theological* account of what preaching 'is'.

Chapter 5 asks a question that may have vexed readers who have been following the various claims of the book – can we read Scripture in the university? I begin by demonstrating how theology's 'travail' is only a replication of the travail or fragmentation of the wider university.[11] After critiquing Philip Davies' account of the Bible's role in the modern university, I seek to re-imagine the teaching of theology and re-conceive the university as a space in which participative reading of Scripture might prosper.

Throughout, this book supposes that the lenses needed to see Scripture will be found by keeping in close company with the church and with a host of eclectic theologians.[12] Keeping within this company draws us closer to the sheer strangeness of God's gospel, a gospel wed to Scripture. As such every invitation to *see* Scripture in terms of the actions and lives of which it is part, and in which it is intelligible, carries with it the warning of Gregory of Nazianzus: 'For one who is not pure to lay hold of pure things is dangerous, just as it is for weak eyes to look at the sun's brightness.'[13]

11.   Nicholas Wolterstorff, 'The Travail of Theology in the Modern Academy' in Miroslav Volf, Carmen Krieg and Thomas Kucharz (eds), *The Future of Theology: Essays in Honour of Jürgen Moltmann* (Grand Rapids: Eerdmans, 1996), pp. 35–46.

12.   I therefore concur with R. R. Reno, 'Theology and Biblical Interpretation' in Michael Root and James J. Buckley (eds), *Sharper Than a Two-Edged Sword: Preaching, Teaching and Living the Bible* (Grand Rapids: Eerdmans, 2008), pp. 1-21 (esp. 17–21), who argues that it is more important to recover the conversation between theology and Scripture, rather than Scripture and biblical studies.

13.   Gregory of Nazianzus, *Theological Orations* 27.2. Cited and translated in John J. O'Keefe and R. R. Reno, *Sanctified Vision: An Introduction to Early Christian Interpretation of the Bible* (Baltimore/London: The Johns Hopkins University Press, 2005), p. 147.

# Chapter 1

## LOCATING SCRIPTURE

### Introduction: Questions and Proposals

A very theological proposal in relation to Scripture is implicated in asking a series of interlocked and overlapping questions. What is Scripture? What is God doing with Scripture? How is Scripture best positioned alongside and within the church's doctrine, worship and practices? In what kind of time is Scripture a participant? Each of these questions fall within the task of offering an account of Scripture's *location*, whose own overarching question is the following: in the context of *what kinds of action* is Scripture intelligible? Such a question is a disabusing reminder that Scripture is not a text explicable wholly by reference to human agency, for example, in the investigations prioritized by historical critical scholars. The kinds of action in which Scripture is participant, actions which this book intends to trace, invite us to look beyond the explanations proffered by a historicism which confidently runs along the tracks of immanent causality. If Jesus is who the church has claimed him to be then the implications for the reading of Scripture, and the understanding of history, cannot be incidental but of enduring interpretative significance. What history 'is' is not a subject on which a theologian can afford to be neutral. These provocations indicate that a very theological proposal in relation to Scripture is resourced by chasing the implications of a set of dogmatic claims: Scripture is a text constituted by divine action; Scripture is a text through which is conveyed the gospel of reconciliation; worship and practice leavens this text through the people of God: and such a people are trained to see Scripture's location in time. To be sure, Scripture is not just 'again and again' taken up into God's eccentric action and expelled into the church but also 'more and more' taken into God's reconciling action.[1] If a theological account of Scripture

---

1. The phrase 'again and again' is borrowed from criticisms that George Hunsinger makes of Barth's overly punctiliar account of the Christian life. See George Hunsinger, *Disruptive Grace: Studies in the Theology of Karl Barth* (Grand Rapids: Eerdmans, 2000), p. 274–75. The language of 'more and more' is a reminder of Calvin's account of the Christian as being engrafted into Christ so that we 'may grow more and more together with him'. See John Calvin, *Institutes of the Christian Religion*, IV.xvii.33 (trans. F. L. Battles; Library of Christian Classics, XX; Philadelphia: Westminster Press, 1960), p. 1407. The Christian life and scriptural reading are mutually informing practices – as we shall see throughout this book, there can be no talk of 'using' Scripture because

represents a series of interwoven claims and practices – such as I have indicated – then to pick these apart will only cause church situated reading to wither.

Christian reading and the location of Scripture as this kind of unique text
therefore requires the conformity of our minds to a specific object(s) of attention. Moreover, theological decisions as to the place and status of Scripture
have a determinative role in shaping our use and understanding of those reading approaches that are *not* primarily shaped by theological convictions. Local
hermeneutics precedes general hermeneutics. One cannot dogmatically locate
Scripture *after* one has done the work of historical criticism, as if to imply that
Scripture's status in the purposes of God is an optional extra for the work of
theology.[2] If correctly locating Scripture in the purposes of God, the life of the
people of God and theological work is 'everything', it will be by beginning
from a determinedly local perspective that one can then broaden out to consider more general approaches to Scripture.[3] The problem with those approaches
which bracket out divine agency – consideration of what God is doing with
Scripture and the church – at the outset of their scriptural reading is that this
begins by setting up the divide between the Bible and theological/ecclesial
interpretation, a ditch over which it is assumed we then have to leap by means
of our intellectual or hermeneutical agility. As suggested in the Introduction,
when we find ourselves faced with the task – 'how do we relate Scripture to
theology or the life of the church?' – this is usually a sign that where and how
we have started out is at fault.[4] Another way of saying this is that a theological
proposal in relation to Scripture is not content to commence with the assumption that Jesus' Lordship is dispensable or optional to understanding Scripture
and so remains under-resourced by those reading perspectives that appear to
operate as if 'Christ had never become incarnate, died, risen, ascended to
heaven, and sent His Spirit'.[5] But if Christ *is* truly Lord, a theological location
of Scripture is compelled to pursue the implications of this claim for our understanding of scriptural reading. In this setting, the doctrine of providence is as

how the Christian lives cannot be so easily disentangled from their reading of Scripture. This is a
way of saying that virtues sustained by what Christians do are essential to 'good' scriptural reading.
For an integrated account of practices in the Christian life and theological education, see Craig
R. Dykstra, 'Reconceiving Practice' in Barbara G. Wheeler and Edward Farley (eds), *Shifting
Boundaries: Contextual Approaches to the Structure of Theological Education* (Louisville:
Westminster John Knox, 1991), pp. 35–66.

2.    Indeed, it is necessary to recognize that those interpretations that are centred purely
on Scripture's human authorship '*already* have a theological dimension', albeit indirectly: Daniel
J. Treier, *Virtue and the Voice of God: Toward Theology as Wisdom* (Grand Rapids: Eerdmans,
2006), p. 130 (emphasis added).

3.    Stephen E. Fowl, 'The New Testament, Theology, and Ethics' in Joel B. Green (ed.), *Hearing
the New Testament: Strategies for Interpretation* (Grand Rapids: Eerdmans, 1995), pp. 394–410 (399).

4.    Mark Alan Bowald, *Rendering the Word in Theological Hermeneutics* (Aldershot: Ashgate,
2007), p. 41.

5.    John Howard Yoder, 'If Christ is Truly Lord' in *The Original Revolution: Essays on Christian
Pacifism* (Scottdale: Herald, 2003), pp. 52–84 (77).

much a claim about the meaning, ordering and our reading of Scripture as it is about the form of God's revelation in Christ.[6] In abbreviated form therefore: if Christians claim Christ to be Lord, what are the implications of this Lordship for locating Scripture?

In a welcome move, a number of recent writers have encouraged us to afford divine agency a decisive role in our understanding both of what Scripture is and our role as readers of *this* text. '"What Scripture says" or "how the community reads" is, then, awkward, and shorthand language for a constellation of theological assertions which orbit around divine agency', is how one recent writer begins his study of theological hermeneutics.[7] In this register, talk of God in relation to Scripture is not merely the *result* of exegesis. God's agency is rather accorded significance *throughout* ecclesial reading of Scripture. Doctrine, which we might be tempted to accord little role in our understanding of Scripture,[8] must be seen not just to arise from the toil of scriptural reading (the kind of reading I evince in Chapter 3) but also must be crucial for *how* we read Scripture itself. David Gibson argues in this vein that Barth's reading of Scripture was christologically 'intensive', the very nature of his reading of the scriptural teaching on election being decisively informed by the prior reality of Christ.[9] Looking to doctrine as that which is both rooted in Scripture (the organic metaphor not being incidental) *and* as that which switches back to make intelligible the very practice of scriptural reading itself is why there is little option other than beginning in the middle of the church's convictions and practices.[10]

Precisely because I am aware that I can only begin in the middle, this chapter is *also* deeply indebted to those who have sought to displace talk of (general) hermeneutics by emphasizing the priority of the church. Too often, I hold, an emphasis on God's action and attention to the church are seen as competitive, and in this chapter I resist separating the two: an emphasis on God's action implicates us in attending to the people of God. Attentive to Scripture's immersion

6. See Serene Jones, 'Graced Practices: Excellence and Freedom in the Christian Life' in Miroslav Volf and Dorothy C. Bass (eds), *Practicing Theology: Beliefs and Practices in Christian Life* (Grand Rapids: Eerdmans, 2002), pp. 51–77 (75).

7. Bowald, *Rendering the Word*, p. 2. See also John Webster, 'Resurrection and Scripture' in Andrew T. Lincoln and Angus Paddison (eds), *Christology and Scripture: Interdisciplinary Perspectives* (LNTS, 348; London: T&T Clark, 2007), pp. 138–55, and Wood, *Barth's Theology of Interpretation*.

8. A trait observed by John Webster in his 'Hermeneutics in Modern Theology: Some Doctrinal Reflections' in *Word and Church: Essays in Christian Dogmatics* (Edinburgh: T&T Clark, 2001), pp. 47–86.

9. David Gibson, *Reading the Decree: Exegesis, Election and Christology in Calvin and Barth* (T&T Clark Studies in Systematic Theology; London: T&T Clark International, 2009).

10. See Nicholas Lash, *Believing Three Ways in One God: A Reading of the Apostle's Creed* (SCM Classics; London: SCM, 2002), p. 2: 'Theologians spend much time arguing where they should *begin*. This is a largely futile exercise because, if one thing is certain in this life, it is that none of us begins at the beginning.'

in both divine action and the church's practices, we can therefore say that the latter helps render visible the text's providential location in God's purposes, for the church is privileged to participate in God's actions. Talk of God's providence is made visible by a church that reads Scripture with an alertness to its figural thrust, with the virtue of patience and with lives that imitate Jesus' nonviolence. Providence is not just something the church thinks, but it is (and must be seen to be) intertwined with the church's reading of Scripture, *how* it reads Scripture and the kinds of practices such reading generates. When one begins in the middle of the claim that

> God's action is uniquely present in, with, and under this text in a way that it is not for any and all others,' it is easier to recognize that scriptural reading, as a church activity, is a *sui generis* activity.[11]

Having placed the reader quite deliberately in the middle of a series of claims, I can now set out how this chapter will plot the location of Scripture. How may we fittingly understand Scripture's place within the action of the triune God *and* the life of the church?

First, with the help of the Scottish Congregationalist theologian P. T. Forsyth, we shall locate Scripture within the wider field of God's redemptive action, God's irrepressible desire that his creatures might live in fellowship with him. Forsyth reminds us that Scripture is not a text that arises out of our best religious sentiments but is a text *constituted* by divine action. Scripture is first and foremost co-opted into a very specific *gospel* action.

Second, we shall see the fruits of locating Scripture in an account of time broadcast to the world and cultivated in members of the church by the liturgy and the church's practices. Here, at the instigation of Stanley Hauerwas, we turn decidedly to the church. We should not suppose, however, that locating Scripture in the action of God and the life of the church marks a two-stage attempt to place Scripture in a wholly divine region of activity (the gospel) and then a wholly human region of activity (the church). This chapter is not an attempt to offer a doctrine of Scripture 'from above' and then a doctrine 'from below'. Indeed, such a competitive account would only trade on asymmetrical impulses that I shall criticize. It is necessary to remember that the church, as a people brought into being by God, is a region of divine activity continuous with the eccentric action of the gospel.[12] When we move to the community of

---

11.   Bowald, *Rendering the Word*, p. 23.

12.   Have I not just 'collapsed' Scripture into the church and so stilled its slaying power? Since I know of no way in which we can understand Scripture theologically other than in company with the convictions and practices of the church (Robert W. Jenson, 'Hermeneutics and the Life of the Church' in Carl E. Braaten and Robert W. Jenson (eds), *Reclaiming the Bible for the Church* (Edinburgh: T&T Clark, 1996), pp. 89–105 thus rightly says 'there can be no reading of the Bible that is not churchly' (98)), it is incumbent that the church's doctrines (Jesus' risen agency) and the church's practices (communal receptivity of the Spirit, confession of sins and accountability to one another) protect the church from itself. What matters is not imposing a model of Scripture's

the reconciled, we are paying no less attention to the reconciling divine action which generates Scripture. 'Whether we are to say that God uses the gospel to gather the church for himself, or that God provides the church to carry the gospel to the world, depends entirely on the direction of thought'.[13] Appeal to the church is not then a general appeal to sociality or human togetherness but a reminder that *this people* is the particular form of salvation that the gospel takes, a gospel housed in *this* text: Scripture. God works the gospel through Scripture and then works Scripture through the church. The church *is* the embodiment of the good news which Scripture conveys – God's determination to live in fellowship with those who were estranged from him (Eph. 2.14).[14] Attempts to locate Scripture theologically do not need therefore to balance out overused categories 'from above' and 'from below'. Rather, locating Scripture theologically is a matter of seeing the interwoven aspects of Scripture's vertical and horizontal locations. God works through Scripture so that we might be drawn to participate in the new life he makes possible through his Son.

## Scripture and the Gospel: Locating Scripture with the Help of P. T. Forsyth

Piecing together the diffuse work of P. T. Forsyth (1848–1921),[15] helps us begin to answer the following question: in the context of *what kinds of action* is Scripture intelligible? Forsyth furnishes us with a doctrine of Scripture grounded in a determined attention to the lively and prevenient activity of the triune God.

Like Karl Barth (to whom he has often been compared), Scripture was central to Forsyth's reorientation from the confines of liberal theology to the spaciousness of what he termed the 'positive gospel'.[16] Forsyth's redirection from being a 'lover of love' to an 'object of grace' sprang from his exposure to

---

independence upon the church but for the church to work out practically, and so learn to see, how Scripture's ministry is sustained by its practices and convictions. The church shares in the authority of Scripture and it is through processes of testing one another that the people of God protect themselves from a fissiparous individualism. See Gavin D'Costa, 'Revelation, Scripture and Tradition: Some Comments on John Webster's Conception of "Holy Scripture"', *IJST* 6 (2004), pp. 337–50 (342).

13. Robert W. Jenson, *Systematic Theology*, Vol. 1 (2 vols; New York: Oxford University Press, 1997), p. 5.

14. See William T. Cavanaugh, 'Pilgrim People' in David Matzko McCarthy and M. Therese Lysaught (eds), *Gathered for the Journey: Moral Theology in Catholic Perspective* (Grand Rapids: Eerdmans, 2007), pp. 88–105, and Treier, *Virtue and the Voice of God*, p. 200 for more on the scriptural importance of the 'people of God'.

15. Space precludes me from entering into a detailed biography of Forsyth, minister in a number of English pastorates for 25 years, and College Principal for 20 years. For more biographical details see William Lee Bradley, *P.T. Forsyth: The Man and His Work* (London: Independent Press, 1952).

16. Robert McAfee Brown, *P.T. Forsyth: Prophet for Today* (Philadelphia: Westminster, 1952), pp. 20–21. Along with many other students of Forsyth, I think the language of 're-orientation', in

the gospel for which he said Scripture was a 'shrine'.[17] The language of Forsyth consistently reinforces this commissioned role of Scripture in service of the gospel. The Bible is a 'humble vassal' bearing the gospel[18] or a 'field' into which the objective gospel has been ploughed.[19] The 'positive gospel', mediated by the New Testament in particular, is the apostolic insight into the significance of the Jesus-event; it is 'a certain interpretation of Christ which is given in the New Testament, a mystic interpretation of a historic fact. It is the loving, redeeming grace of a holy God in Christ'.[20] The gospel is therefore two-sided: it is both the outgoing of God's holy love *and* the apostolic interpretation of this divine action. The New Testament faith, which Forsyth consistently counsels the church to be resourced by, is that the actions of Jesus were the actions of God among us. Thus, in the hands of Paul the apostle the historical reality of Jesus' death on a Roman cross is seen for what in truth it *is*: the atoning death of God in Christ.

Forsyth's decisive positioning of Scripture in service to the apostolic gospel gave him notable freedom with regard to two prevailing sources of authority, which are just as present today as they were in Forsyth's time: biblical infallibility and biblical scholarship. Evangelical authority, Forsyth implores, is not secured by shielding the Bible from legitimate scrutiny but by turning with renewed concentration and vigour to that for which Scripture acts as conduit: the gospel. Christians who believe not in an infallible Bible, but in an impregnable gospel, need not be unsettled by the perceived critical plunders of scholarship. Authority in the church is a permanent correlate of the 'moral reality rising from the experience of forgiveness in the Gospel and from the certainty that Christ has there done on us a work that none but God could do'.[21]

Likewise, Forsyth encouraged the church to graduate from notions of the Bible's verbal inspiration, even if it was a distinctive tenet of Reformation thought. 'To the Bible as the Reformers read it we can never, indeed, return', Forsyth gravely intoned.[22] Notions of plenary inspiration relied upon theories that stultified the relationship between the Word and the Spirit.

---

preference to 'conversion', better articulates Forsyth's gradual immersion within the positive gospel.

17. P. T. Forsyth, *Positive Preaching and the Modern Mind* (Biblical and Theological Classics Library; Carlisle: Paternoster, 1998), p. 177; P. T. Forsyth, *Faith, Freedom and the Future* (London: Independent Press, 1955), p. 171.

18. P. T. Forsyth, 'The Grace of The Gospel as the Moral Authority in The Church' in *The Church, The Gospel and Society* (London: Independent Press, 1962), pp. 65–127 (68).

19. P. T. Forsyth, 'The Place of Spiritual Experience in the Making of Theology' in *Revelation Old and New: Sermons and Addresses* (John Huxtable (ed.); London: Independent Press, 1962), pp. 68–80 (80).

20. P. T. Forsyth, *The Person and Place of Jesus Christ* (London: Independent Press, 1946), p. 3.

21. P. T. Forsyth, *The Justification of God: Lectures for War-Time on a Christian Theodicy of God* (London: Duckworth, 1916), p. 89.

22. Forsyth, *Faith, Freedom and the Future*, p. 132.

Verbal inspiration risks slighting the Spirit's present action upon Scripture, rendering Scripture merely a 'mechanical creation' running on fuel deposited there and then rather than having its location in a present reality continually at work through the Spirit.[23] 'The Gospel is always the Spirit in action, not from afar, not from an old inspired past which never loses its force but from the direct present using that timeless past.'[24] Conversion to the gospel is not the legacy of an inspired past but the operation of the Spirit in the present. The Spirit keeps us at once bound to the historic act of God in Jesus Christ while simultaneously operating as this singular event's 'continuity, amplification, and its individualisation'.[25] Danger lay in divorcing the Word and Spirit: not only would the Word become calcified, but the Spirit would have warrant to wander free of the Word and mutate into an adjunct of our evolutionary or subjective predilections. Wrenched apart from the Spirit, the Bible is de-historicized and, instead of being read in tune with the apostolic revelation, the text is 'brought to the bar of the inspiration it creates'.[26] This is to succumb to religious impressionism, namely enlisting the Bible to a spiritual experience created within us, rather than exposing ourselves to Scripture's regenerative gospel. The risen and present Christ, whose objective and completed work is the abundant energy acting on the Bible, works in us through the Spirit's stewardship. 'It is the living matter and content of the ageless Word that is brought livingly home to us by the personality of the Spirit.'[27]

Verbal inspiration was therefore replaced with talk of personal or apostolic inspiration: 'it is not, strictly speaking, the Bible that was inspired, but the souls of the men whose writings fill it'.[28] Indeed, Paul was 'inspired before his Epistles were' and he was 'more inspired than Romans'.[29] Forsyth therefore offers what might be called an ontology of the apostles, a theological account of who they are and how their writings are to be understood, both of these accounts firmly in relation to the saving action of God.[30] For Forsyth,

> the Apostles were not panes of bad glass, but crystal cups the Master filled. They were not mere mediums even, but sacraments. They were not mere channels but agents, not

---

23. Forsyth, *Faith, Freedom and the Future*, p. 33.
24. Forsyth, *Faith, Freedom and the Future*, p. 30.
25. Forsyth, *Faith, Freedom and the Future*, p. 11.
26. Forsyth, *Faith, Freedom and the Future*, p. 130.
27. Forsyth, *Faith, Freedom and the Future*, p. 30.
28. P. T. Forsyth, *Christ on Parnassus: Lectures on Art, Ethic and Theology* (London: Hodder and Stoughton, 1911), p. 243. See also Forsyth, *Person and Place of Jesus Christ*, p. 139; P. T. Forsyth, *Theology in Church and State* (London: Hodder & Stoughton, 1915), p. 71.
29. Forsyth, *Theology in Church and State*, p. 37.
30. In this connection, see the helpful essay of C. Stephen Evans, 'Canonicity, Apostolicity, and Biblical Authority: Some Kierkegaardian Reflections' in Craig Bartholomew, Scott Hahn, Robin Parry, Christopher Seitz and Al Wolters (eds), *Canon and Biblical Interpretation* (Scripture and Hermeneutics Series, 7; Milton Keynes: Paternoster, 2006), pp. 146–66.

> vehicles of Christ but members of Him. They did not merely take their departure from
> Jesus, they had their life, and function, and truth in Him always.[31]

The apostolic issue is the work of the Spirit as 'the returning expositor and translator into history' of Jesus' work.[32] The uniqueness of the apostles is not their historical proximity to Jesus – plainly other people enjoyed historical encounters with Jesus – nor does their uniqueness lie in the quality of their faith, or their particular experience of redemption. The certainty which the New Testament conveys is not a matter of the religious experiences of the apostles. Rather, the apostles' uniqueness was their instruction by the Spirit of the risen Christ whose office was 'not enlarging the revelation in matter but . . . opening its interior'.[33] Their charism was Christ *himself* opening his final revelation out in them, and their writings are the textual extensions and expositions of his work, a work that could not remain dumb and inert.[34] Inspiration is therefore positioned by Forsyth at the frontier with revelation. Inspiration is a subjective state experienced by the biblical writers, 'an exalted state of the spiritual and imaginative faculties',[35] whilst revelation is the objective and saving action of Christ. Faithful reading is the careful sifting out of the decisive revelation from amidst the Bible's fallible inspired writings:

> The same molten state of inspiration holds suspended in it both gold and dross, both
> passing error and permanent eternal truth; and a great amount of inspiration will yield
> sometimes only a percentage of real and eternal revelation. To take the Bible as a
> whole, it is the record of a vast and voluminous inspiration, which fused up in its heat
> a whole mass of human interests, passions, beliefs, ambitions, and errors; but it is not
> impossible, as every Christian knows, to extract from the mass the pure gold of the
> historic, superhistoric, and eternal revelation of the holy love and free grace of God in
> Christ Jesus our Lord.[36]

---

31.  P. T. Forsyth, *The Principle of Authority in Relation to Certainty, Sanctity and Society: An Essay in the Philosophy of Experimental Religion* (London: Independent Press, 1952), pp. 134–35.

32.  Forsyth, *Principle of Authority*, p. 131.

33.  Forsyth, *Person and Place of Jesus Christ*, p. 164.

34.  See John H. Rodgers, *The Theology of P.T. Forsyth: The Cross of Christ and the Revelation of God* (London: Independent Press, 1965), p. 104: 'The deed is only fully itself in that it communicates its significance to man.'

35.  Forsyth, *Christ on Parnassus*, p. 243.

36.  Forsyth, *Christ on Parnassus*, pp. 243–44. Thus, the authority of Scripture is not located in its inspiration, but rather in its commissioned role in conveying the gospel – the action which first pulverizes and then recreates our soul. This correct attitude to Scripture will mean that we strain the writings written by inspired authors for the revelation that lies within. It is this revelation which is the 'creative interior' of Paul's writings, for in this vital centre we have 'not an account of the Christian consciousness but of God's revelation which creates that consciousness; a revelation which, indeed, emerges in man's consciousness always, and in its terms, but is not identical with it, and does not arise from it': Forsyth, *Theology in Church and State*, p. 9.

The New Testament therefore has a decisive location in the extension of the gospel. Indeed, Jesus' work is completed *only* with the interpretation of himself through the apostles, whose issue is 'part of the action . . . and not a searchlight thrown on it from without'.[37] Neither the record of Jesus' impressive personality nor an insight into the spiritual mores of the apostles, the New Testament is decisively fixed within the act of Jesus' self-revelation.[38] The apostolic records are indeed 'acts within his [Jesus'] integral and historic act of redemption' and so they are 'sacraments' more than they are 'sources' to be quarried by scholars.[39] The apostolic issue 'partakes of the authority of that revelation whom they interpreted'.[40] Whilst the synoptic Gospels alone could not found the church, this need not be a worry for the apostolic gospel can make sense of the synoptic witness.[41] The twofold witness within the New Testament, the synoptic and the apostolic, is not then to be sundered – or plundered – by the historical critics. Indeed, in his *The Person and Place of Jesus Christ*, Forsyth attempts to narrow the perceived gap between the synoptic and the Johannine witness to Jesus, staking much on the so-called 'Johannine thunderbolt': 'no one knows the Son except the Father, and no one knows the Father except the Son, and anyone to whom the Son chooses to reveal him' (Mt. 11.27).[42] In this declaration, Jesus reveals an awareness of his pre-existent Sonship, pointing to the congruity between Jesus' teaching and the apostolic gospel.[43] Just as in John, Jesus seems here to be preaching *himself* for *he* is the gospel: the eternal Son revealing the eternal Father. Little wonder that Forsyth says Mt. 11.27 'is the Fourth Gospel *in nuce*',[44] providing the 'centre of gravity' for the synoptic insight.[45] Forsyth consistently argues that there is no disjunction between the teaching of Jesus and the apostolic interpretation of Jesus. The Jesus who remains largely silent in the synoptic Gospels, as with all 'great doers', breaks his silence in Paul's epistles and 'becomes his own divine scholiast'.[46] Liberal proposals that the apostles were unfaithful to Jesus' teaching and imported a whole array of concepts foreign to Jesus himself betray

---

37. Forsyth, *Principle of Authority*, p. 131.
38. Forsyth, *Person and Place of Jesus Christ*, p. 151.
39. Forsyth, *Person and Place of Jesus Christ*, p. 172. See Forsyth, *Principle of Authority*, p. 141, for Forsyth's definition of a sacrament as that which comes 'to abolish time and space, and give us direct contact with Him in a mediate immediacy'.
40. Forsyth, *Person and Place of Jesus Christ*, p. 155.
41. Forsyth, *Person and Place of Jesus Christ*, pp. 142–43; P. T. Forsyth, *Rome, Reform and Reaction* (London: Hodder & Stoughton, 1899), pp. 76–77.
42. According to Robert Benedetto, *P.T. Forsyth Bibliography and Index* (Westport: Greenwood Press, 1993), p. 76, Forsyth makes some 12 references to Mt. 11.27 in his books. Unless stated otherwise all translations are from the NRSV.
43. Forsyth, *Person and Place of Jesus Christ*, pp. 111–14.
44. Forsyth, *Person and Place of Jesus Christ*, p. 116.
45. Forsyth, *Theology in Church and State*, p. 28.
46. P. T. Forsyth, *The Cruciality of the Cross* (London: Independent Press, 1948), p. 16.

a lack of faith in the Spirit's work of binding together history and faithful expansion.[47]

The conviction that the apostles were powerfully co-opted into God's reconciling action also resourced Forsyth's attitude towards biblical scholarship. *How* we read the Bible is a correlate of the actions of which Scripture is a part. To confine the Bible to a rational veracity would install an intellectual hierarchy and misread the Bible as a historical source rather than a sacramental agent.[48] Forsyth consistently warned of the dangers of rationalism, an attitude which forgets that 'the judges of Christian truth are not, in the first place, reasonable men, but redeemed men'.[49] 'Grace', Forsyth reminds us, 'is not irrational in the sense of being foreign to reason, but it is not in the reason of it that its authority resides.'[50] The principal function of the Bible is not for it to be scrutinized, but for it to examine us. Thus the reality which the New Testament was created by is best 'expounded by a mind that has experienced its creative change'.[51] The reader who appreciated this would know that the gulf between the reader and the text is not one decisively traversed by intellectual apparatus but by the holy God who reaches out to sinful humanity. To adopt the words of John Webster in his discussion of the biblical hermeneutics of Dietrich Bonhoeffer and Karl Barth, the real difficulty in reading Scripture 'is spiritual and therefore moral; it is our refusal as sinners to be spoken to, our wicked repudiation of the divine address, our desire to speak the final word to ourselves'.[52] The rupture between the reader of Scripture and God is met by the gospel: the forgiving *action* of the holy Father in his Son, Jesus Christ. Readers of Scripture attuned to *this* reality find themselves in a place of remarkable freedom in relation to critical modes of reading Scripture. The Christian reads Scripture in a sphere of autonomous and regenerative grace, a topic about which A. M. Hunter wrote powerfully in his study of Forsyth:

> The man who has never experienced this divine act [God's central act in Christ] in his own life has no rights to judge it by methods which, however valid in other fields, do not apply to the experienced fact of grace. In short, the Christian gospel cannot have anything else for its criterion. It is spiritually autonomous.[53]

---

47.  Forsyth, *Cruciality of the Cross*, p. 49.
48.  Forsyth, *Faith, Freedom and the Future*, p. 75; P. T. Forsyth, *The Church and the Sacraments* (London: Independent Press, 1947), p. 132.
49.  P. T. Forsyth, 'Mystics and Saints', *The Expository Times* 5 (1894), pp. 401–04 (402).
50.  P. T. Forsyth, 'Authority and Theology' in *The Gospel and Authority: A P.T. Forsyth Reader* (Marvin W. Anderson (ed.); Minneapolis: Augsburg, 1971), pp. 130–47 (140).
51.  P. T. Forsyth, 'Regeneration, Creation, and Miracle', *The Methodist Review Quarterly* 63 (1914), pp. 627–43 (631).
52.  Webster, *Word and Church*, p. 109.
53.  A. M. Hunter, *P.T. Forsyth – Per Crucem ad Lucem* (London: SCM, 1974), p. 54.

Forsyth's conviction is that the gospel dislodges any human critical faculties in which we may seek to fix authority.[54] In every attempt to tame Scripture – through ecclesial institutionalism, creedalism or scholarship – the Bible reveals itself as a 'Trojan horse',[55] a text whose subversive principle *within* is always greater than any attempt to master it from without. Those concerned by the incursions of biblical criticism may, then, be of good cheer, for the Bible contains within it a gospel which the 'dissector's knife' cannot reach,[56] and scholars lack 'the power to reconstruct the Gospel in the Bible; and that Gospel has the power to reconstruct both Bible and Church'.[57] If the Bible is read for what it *is* – 'the exposition of a long action and a final act of grace' – criticism will not rock this truth.[58] Faith is therefore Scripture's 'native air, in which it expands, reveals and bestows its true soul'.[59] Biblical criticism has a restraining leash kept on it insofar as its findings are tested according to evangelical principles, their 'compatibility with the central life and experience of redemption which makes the Church'.[60] With the right perspective on biblical scholarship, biblical scholars can, of course, be enlisted in the theological endeavour as 'assessors and advisers'.[61] Biblical scholarship, after all, was a gift of the Holy Spirit.[62] The biblical reader, Forsyth warned, has nothing to gain by denying the validity of biblical criticism. Nevertheless, the reader of Scripture is best fixing their faith beyond the reach of biblical scholarship by returning 'to the Epistles for the key of the Gospels, for the evangelical secret, and the principle of the Highest Criticism of all'.[63]

With this attention to the action of the gospel, there is no sense of Forsyth being careless with regard to the historical reality of God's action. However, the crucial matter remains always how God in Jesus Christ's history is interpreted, and here Forsyth's reading companions to the Gospels are not surprisingly

54. Leslie McCurdy, *Attributes and Atonement: The Holy Love of God in the Theology of P.T. Forsyth* (Paternoster Biblical and Theological Monographs; Carlisle: Paternoster, 1999), p. 78. For Forsyth's unwillingness to promote rationalism over revelation see P. T. Forsyth, 'Revelation and the Person of Christ' in *Faith and Criticism: Essays by Congregationalists* (no editor cited; London: Simpson Low Marston, 1893), pp. 95–144 (109).

55. Forsyth, *Rome, Reform and Reaction*, p. 108.

56. Forsyth, *Theology in Church and State*, p. 69.

57. Forsyth, *Rome, Reform and Reaction*, p. 225. See also Forsyth, *Person and Place of Jesus Christ*, p. 318: 'The judgement of the cross criticises all criticism, and the finality of its felt salvation is the rock impregnable.'

58. Forsyth, *Positive Preaching and the Modern Mind*, p. 170.

59. P. T. Forsyth, 'Treating the Bible Like Any Other Book', *The British Weekly* (15th August 1901), pp. 401–02 (401).

60. Forsyth, *Person and Place of Jesus Christ*, p. 49.

61. Forsyth, *Rome, Reform and Reaction*, p. 224.

62. Forsyth, *Church and the Sacraments*, p. 36; P. T. Forsyth, *The Work of Christ* (London: Independent Press, 1946), pp. 33–34.

63. Forsyth, *Person and Place of Jesus Christ*, p. 318.

the epistles with their kerygmatic interpretation of Jesus' significance. Scripture's decisive location is not the historical context from which the texts arose, but always the gospel.

> Fact, history, is quite necessary, but it is the nature, the interpretation, the theology, of the historic fact, the nature of its purpose and action, that tells. It is the eloquence of the fact, or let me rather say its vitality, its conductivity, its conveying power. It is fact as sacramental.[64]

Historical study of Jesus risks confining our attention to Jesus within a limited time frame. The more urgent task is however to ground one's life and thought in what, through Jesus, is continually expansive.

> Christ himself arose at a point within human history and stands at a particular moment of it. And the whole business of history is to give Christ His eternal place in the whole course of history . . . to let loose the eternity locked in those brief thirty years, and give it its ruling place in all the affairs of time.[65]

Forsyth is keen on giving the example of the cross on which Jesus died. That Jesus was crucified on a Roman cross is historic, but that this act is the decisive act of a holy God is super-historic. The gospel is based in history, but it is not confined to the investigations of historical scholars,

> the Person of Christ which is to be the foundation of living faith must be something else than the residuary legacy of historical research . . . we must found anything so real as eternity on a historic fact; but one too creative of history to be given by history alone.[66]

As a consequence of these convictions, Forsyth directed that the Bible was neither a document of doctrinal orthodoxy nor a statute book of ethics. The one who speaks from within the biblical interior is fittingly resourced by the gospel 'upon which all [biblical] texts crystallize and fall into their graded place'.[67] Reading the Bible out from this centre gives readers the appropriate blend of finality and sequacity. The gospel 'is not something to stand on, but something to live from . . . [i]t is more than ground that will not give way; it is a source

---

64. P. T. Forsyth, 'Unity and Theology: A Liberal Evangelicalism the True Catholicism' in *Towards Reunion: Being Contributions to Mutual Understanding by Church of England and Free Church Writers* (no editor cited; London: Macmillan, 1919), pp. 51–81 (64).

65. P. T. Forsyth, 'The National Aspect of Missions' in *Missions in State and Church: Sermons and Addresses* (New York: A.C. Armstrong, 1908), pp. 167–93 (184–85).

66. P. T. Forsyth, 'The Inner Life of Christ', *The Constructive Quarterly* 7 (1919), pp. 149–62 (152–53).

67. P. T. Forsyth, 'The Need for a Positive Gospel', *London Quarterly Review* 102 (1904), pp. 64–99 (80).

that will not fail or dry'.[68] Forsyth's own reading of the Bible demonstrated this 'positive core' and 'flexible casing': He had little or nothing invested in the synoptic Gospels' presentation of the virgin birth, and he consistently argued that the finished work of the cross was the source of Christian ethics rather than the occasional precepts of the Sermon on the Mount.[69] Ethical action fuelled by Jesus' teaching would soon find itself running on empty; only the cross has resources enough to fund our moral behaviour. Again, Forsyth is as good as his own counsel; in *The Christian Ethic of War*,[70] written in the midst of the First World War, Forsyth excoriates those who justified pacifism on the basis of the Sermon on the Mount.[71]

How then was the Bible to be located within the church and the work of theology? The Bible is indispensable to theological thought because it is the source of the apostolic kerygma. Verses like 2 Cor. 5.19, Rom. 1.17 or Jn 3.16 were in service to what Forsyth understood as unshakeable 'dogma'. In such verses the church is confronted with a truth that is 'absolute, final and essential'.[72] The church speaks on the basis of these statements whose 'creative interior' is the action of God for humanity, whose guiding idea is not human thoughts about God but God's decisive dealing with humanity.[73] In Forsyth's understanding therefore, 'dogma' points not to the immovable creeds of the church. On the contrary, the apostolic kerygma evident in verses like 2 Cor. 5.19 serves dogma: 'God in his gracious turning to man in Jesus Christ'.[74] Doctrine, in this setting, is subordinate to dogma and marks the church's release of dogma's pressure; it is the space into which dogma expands. Doctrine is the energy of dogma expressed in the church's understanding, appropriate to the particular time and place it finds itself in, as in the historic creeds of the church.[75] The authority of a creed is therefore of a lower order from the authority of the dogma enclosed in the apostolic witness: doctrine is 'faith's

---

68. Forsyth, *Principle of Authority*, p. 36.

69. P. T. Forsyth, 'Orthodoxy, Heterodoxy, Heresy, and Freedom', *Hibbert Journal* 8 (1910), pp. 321–29 (322).

70. P. T. Forsyth, *The Christian Ethic of War* (London: Longmans, Green, 1916).

71. Forsyth's instincts are right here, but I believe his conclusion to be mistaken. Unless we are to subscribe to an unsustainable prescriptive reading of Scripture, the Sermon on the Mount alone cannot indeed warrant a pacifist perspective. Moreover, Forsyth is right to think that Christian ethical action is never fuelled by Scripture alone but is always nested in a wider region of divine-human action. Had, however, Forsyth attended to the overall narrative of Jesus' life, this would have encouraged him to see the peaceable nature of Jesus' life, explicated by his teaching. Attention to the length of Scripture is important here. Forsyth was notoriously inattentive to the shape and form of Jesus' life.

72. Forsyth, *Theology in Church and State*, p. 17.

73. Forsyth, *Theology in Church and State*, p. 9.

74. Rodgers, *Theology of P. T. Forsyth*, p. 85.

75. Forsyth, *Theology in Church and State*, pp. 46–50.

thermometer for guidance rather than its governor for obedience'.[76] Forsyth's location of Scripture in relation to doctrine will serve us well in Chapter 3.

As can be seen from our explorations thus far, Forsyth first and foremost locates Scripture in relation to *God's* activity, an action best regarded as 'not merely a gospel of definite truth but of decisive reality, not of clear belief but of crucial action'.[77] This plea that we attend to the lively activity of God – rather than a series of propositional truths *about* God – explains Forsyth's resistance to dry-freezing Scripture and regarding it as little more than 'an arsenal of Christian evidences'.[78] Scriptural reading is to resist having commerce with stupefied orthodoxies. Christian faith is not ultimately faith in doctrines but rather a faith in those realities and powers which Scripture and doctrine attempt to articulate.[79] The power of Jn 3.16 is not that it is a message about God's love for us; it points to God's love enacted for us. Finely-wrought doctrinal systems are prone to misunderstand faith as an intellectual assent to truths articulated, rather than the soul's 'direct contact with Christ crucified'.[80] Biblical readers who domesticate the Bible into systems of orthodoxy are liable to forget that it is the theologian's 'hard and high fate to cast himself into the flame he tends, and be drawn into its consuming fire'.[81] To be 'biblical' is therefore to apprehend that Scripture's core

> is not a crystallization of man's divinest idea, it is not even a divine declaration of what God is in himself; it is his revelation of what he is *for us* in actual history, what he for us has done, and forever does.[82]

Being biblical is a matter of apprehending correctly God's redemptive activity *into which Scripture has been drawn and is now located.*

> No belief is scriptural simply because it be met with in the Bible. We do not believe in the contents of the Bible, but in its content, in what put it there, and what it is there for. For it is a means, and not an end. We believe in the Gospel, the Gospel of God's Grace justifying the ungodly in Christ's Cross and creating the Bible for that use.[83]

Scripture is located by the gospel, before it is located by us.

---

76. Forsyth, *Theology in Church and State*, p. 57.
77. Forsyth, 'The Need for a Positive Gospel', pp. 70–71.
78. Forsyth, 'The Evangelical Churches and the Higher Criticism' in *Gospel and Authority*, pp. 15–53 (26).
79. Forsyth, *Theology in Church and State*, p. 99.
80. Forsyth, *Rome, Reform and Reaction*, p. 172.
81. Forsyth, *Cruciality of the Cross*, p. 169.
82. Forsyth, 'The Evangelical Churches and the Higher Criticism', p. 23.
83. Forsyth, *Theology in Church and State*, p. 81.

## *Extending the Location of Scripture*

P. T. Forsyth reminds us that Scripture is fittingly located within the realm of God's gospel action. Located thus, the church recognizes that Scripture occupies a space like no other text. What Forsyth has to say about who the apostles were or the authority of historical criticism is ordered by this non-negotiable location of Scripture, elaborating some of the claims about the priority of local hermeneutics with which this chapter commenced. Moreover, Forsyth's assertions about Scripture's relation to divine action helpfully distinguishes between revelation and text, binding them to one another, although not confusing them with one another. We thus avoid the thickets of elevating Scripture to an inappropriate status or of foreclosing the freedom of God to act upon us anew. The priority must be *God's* use of the text. Equally, Forsyth reminds us, the reliability of Scripture is a question not of its verbal imperfections but a matter of Scripture's relationship to the triune God who elects it into his service. What T. F. Torrance calls the 'double place' of Scripture – its location both in the redeeming action of God and a world in need of redemption – is a way of recognizing the peculiar problem of Holy Scripture and its peculiar place. Holy Scripture is assumed by Christ to be his instrument in conveying revelation and reconciliation, and yet Holy Scripture belongs to the sphere where redemption is necessary. The Bible stands above the church, speaking to the church the very Word of God, but the Bible also belongs to history which comes under the judgement and the redemption of the cross.[84]

Scripture is thus located in God's movement outwards to embrace and call people into the gospel action. The reconciling action of the gospel is the sphere which initially and decisively renders Scripture intelligible: 'true hearing of the Word of God coming to us through the human words of the Bible which is faithful to those words can take place effectively only within the sphere of reconciliation to God'.[85] Scriptural reading is not an activity which can be allowed to wander far from our restored relationship with God made possible by the gospel.

Notwithstanding these notes of appreciation for Forsyth's location of Scripture, there are some problems in his account of Scripture. One disturbing lacuna at the heart of Forsyth's location of Scripture is his reticence on the Old Testament. Readers will have noticed that whilst Forsyth confidently locates the New Testament in relation to the gospel action, he says very little about the Old Testament. Such reticence threatens to relegate the Old Testament to a moment of salvation history now past and fails to see how Christ's resurrection

---

84.   Thomas. F. Torrance, *Theology in Reconstruction* (London: SCM, 1965), p. 138.

85.   Torrance, *Theology in Reconstruction*, p. 142. See also T. F. Torrance, 'Introduction: Biblical Hermeneutics and General Hermeneutics' in *Divine Meaning: Studies in Patristic Hermeneutics* (Edinburgh: T&T Clark, 1995), pp. 5–13.

fills full the Old Testament as a *continuing* witness to Christ. As we shall see figural reading, a reading sustained by the liturgy and practices of the church, is a way of recognizing the Old Testament's location in the gospel action. A sustainable figural reading depends upon a clear idea of what time is in the purposes of God and an appreciation that, to borrow Forsyth's words, to understand history we must 'give Christ His eternal place in the whole course of history . . . let loose the eternity locked in those brief thirty years, and give it its ruling place in all the affairs of time'.[86] We shall emphasize the contribution of figural reading at various points within this book.

Forsyth's doctrine of Scripture as a commissioned text can be profitably placed alongside the work of a contemporary theologian, John Webster, and his robust location of Scripture within the action of God.[87] What might we learn about some of the shortcomings of a 'divine action' location of Scripture by drawing Webster alongside our reading of Forsyth? Both Forsyth and Webster certainly place a strong emphasis on the action of God, both steer well clear of making claims about the imperfections of the text and both prioritize God's deployment – 'annexation' in Webster's case – of the scriptural text in the communication of the reconciling gospel. But both accounts share a common problem: their accounts of Scripture's relationship to the church are frustratingly disembodied and set at a distance from the church's dense, timeful practices. Both Forsyth and Webster raise the spectre of *episodic* accounts of Scripture's action on and among us: such accounts are insufficiently wedded to the horizontal time which we inhabit and so make it hard for the church to see how Scripture and God's action *consistently* relate one to another through and in time. It is indicative, for example, that in one of his many accounts of God's action in relation to Scripture, John Webster narrates Scripture's interaction with Christians by recourse to such words as 'episode', 'event' and 'incident'.[88] Whilst such language is doubtless useful in prioritizing *God's* use of Scripture and securing the freedom and the transcendence of the Word, there is a risk of abstracting scriptural reading, and God's involvement in the transformation of such reading, from the 'limits and relativities' of the history we inhabit.[89] It is by locating Scripture in the church, and following through the implications of such a location that we will be helped to uproot our mundane expectations of time and invited to see that the world is figurally constituted. I suspect that Forsyth's near silence on the Old Testament has its origins somewhere near his reluctance to follow through his own insight that time is

---

86.   Forsyth, 'The National Aspect of Missions', pp. 184–85.

87.   See, for example, John Webster, *Holy Scripture: A Dogmatic Sketch* (Current Issues in Theology; Cambridge: Cambridge University Press, 2003).

88.   John Webster, 'Texts: Scripture, reading, and the rhetoric of theology', *Stimulus* 6 (1998), pp. 10–16 (11, 13, 14).

89.   Nathan Kerr, *Christ, History and Apocalyptic: The Politics of Christian Mission* (Theopolitical Visions; Eugene: Cascade, 2009), p. 81.

constituted by the gospel. Equally, Webster's emphases upon the episodic nature of Scripture's action on readers, of a piece with his enthusiasm for the 'clarity' of Scripture,[90] are of little support to a figural reading of Scripture which prioritizes talk of participation.[91] To avoid this episodic language – correlative with a punctiliar account of God's action on Christians – Scripture's life needs to be located very firmly within the life of the people of God. If we do otherwise and locate Scripture's action on us in an isolated series of moments, we risk reducing Scripture's action and our reading of it 'to something that cannot essentially be *narrated*'.[92] In other words, in episodic accounts of God's relationship to Scripture, the text is not sufficiently set within our time. It is as if the church's reading with Scripture has 'no existence in real time'.[93] This is *not* a plea for the theological significance of historical criticism. Attending to Scripture's *participation* in the worship and liturgy of the church is more radically historical – more attentive to time – than the historical critics and can help counter that which John Webster rightly opposes, namely 'a competitive understanding of the transcendent and the historical'.[94] *Co-ordinating the life of Scripture with the life of the church invites us to locate Scripture in its proper liturgical setting, a setting which reworks what we imagine time to be.* Such a determination to locate Scripture in the church takes its rise from the wider aims of this book – to draw attention to the necessarily local aspects of scriptural reading.

All accounts of Scripture are inseparable from accounts of the church. As we apply this rule to Webster's account of Scripture, it is hard to shrug off the feeling that he ends up imposing a 'blueprint' of Scripture's authority upon the church in abstraction from how the Spirit helps the church work out, see and imagine both what Scripture is and the times of which it is part. The term 'blueprint' is one I borrow from Nicholas M. Healy who worries in a related manner about what he calls 'blueprint ecclesiologies'. Such models of the church imply 'that it is necessary to get our *thinking* about the church right first, after which we can go on to put our theory into practice'. The effect is, Healy avers, an entrenchment of the disjunction between 'theoretical and practical reasoning'.[95] Healy's point can be transferred to doctrines of Scripture abstracted from

---

90. Webster, *Holy Scripture*, pp. 91–101.

91. See Levering, *Participatory Biblical Exegesis*.

92. Jenson, *Systematic Theology*, Vol. 1, p. 169.

93. Oliver O'Donovan, *Church in Crisis: The Gay Controversy and the Anglican Communion* (Eugene: Cascade, 2008), p. 13. O'Donovan makes this criticism of liberal theology's inability to interpret the situation in which we currently find ourselves.

94. Webster, *Holy Scripture*, p. 21. Similar concerns to mine are voiced by D'Costa, 'Revelation, Scripture and Tradition', p. 347.

95. Nicholas M. Healy, *Church, World and Christian Life: Practical-Prophetic Ecclesiology* (Cambridge Studies in Christian Doctrine, 7; Cambridge: Cambridge University Press, 2000), p. 36. I suspect that Healy would charge John Webster's, 'On Evangelical Ecclesiology', *Ecclesiology* 1 (2004), pp. 9–35 with representing a 'blueprint ecclesiology'.

attention to the church as a region where, as in Scripture's original constitution, divine and human agency meet in a transforming encounter.

Scripture's authority in the church is indeed *given* (not generated), but the process of *receiving* Scripture and 'working it out' needs rather more attention than Webster is willing to give consideration. Unless attention is paid to the church's life as an aid to locating Scripture – as this study will endeavour to do throughout – we are at risk of simply not recognizing the text spoken of by Webster. Locating Scripture 'is not a doctrinal theory that can be worked out without close attention to the concrete life of the church'.[96] Although Webster rightly warns us away from competitive understandings of the text's relationship to God and location within history, it would seem that he is not immune to such temptations when he sketches Scripture's relationship to the church. Placing great emphasis on divine agency – especially the Holy Spirit – Webster advocates that talk of 'interpreting' Scripture should be replaced with the less hermeneutically anxious term 'reading'.[97] But surely this is to imply that interpretation cannot itself be sanctified by God, in the same manner that the human texts of the Bible are enlisted into the service of the gospel? One is left wondering precisely what is left for human agency aside from receptivity (which, I agree with Webster, is not passive).[98] By hindering his readers from exploring how we *learn* to read Scripture through the time God gives us, Webster ends up not sufficiently protecting himself from the risks of a one-sided account of interpretation. In other words, Webster falls into the same trap he had earlier warned against, of pitting human agency in competition with divine agency.

Avoiding an overly anxious 'division of labour' between what is deemed 'practical' and what is 'theological',[99] the next section of this chapter emphasizes that revelation has its necessary correlate in the interpretative practices of the church. The necessary emphasis on Scripture's location in God's action, emphasized by Forsyth and Webster, needs to be complemented by attention to the church but only because the church provides us with resources to understand God's action. Put simply, to understand the practices of the church – practices as mundane as reading – we need to see how 'God acts in our acts'.[100] By attending to the church, we can see the time in which Scripture is located and so re-imagine the shape of time. What we might call a 'concursive imagination', aware that participation in the life of the church is an exercise in

---

96. Healy, *Church, World and Christian Life*, p. 50.
97. Webster, *Holy Scripture*, pp. 86–87.
98. Webster, *Holy Scripture*, pp. 68–106. I owe this point to a paper presented by Sean Winter at the 2008 British New Testament Conference entitled 'Interpretive Pluralism in Theological Perspective: The Contribution of Karl Barth' and the subsequent conversations afterwards.
99. Healy, *Church, World and Christian Life*, p. 66.
100. Craig Hovey, *To Share in the Body: A Theology of Martyrdom for Today's Church* (Grand Rapids: Brazos, 2008), p. 30.

formation, sees Scripture as God would have us see it and need not be, as John Webster would charge, an exercise in self-assertion or creativity.[101]

## Scripture, Time and the Church

In the emphasis I now expand on – the location of Scripture in the time of the church – I am clearly motivated by what might inadequately be termed a 'postliberal' emphasis on Scripture's ecclesial setting, with Stanley Hauerwas an especially important stimulus. Hauerwas exemplifies the importance of starting from within the church, and its practices and performances, in order to understand aright Scripture and its relationship to theology and ethics. Journeying with Hauerwas in this location of Scripture, I will follow 'the direction in which he points' by picking up what I can of the language he speaks and extending the implications of his writings.[102] To deploy an image which I alluded to in the Introduction to this book, and one that is important in Hauerwas' first book, *Vision and Virtue*,[103] by pointing to the visibility of the church Hauerwas reminds us that the church can help us *see* the lives and actions of which Scripture is a part.

For Stanley Hauerwas, Gilbert T. Rowe Professor of Theological Ethics at Duke Divinity School, the community of the faithful is accorded prime significance in the reading of Scripture: 'the Bible without the community, without expounders, and interpreters, and hearers is a dead book'.[104] So although he would rightly resist such restrictive labels, Hauerwas can nonetheless be positioned within that postliberal strain within theology which sees the church as an indispensable companion to understanding Scripture. Samuel Wells' pronouncement that 'Scripture . . . not only identifies God: it identifies God's people' is neatly representative of this desire to see church and Scripture as intertwined, implicated within one another and mutually informing.[105] Church-centred reading of Scripture, in Hauerwas' hands, sits lightly in relation to presumptions that the meaning of a text is equivalent to establishing the (always putative) authorial intention. 'Good' reading of Scripture is faithful

---

101. Webster, *Holy Scripture*, p. 97–99.

102. Samuel Wells, *Transforming Fate into Destiny: The Theological Ethics of Stanley Hauerwas* (Eugene: Cascade, 2004), p. 2.

103. Stanley Hauerwas, *Vision and Virtue: Essays in Christian Ethical Reflection* (Notre Dame: Fides Press, 1974).

104. Hauerwas, *Peaceable Kingdom*, p. 98. See also Stanley Hauerwas, *A Community of Character: Toward a Constructive Christian Social Ethic* (Notre Dame: University of Notre Dame Press, 1981), p. 55: 'Without that community [the church], claims about the moral authority of Scripture – or rather, the very idea of Scripture itself – make no sense'.

105. Samuel Wells, *God's Companions: Reimagining Christian Ethics* (Challenges in Contemporary Theology; Oxford: Blackwell, 2006), p. 17.

before anything else and builds up the church.[106] Worrying little about 'meaning', Hauerwas simply reads Scripture 'as an aid for the church to "muddle though"'.[107]

Hauerwas can help us locate Scripture if we trace the implications of reading two very 'Hauerwasian' pronouncements alongside one another. First, Hauerwas opens his recent commentary on Matthew's Gospel with the statement that 'this commentary is guided by the presumption that the church is the politics that determines how Matthew is to be read'.[108] Second, towards the end of his Gifford lectures, Hauerwas (infamously) claims that 'the truth of Christian convictions depend[s] on the faithfulness of the church'.[109] How would the church see Scripture if it followed the logic of these statements? Specifically, I wish to exploit these two statements by exploring how the *time* which the church inhabits and conveys can help us locate Scripture.

Scott Bader-Saye is right to say that, 'the ways we experience, name, and interpret time contribute to the kinds of communities we imagine and inhabit'.[110] The school for Christian imagination is worship, for 'the training we receive in worship . . . enable[s] us to rightly see the world and to perceive how we continue to be possessed by the world'.[111] The very act of 'taking time' to worship, a phrase redolent of our commodification of time and tendency to see time as 'ours',[112] is itself a political and countercultural act. Worship is a statement that we are not free to do as we wish with time, but we are to understand time as *gifted*. Christians view time not through the prism of scarcity but through the prism of providence, the assurance that God is an agent within time and that time is not devoid of his promise. Liturgical time – as time that is first received – is a corrective to the notion that we must master time or be mastered by it. Worship – in which scriptural reading is most fittingly enclosed – is therefore

---

106. Stanley Hauerwas, *Matthew* (Brazos Theological Commentary on the Bible; Grand Rapids: Brazos, 2006), p. 145.

107. Stanley Hauerwas and James Fodor, 'Remaining in Babylon: Oliver O'Donovan's Defense of Christendom', *SCE* 11 (1998), pp. 30–55 (42). For this kind of hermeneutical pragmatism see Jeffrey Stout, 'What is the Meaning of a Text?', *New Literary History* 14 (1982), pp. 1–12.

108. Hauerwas, *Matthew*, p. 30.

109. Stanley Hauerwas, *With the Grain of the Universe: The Church's Witness and Natural Theology* (Grand Rapids: Brazos, 2001), p. 231. See the clarification of Stanley Hauerwas, 'Hooks: Random Thoughts By Way of a Response to Griffiths and Ochs', *Modern Theology* 19 (2003), pp. 89–101.

110. Scott Bader-Saye, 'Figuring Time: Providence and Politics' in Randi Rashkover and C. C. Pecknold (eds), *Liturgy, Time, and the Politics of Redemption* (Radical Traditions; Grand Rapids: Eerdmans, 2006), pp. 91–111 (98).

111. Stanley Hauerwas, *In Good Company: The Church as Polis* (Notre Dame: University of Notre Dame Press, 1995), p. 156.

112. Wells, *Transforming Fate into Destiny*, pp. 148–49.

an occasion for re-imagining our participation in time. Hauerwas and Willimon sum up these sentiments when they write:

> Christian politics is constituted by the worship of the true God found in Jesus Christ. It is politics that assumes we have all the time in the world, eternity, in a world of deep injustice and pain, to take time to worship…Sunday worship is thus a radical protest from the world's time, a time when we literally take time to rejoice that in Jesus Christ God has made our time his own.[113]

Christian worship makes plain the difference of the Christian apprehension of time.[114] In being enfolded in a story not of our devising modernity's attempt to 'defeat time' is rudely confronted.[115] Time is not causal – 'just one damn thing after another' – but eschatologically directed; time and history are ruled now by the cross and empty tomb.[116] Time, 'what really *is*, is constituted by Jesus' history'.[117] Such time is apocalyptic time, and apocalyptic worshippers are confident that everything that needs to be done has been done for us in the life, death and resurrection of Jesus Christ. God's irrepressible presence in the world helps us exchange a view of history as 'a seamless web of causal relations' for a view of '"how things are"'.[118] As we will see in the next chapter, such a distinctively Christian understanding of time is correlative with the patient virtues it nurtures in Christian lives. Patience is nothing less than the practical response to God's providential ordering of the world. Liturgy – a training ground for patience – is an invitation to participate in time as it truly is and to shape a counter-imagination to regnant models of time.[119]

We can point to three ways in which Scripture, church, liturgy and time co-inhere and mutually inform one another.

(1) Worshipful practices such as the reading and rereading of Scripture through lectionary cycles are themselves timeful, and so moral, exercises. As Rowan Williams points out the reading and hearing of a scriptural text, like a symphony, cannot be rushed, compressed or abridged without fundamentally

---

113. Stanley Hauerwas and William H. Willimon, *The Truth about God: The Ten Commandments in Christian Life* (Nashville: Abingdon, 1999), p. 65.

114. Wells, *Transforming Fate into Destiny*, pp. 141–63.

115. Stanley Hauerwas, *The State of the University: Academic Knowledges and the Knowledge of God* (Illuminations: Theory and Religion; Oxford: Blackwell, 2007), p. 37.

116. Hauerwas, *State of the University*, p. 155.

117. John Webster, '"Assured and Patient and Cheerful Expectation": Barth on Christian Hope as the Church's Task', *Toronto Journal of Theology* 10 (1994), pp. 35–52 (40).

118. Stanley Hauerwas with Jeff Powell, 'Creation as Apocalyptic: A Tribute to William Stringfellow' in Stanley Hauerwas, *Dispatches from the Front: Theological Engagements with the Secular* (Durham: Duke University Press, 1994), pp. 107–15 (109).

119. Stanley Hauerwas, *Performing the Faith: Bonhoeffer and the Practice of Nonviolence* (London: SPCK, 2004), p. 97–99.

altering its claims on us. If a reader at a Palm Sunday service boiled the Passion narratives down to a few 'key points' we would, rightly, feel somewhat short-changed.[120] Christians participate first in the narrative, not in the application of its 'lessons'. As Peter Candler has stated, in order to 'read well, then, one must take time, one must learn to remember, and one must make a certain progression through a text – a progress which is one of gaining knowledge, but also one of drawing nearer to wisdom'.[121] Properly then, the church does much more than 'take' time to read Scripture – receiving the time God gives us to read Scripture is the church's thankful giving of time back to God 'by the way we use it'.[122] Moreover, the church is not in the business of just reading Scripture, but *rereading* it, knowing that there is no point at which we could ever dispense with the text itself. The time the church sets aside to re-read Scripture is a reminder not just that the church can never finish reading Scripture, but also that its understanding is something acquired over time. The church's liturgical repetition of Scripture is not a returning again and again to the same 'meaning' but rather a deepening or a chastening encounter with the triune God who providentially orders the texts of Scripture. This re-reading of Scripture can be as much a rebuke as it can be a confirmation of what we think; reading Scripture under the pressure of eschatological time does not view growth in understanding as inevitable. Appropriate care must be taken here that we do not contradict the eschatological presence of Christ around which our reading constellates by lurching into the interpretative equivalent of an 'evolutionary eschatology' that presumes our advance or progress.[123]

(2) The time made known by liturgy and the practices of the church help re-imagine the time into which Scripture is drawn and of which it is part. 'Worship is the communal cultivation of an alternative construction of society *and of history*.'[124] Through worship we come to learn that there is more at play than

---

120.   Rowan Williams, *On Christian Theology* (Challenges in Contemporary Theology; Oxford: Blackwell, 2000), p. 51, and Rowan Williams, *Open to Judgement: Sermons and Addresses* (London: Darton, Longman and Todd, 1994), pp. 247–50. Hauerwas, *Performing the Faith*, pp. 104–05, draws upon Williams to make this point about the timeful aspect of music. I am building upon them both to point to the role that scriptural reading plays in the liturgy's re-imagination of time.

121.   Candler, *Theology, Rhetoric, Manuduction*, p. 9.

122.   Ben Quash, 'The *Trisagion* and the Liturgical Untilling of Time' in Rashkover and Pecknold (eds), *Liturgy, Time, and the Politics of Redemption*, pp. 141–63 (159).

123.   Karl Rahner, 'A Fragmentary Aspect of a Theological Evaluation of the Concept of the Future' in *Theological Investigations*, Vol. X (trans. David Bourke; 23 vols; London: Darton, Longman and Todd, 1973), pp. 235–41 (236).

124.   John Howard Yoder, *The Priestly Kingdom: Social Ethics as Gospel* (Notre Dame: University of Notre Dame Press, 2001), p. 43 (emphasis added). Yoder's statement that worship offers an *alternative* construction of time and history is a helpful reminder of how moderns are shaped to see history as a more decisive category than providence. See Stanley Hauerwas, *Wilderness Wanderings: Probing Twentieth-Century Theology and Philosophy* (Radical Traditions; London: SCM, 2001), p. 46 n. 6. See also Charles Taylor, *A Secular Age* (Cambridge, MA: Belknap

just the horizontal succession of events. When time, as it is in modernity, is understood without reference to God then it is easy for God to become extrinsic to time, and so somebody we subsequently labour to fit in to our stunted imagination of time. But time is *constituted* by the cross and resurrection and liturgy is the invitation to participate in the scripturally figured world.[125] It is the events of Jesus' life, death and resurrection that fill full Scripture with meaning: 'beginning with Moses and all the prophets, he [the risen Jesus] interpreted to them the things about himself in all the scriptures' (Lk. 24.27). Correspondingly, liturgical imagination is a way of remembering that 'Israel and the church are not characters in a larger story called 'world,' but rather world is a character in God's story'.[126] If all time acquires its meaning in relation to God's activity in Israel and Jesus' cross and resurrection, then it is around these events that Scripture is to be read, rather than views of time and history framed apart from attention to the resurrected presence of Christ in the church. Hauerwas may be being deliberately provocative when he insists that '[w]ithout the church the world would have no history',[127] but his point is an important one. We do not naturally see time for what it is and only with the training of the church's worship can we hope to apprehend time as it truly is in the light of the resurrection This alternative understanding of time is not of course created by worship: the rule here is that convictions about the nature of reality must always have their visible manifestation.

Worshipful practices such as figural reading and preaching are therefore faithful to the providential action in which Scripture is located. In this form of reading, one narrated event or person is read in the light of a perspective offered by a later narrated event or person. Scripture has a pattern and is not the narration of one random event after another. For example, placing the baptism of Jesus as a coordinating event of the triune God invites us to look back to the deliverance of Israel through the waters of the Red Sea (which in turn is an anticipation of Christ in the waters of the Jordan) and forward to our own

---

Press of Harvard University Press, 2007), p. 59: 'Our encasing in secular time is also something we have brought about in the way we live and order our lives . . . the disciplines of our modern civilized order have led us to measure and organize time as never before in human history. Time has become a precious resource, not to be "wasted" . . . We have constructed an environment in which we live a uniform, univocal secular time, which we try to measure and control in order to get things done.' If Taylor's account is so, it is incumbent upon Christians not to suppose that they can overcome the accounts of time germane to modernity, but to *see* how Christian convictions and practices embed Scripture within a rather different account of time.

125. See Charles Taylor, *Philosophical Arguments* (Cambridge, MA: Harvard University Press, 1995), p. 310 n. 17.

126. Stanley Hauerwas, *Sanctify Them in the Truth: Holiness Exemplified* (Edinburgh: T&T Clark, 1998), p. 192.

127. Stanley Hauerwas, *Christian Existence Today: Essays on Church, World, and Living in Between* (Grand Rapids: Brazos, 2001), p. 61.

baptismal participation in the life of the church (Romans 6).[128] In this mode of reading events at different times are not carelessly collapsed into one another, but rather their participation in a common history is apprehended. It is in this way that figural interpretation is a hermeneutic of resistance against the idea that 'each moment stands utterly unconnected from the moments around it – that every moment is self-enclosed'.[129] To read figurally is to apprehend that Scripture is a single text which has its point of unity in the life, death and resurrection of Jesus.

The people who help make this conviction visible are the church, those who lead lives that witness to the truthfulness of God's providential figuring of the world. That we have lost grip of Scripture's figural unity is surely correlative with an equal loss of a sense of how God's providential activity stands ready to reorder our understanding of time and our lives. A practical appearance of the doctrine of providence would surely be the church's willingness to embrace its status as people 'not in charge'.[130] The church must be the people who make visible the claim that Scripture is a figural text, a claim clearly made in the wake of Hauerwas' assertion that 'the truth of Christian convictions depend[s] on the faithfulness of the church'.[131] If talk of history has been denuded of its providential categories, responsibilities for this forgetfulness must lie with a church that has not sufficiently heeded that 'biblically the meaning of history is carried first of all, and on behalf of all others, by the believing community'.[132] It is worth noting well that none of this detracts in any way from what we learned in the opening part of this chapter. As people formed by the liturgy, the church comes to see that Scripture is a figurally charged text and so *is itself* a participant in the drama of salvation. Scripture is elected to participate in a quite specific field of divine activity to which human action must correspond. 'You search the scriptures because you think that in them you have eternal life; and it is they that testify on my behalf' (Jn 5.39). When reading Scripture, the church is therefore 'asked to engage a kind of map that traces the work of God in history . . . apprehension [of which] provides a living structure to the

---

128.   A reading offered by Joseph Ratzinger, *Jesus of Nazareth: From the Baptism in the Jordan to the Transfiguration* (trans. Adrian J. Walker; London: Bloomsbury, 2007), pp. 15–20. See Angus Paddison, 'Following Jesus with Pope Benedict' in Adrian Pabst and Angus Paddison (eds), *The Pope and Jesus of Nazareth* (Veritas; London: SCM, forthcoming) and the discussion of typological readings of baptism in the hands of Cyril of Jerusalem in O'Keefe and Reno, *Sanctified Vision*, pp. 78–82.

129.   Ben Quash, 'Making the Most of the Time: Liturgy, Ethics and Time', *SCE* 15 (2002), pp. 97–114 (106). Earlier in this essay, Quash offers a helpful definition of liturgy as 'the embodiment of worship in words, gestures, actions, habits and exchanges' (97).

130.   John Howard Yoder, 'On Not Being in Charge' in *The Jewish-Christian Schism Revisited* (Radical Traditions; Michael G. Cartwright and Peter Ochs (eds); London: SCM, 2003), pp. 168–79.

131.   Hauerwas, *With the Grain of the Universe*, p. 231.

132.   John Howard Yoder, *The Royal Priesthood: Essays Ecclesiastical and Ecumenical* (Michael G. Cartwright (ed.); Scottdale: Herald, 1998), p. 118.

actual life of the world in which the [church] lives'.[133] If Scripture 'is part of the drama itself, moving along with it' then such a claim becomes intelligible through the lives of people who have become transparencies for their convictions.[134]

Two further things can be said here about the claim that the figural nature of Scripture is rendered visible by the lives of the people of God.[135] To say this is to be reminded that the main obstacle in understanding Scripture is not our lack of scholarly apparatus but our performance, our resistance to align ourselves with the deepest impulses of the text itself. One cannot divorce the shape of our lives from interpretation.[136] Second, there is the implication that Scripture's figural shape can *only* be discerned from within the church because the church provides the necessary backdrop of practices and lives which fill out this claim. The claim that outside of the church there is no interpretation and no understanding of Scripture is easily misunderstood as a statement of arrogant exclusivism, yet the claim is essentially that only in the church can the claims of and about Scripture *be seen* to make sense. It is a claim about the translatability of the doctrine of providence apart from the visibility of lives ordered to Scripture's providential location.

(3) As should be quite clear by now, liturgy's re-imagination of time holds in unity the church and Scripture. Reading Scripture in the church therefore allows us to be *more* historical than the historical-critics. Much historical criticism is motivated by the earnest assumption that the hard, scholarly work spent in recovering the form of the New Testament church stands a good chance of being automatically relevant for the church today.[137] Faithfulness to the scriptural narrative is not however a matter of nervously applying original features of the narrative to our context, but living out the story in our context.[138] This is carried out in the belief that the people and events of Scripture are in continuity, but are not *identical*, with the church today. Stanley Hauerwas writes of the

133. Ephraim Radner, *Leviticus* (SCM Theological Commentary on the Bible; London: SCM, 2008), p. 25. In the original quotation Radner referred just to 'the reader'.

134. Hans Urs von Balthasar, *Theo-Drama: Theological Dramatic Theory*, Vol. II (trans. Graham Harrison; 5 vols; San Francisco: Ignatius, 1990), p. 112.

135. Note here the important work of Ephraim Radner who argues that the church's weak understanding of Scripture's providential depth is correlative to allowing the mutually informing relationship between Church and Scripture to be loosened. What we have lost sight of, Radner claims, is 'the conviction that the historical experience of the Christian community, because of its conformity to the scriptural narrative and claims, provided, the window of access to a clear knowledge of Jesus Christ': Ephraim Radner, *Hope Among the Fragments: The Broken Church and its Engagement of Scripture* (Grand Rapids: Brazos, 2004), p. 170.

136. Stanley Hauerwas, *Unleashing the Scripture: Freeing the Bible from Captivity to America* (Nashville: Abingdon, 1993), p. 8.

137. For similar worries about the New Testament being read as a blueprint for contemporary ecclesiology, see Dale Martin, *Pedagogy of the Bible: An Analysis and Proposal* (Louisville: Westminster John Knox, 2008), pp. 74–75.

138. Cf. Wells, *Transforming Fate into Destiny*, p. 153.

lofty ambitions sometimes harboured by historical critics who invest their historical work with theological significance:

> The assumption that we should if we could get back to the "original language or mean-ing," or discover "what the first hearers heard," sometimes implies that at one time someone got it right. History done in the objectivist mode turns out to be the expression of mythological assumptions quite foreign to Christian practice.[139]

Attempts to recreate any supposedly 'pure' church of the New Testament neglect the much more important task of discerning what, as disciples, we must do now in extending the narrative. Being 'a New Testament church' is not a matter of doing what the Corinthian or Thessalonian Christians did, but doing what they did in a manner appropriate to our context. This is the skill of living in time faithfully. Therefore, attempts to recreate the Thessalonian church in our context signals a lack of belief that we are not already part of the same history. Such tactics ignore the necessarily Christian (and so local) claim that 'the community from which Scripture comes and which is its immediate com-munity of interpretation is simply the same community'.[140] The same, yes, but at different periods within history.[141]

The Christian journey is not a venture back to some ideal church but forward in the hope that God will sustain our efforts to be faithful. Assumptions that a New Testament church (or indeed any other time in the church's history) got things just right signals an irresponsible evasion from time itself. To view ecclesial time as one of declension is just as unhelpful as viewing time as inevi-tably progressive. Being faithful readers of Scripture is less a matter of being faithful to putative origins and more a matter of participating and going on faithfully in the life which the Jesus of the Gospels makes possible. Here the benefits of starting in the middle become apparent: the movement of scriptural readers is from 'the narratively rendered identity of God in Jesus Christ to the identity of the church as a character in that *ongoing story*'.[142] Truth, in this approach, is free to be eschatological rather than 'archaeological'.[143]

---

139.  Hauerwas, *In Good Company*, pp. 220–21.

140.  Jenson, 'Hermeneutics and the Life of the Church', p. 104.

141.  The loss of time as shot through with possibilities of figural participation in the scriptural world is wrapped up in the social imagination of the nation-state, as Benedict Anderson, *Imagined Communities: Reflections on the Origin and Spread of Nationalism* (London: Verso, rev. edn, 2006), pp. 22–24 argues (it is no coincidence that the cover of Hauerwas' *Unleashing the Scrip-ture: Freeing the Bible from Captivity to America* has a picture of the US flag keeping Scripture closed). As moderns, we balk now at medieval representations of the nativity replete with figures in dress contemporary to the time of production and the simultaneity thus being assumed.

142.  Charles L. Campbell, *Preaching Jesus: New Directions for Homiletics in Hans Frei's Post-liberal Theology* (Grand Rapids: Eerdmans, 1997), p. 230 (emphasis added). To be sure, the God who is revealed in Jesus Christ is the God of Abraham and Isaac, as all figural readers would appreciate.

143.  John B. Thomson, *The Ecclesiology of Stanley Hauerwas: A Christian Theology of Liberation* (Ashgate New Critical Thinking in Religion, Theology, and Biblical Studies; Aldershot: Ashgate, 2003), p. 134.

That faithfulness to the story is often judged by our faithfulness to its origins, rather than its eschatological direction, is an indication that much scriptural reading in the church is still determined by something other than the continuity of the story which stretches from Israel to Jesus and the church. In historical criticism, a general hermeneutical approach that generations of preachers and clergy have been uncritically (!) taught, past and present *necessarily* remain divorced. Historical critical readings of Scripture, although they are immensely varied, have in common a 'discernment that the real world in which we ineluctably exist is not the biblical stories' world'.[144] Time sets us at a distance from the biblical world. Some historical critics even confuse their professional preoccupation – the maintenance of the distance between 'their' world and 'our' world – with the Word of God itself. To assume that we are set at a distance from Scripture is to neglect the vantage point offered by the church and the communion of the saints. It is to invest in a notion of time and history that we need not accept wholly. Readers of Scripture in the church have resources to resist the claim of historical critics that time alienates us from Scripture. Time, in an ecclesial setting, faithfully mediates and conveys the narrative of Scripture. Time, far from signalling an alienation from the scriptures, is the opportunity given by God that we might faithfully step into the narrative, participate in it and extend it.

## Conclusion

What then may we say about the location of Scripture? The company we have kept in this chapter reinforces the variety of actions and convictions in which Scripture is fittingly embedded. All the voices I have drawn from, in different ways, tell us that hermeneutics need not take the place of attention to doctrine and the church. Forsyth, for example, counsels us to attend to history as it is revealed by the gospel borne within Scripture, and to not allow immanent history to impose its principles on the gospel. Forsyth's insight – Scripture's location in the history and time of the gospel action – has been a particular preoccupation of this chapter, and one that I have sought to extend.

It needs to be recognized that recent advocates of the importance of divine agency to the theological depiction of Scripture – some of whom were cited at this chapter's head – have voiced a fair degree of suspicion about the ecclesial emphases of Hauerwas and those associated with him. According to Donald Wood, for example, much postliberal, ecclesial interpretation borrows heavily from social science categories and imposes general reflections on reading communities upon the special circumstances of the church. The fear is twofold: first, that much theological weight is resting upon foundations based in little more than ethnography and, second, that doctrine is not allowed to describe

---

144.   Hans W. Frei, *The Eclipse of Biblical Narrative: A Study in Eighteenth and Nineteenth Century Hermeneutics* (New Haven: Yale University Press, 1974), p. 227.

in any substantive way the shape and manner of Christian interpretation.[145] Certainly, I think Hauerwas is vulnerable to the charge that he is insufficiently clear how what he proposes relates to doctrine. Hauerwas' pervasive suspicion that doctrine divorced from practical witness can be an ally of privatized forms of Christianity is the inspiration behind his insistence that 'theological claims are practical from beginning to end'.[146] But more work needs to be done in setting out the interdependence of *both* Christian convictions and practices. Hence, it has been a concern of this chapter to coordinate his proposals alongside a greater doctrinal clarity. Positioning Forsyth's robust theological location of Scripture is a reminder of a vital emphasis underplayed in some ecclesial locations of Scripture: God's revelation.

The criticisms of the risks inherent to Hauerwas' and Webster's respective locations of Scripture in this chapter are of a piece with my conviction that we still need to work at eliminating competitive understandings of divine and human agency in relation to Scripture. Likewise, we should be careful not to see doctrine and the church as competitors for our attention in the location of Scripture, but rather as implicated in one another. Forsyth's and Webster's divine-action models of understanding Scripture find their complement in a people whose life and worship is orientated to God's use of the text. 'Nearly all the wisdom we possess, that is to say, true and sound wisdom, consists of two parts: the knowledge of God and of ourselves. But, while joined by many bonds, which one precedes and brings forth the other is not easy to discern'.[147] Rather than worrying about getting the order correct among Scripture, doctrine and the church, I propose that it is more helpful to see Scripture, doctrine and church as mutually informing realities. In such a vision, the movement between Scripture and the church will be more complex than a one-way relationship:

> The Bible interprets the church, and the church interprets the Bible. Again, this must be a mutual relationship. We cannot seek refuge in an ecclesiastical positivism. Finally, the last word belongs to the church, but the church must give the last word to the Bible.[148]

---

145. Donald Wood, 'The Place of Theology in Theological Hermeneutics', *IJST* 4 (2002), pp. 156–71 (164–65).

146. Hauerwas, 'Hooks: Random Thoughts By Way of a Response to Griffiths and Ochs', p. 93.

147. Calvin, *Institutes*, I.i.1, p. 35.

148. Joseph Cardinal Ratzinger, 'Biblical Interpretation in Crisis: On the Question of the Foundations and Approaches of Exegesis Today' in Richard John Neuhaus (ed.), *Biblical Interpretation in Crisis: The Ratzinger Conference on Bible and Church* (Grand Rapids: Eerdmans, 1989), pp. 1–23 (23). Cited in Gavin D'Costa, *Theology in the Public Square: Church, Academy and Nation* (Challenges in Contemporary Theology; Oxford: Blackwell, 2005), pp. 140–41. I confess that I cannot locate this citation in my copy of Ratzinger's essay.

Chapter 2

## Scripture, the Church, Ethics: Why We Need No 'and'

### Introduction: The Importance of Knowing Where to Begin

The arguments of the previous chapter continue into this chapter: when considering Scripture's role in our ethical formation and discernment (both of which can only be understood together), we have no place to begin other than the particular reading community that is the church. The decisive location for the reader who wills to participate in the movement and embodiment of the biblical text is not the academy but the church. It is worth remembering this as we turn to a representative biblical scholar's treatment of the Bible's relationship to normative ethical behaviour.

Tom Deidun's article, 'The Bible and Christian Ethics', contained within a textbook on Christian ethics, gives us some clues as to how biblical scholars often view the self-styled 'problem' of relating the biblical writings to Christian ethics.[1] (The essay's location in a textbook confirms that the impediments to reading the Bible theologically begin at an early stage.[2]) Representing the 'standpoint of biblical scholarship', Deidun's article helpfully reinforces the formative power of the biblical guild's working assumptions.[3] Deidun presumes that his role is to set out what the Bible says, before very tentatively proposing how the Bible can be 'used'. As we will see there are a great many problems with this verb 'use' in relation to a theological reading of Scripture – one of the aims of this chapter is to help disentangle our minds from the notion that Scripture is a latent or independent text waiting to be 'used' in crisis situations abstracted from thicker contexts of performance.

Implicitly adopting Krister Stendahl's influential distinction between what the Bible meant and what the Bible means,[4] Deidun works with the two-stage

---

1. Tom Deidun, 'The Bible and Christian Ethics' in Bernard Hoose (ed.), *Christian Ethics: An Introduction* (London: Continuum, 1998), pp. 3–47.

2. On a larger scale, many of Deidun's hermeneutical assumptions are replayed in the comprehensive volume of Richard Burridge, *Imitating Jesus: An Inclusive Approach to New Testament Ethics* (Grand Rapids: Eerdmans, 2007).

3. Deidun, 'Bible and Christian Ethics', p. 4. See Stephen E. Fowl and L. Gregory Jones, *Reading in Communion: Scripture and Ethics in Christian Life* (Biblical Foundations in Theology; London: SPCK, 1991), pp. 17–19.

4. Krister Stendahl, 'Biblical Theology, Contemporary' in G. A. Buttrick and others (eds), *The Interpreter's Dictionary of the Bible* (New York: Abingdon, 1962), pp. 418–32.

move of interpretation and appropriation.[5] In this model, we must first work out what the biblical authors meant, and then we must try and interpret it for our context. At work throughout Deidun's article are a host of assumptions prevalent within the guild of biblical scholarship: the biblical texts are diverse, unrelated to one another, the texts he primarily raises questions about are the 'precepts' not the narratives (what would it mean to be morally trained by Jesus' action in Gethsemane?) and what ethical pronouncements the texts provide always, he says, arise from specific contexts. Deidun implies that the Bible's diversity was only discovered by historical critics, and he asserts that the diversity of the canon throws a spanner in the works, '[f]or if canonicity renders the Bible normative, it must render all of it normative, even when elements in it stand in tension with each other or are mutually exclusive'.[6] But the Bible's diversity was recognized long before historical criticism, and no theologian that I am aware of operates with the assumption that every single text is of the same value and significance. The canon, caught up now in the animation of the resurrection, is a place where the church continually relearns what it is to say that these texts testify on Jesus' behalf (Jn 5.39).[7] The Bible's canonicity is primarily a claim about Christ's relationship to the different texts as commissioned texts, not a claim that all the texts perfectly cohere and say the same things. Contrary to Deidun's assumption that the canon is a statement about the text's *uniformity*, the church enters into relationship with these texts (and not others) as donated texts through which we may come to understand Christ. Put simply, it is clear that what historical critics understand by the canon is bound to be – and should be – different from what the church understands as the canon.[8]

Although there is a fair amount that is helpful in the appropriation section, the division of the essay skews the direction towards historicism: the assumption that origins define meaning. Theological readings of Scripture should however be nervous about being confined by historicist definitions of what the text is. Appreciating that our understanding of what the text *is* impacts upon interpretation, Dale Martin thus argues that the meant/means distinction must be disposed of, for 'students should be taught to think about what Scripture is in a Christian context *before* they are introduced to the practices of historical criticism'.[9] Given all that Deidun has said, it is not surprising that he regards the historical distance between ourselves and the text – rather than the Word of

---

5.   Deidun, 'Bible and Christian Ethics', p. 4.
6.   Deidun, 'Bible and Christian Ethics', p. 9.
7.   See O'Keefe and Reno, *Sanctified Vision*, pp. 24–44.
8.   See John Webster, '"A Great and Meritorious Act of the Church"? The Dogmatic Location of the Canon' in John Barton and Michael Wolter (eds), *Die Einheit der Schrift und die Vielfalt des Kanons/The Unity of Scripture and the Diversity of the Canon* (Berlin: Walter de Gruyter, 2003), pp. 95–126.
9.   Martin, *Pedagogy of the Bible*, p. 102.

God itself or the fact that we do not faithfully enact the Word – as the stumbling block for those who think the Bible can easily be co-opted in contemporary ethical debates. Nor, given the confidence Deidun places in the working assumptions of historicist scholarship, is it unexpected to find Deidun lending the academy a quasi-disciplinary and formative role: 'some of the most virulent forms of bigotry in our own day are promoted by people who have been formed from mother's knee on the Bible unencumbered by biblical scholarship'.[10] It is the academy, not the church, which can school us in right thinking.

Although all of Deidun's conclusions may well be legitimate from within the perspective of biblical scholarship (many biblical scholars would echo Deidun), *his working assumption is that we can talk of Scripture as 'some-thing' capable of being understood in isolation from attention to the lively reality of Christ and the community in whose life it is embedded*. It is because of where Deidun begins – within the working assumptions of a guild that isolates the text from the people who render Scripture intelligible – that the kind of 'problems' he identifies in 'using' the Bible naturally present themselves. Deidun never inquires as to *who* the reader of Scripture is and nor does he raise questions of character, thus implying that such questions of location are peripheral to the task of relating Scripture to ethical performance. But if '[a] theological reading of Scripture . . . cannot be indifferent to the manner of life leading to or resulting from a reading of Scripture' Deidun will always remain an 'eavesdropper' rather than a participant in the biblical world.[11] What if, in our concern to read Scripture *theologically*, we began somewhere different? What if we pursued the implications of Samuel Wells' statement that 'ethics presupposes context'?[12] What if, accordingly, we thought about the relationship between Scripture and ethics from within the life, worship and witness of the church? What if we saw the canon not as a medley of texts which *we* have to somehow put back together but as that which is given to us to make sense of our lives? How might the questions we think face us when attempting to 'use' Scripture in ethics be changed if we turned to the politics of the church? It is these questions that this chapter aims to explore.

Knowing that the place to begin is from within the church is a reminder that when we attempt to relate Scripture to contemporary ethics – rather than just setting out a 'historical' ethics – we are not speaking from nowhere in particular, but somewhere quite specific. Unwittingly or not, Deidun's working assumptions as to the relationship between the Bible and ethics are embedded within a set of assumptions about the nature of ethics, chiefly that one's location is dispensable. But 'ethics' is neither a context-free nor value-free term, and so

---

10. Deidun, 'Bible and Christian Ethics', p. 27.

11. Fowl, 'The New Testament, Theology, and Ethics', p. 406. Cf. Deidun, 'The Bible and Christian Ethics', p. 13.

12. Samuel Wells, *Improvisation: The Drama of Christian Ethics* (London: SPCK, 2004), p. 59.

talking of Scripture and ethics simply makes no sense apart from attention to the people of God and the kind of things such people *do* – worship God, pray, praise, seek peace, speak the truth, serve one another and pursue justice. To assert this is to follow through one of the claims made already in this book – there can be no theological reflection on Scripture without talk of Christ, church or revelation. Just as Christian ethics needs theology to be intelligible, so an ethically engaged reading of Scripture needs considerable theological and ecclesial buttressing. To reject the studied neutrality which Tom Deidun proposes (which, of course is not as 'neutral' as it may appear but is embedded within a wider social setting) is to query the assumption that ethics can come from nowhere and be dislocated from a wider argument as to the nature of the good.[13] One of the tasks of thinking theologically about Scripture – and so from within the *knowledge* generated by participation in the life of the church – is to unmask those forms of reading which seek to keep veiled their politics. This is epitomized by the historical critic who assures us that she is just telling us what the Bible meant. Stanley Hauerwas thus rightly says the issue is not 'whether the Bible should be read politically, but an issue of *which* politics should determine our reading as Christians'.[14]

Theological ethics is, like theological hermeneutics, a distinctly local enterprise. Just as a theological approach to Scripture examines what the church must distinctively say about Scripture – in a manner which no other community *need* say – so too theological ethics is distinguished by its *local concentration*. As John Howard Yoder (who we will turn to later in this chapter) writes,

> we cannot do ethics for everyone . . . Cross-bearing in the hope of resurrection, enemy-love as the reflection of God's love, forgiving as one has been forgiven, behavior change describable as expressing regeneration or sanctification, *do not make sense in the context of unbelief*.[15]

Yoder reminds us that Christian ethics does not find its true home in the chimera of a 'free' universal space which all people can share, removed from the practices of discipleship and worship. Like thinking theologically about Scripture, Christian ethicists are charged with a notably specific vocation. Stanley Hauerwas states with characteristic vigour that

> It is from the church that Christian ethics draws its ethical substance and it is to the church that Christian ethical reflection is first addressed. Christian ethics is not written for everyone, but for those people who have been formed by the God of Abraham,

---

13.   Alasdair MacIntyre, *After Virtue: A Study in Moral Theory* (London: Duckworth, 3rd edn, 2007), p. 23.

14.   Hauerwas, *Unleashing the Scripture*, p. 15 (emphasis added).

15.   Yoder, *Priestly Kingdom*, p. 110 (emphasis added).

Isaac, Jacob, and Jesus . . . Therefore the first social task of the church – the people capable of remembering and telling the story of God we find in Jesus – is to be the church and thus help the world understand itself as world.[16]

In this setting, the church is a visible performance of the Lordship of Christ, and Christian ethics simply cannot afford to begin anywhere else. The point of eliminating the 'and' from this chapter's title, which would make better grammatical sense and is the academic norm, is an invitation to cease thinking of ethics *and* Scripture *and* church, and instead to start thinking of ethics, Scripture, church as inseparable and as implicated in one another.[17] We do not move *from* one to the other, in a linear fashion, for their relationship is interwoven – with Christ, of course, as the apocalyptic presence throughout. The task of behaving ethically in a Christian sense is not a task separable from reading Scripture. But equally, we will not know how to read Scripture unless we are trained through the sustenance of 'an alternative community that tells another narrative, forms other practices, extols other virtues' from those rival stories that surround us.[18] Therefore, eliminating the 'and' in the title of the lectures is emphatically not a statement that all we need is Scripture in matters of ethics. Rather, the removal of the 'and' is a way of saying that Scripture has been misplaced when we think the biggest problem we are faced with is working out *how* Scripture and ethics relates. The biggest problem is not how to relate Paul's world (for example) to our world but whether the church has the skills to disentangle itself from the competing stories of the world and the vision to see the interplay between its attention to Scripture and its ethical performance. That the church can read in this way is the outworking of its joyful confidence that the decisive work is done in Christ making himself present and not in our attempts to leap over well-hewn ditches between the past and the present.

In this chapter, I shall first set out why Christians do not 'use' Scripture. Then I shall turn to John Howard Yoder as an exemplar of the scriptural reasoning we need, after which I shall consider what kind of people the church should expect to be in order to read Scripture faithfully.

16. Hauerwas, *Peaceable Kingdom*, p. 131. To be sure, the church occupies this prominence on the basis of what Christ has done – a doctrinal point always assumed but not sufficiently laboured by Hauerwas.

17. I was obviously influenced by Stanley Hauerwas', 'Worship, Evangelism, Ethics: On Eliminating the "And"' in *A Better Hope: Resources for a Church Confronting Capitalism, Democracy and Postmodernity* (Grand Rapids: Brazos, 2000), pp. 155–62, when writing this paragraph and coming up with my chapter title. Cf. Fowl, 'The New Testament, Theology, and Ethics'.

18. Arne Rasmusson, 'Historicizing the Historicist: Ernst Troeltsch and Recent Mennonite Theology' in Stanley Hauerwas, Chris K. Huebner, Harry J. Huebner and Mark Thiessen Nation (eds), *The Wisdom of the Cross: Essays in Honour of John Howard Yoder* (Grand Rapids: Eerdmans, 1999), pp. 213–48 (235).

## Why Christians Don't 'Use' Scripture

> Asking how ethicists should 'use' Scripture ignores the prior question of how Scripture shapes Christians and the communities to which they belong. It is communities that convey the central stories, symbols and moral convictions that shape the character of their members.[19]

Many books which attempt to relate Scripture to ethics or theology find themselves deploying the verb 'to use'.[20] All too often such method-driven discussions are abstracted from proper consideration of how the church itself is a school in which we learn to read faithfully. To ask 'how should we *use* Scripture ethically?' is to imply that readers first draw off a 'meaning' of Scripture that they can neatly 'apply' to particular contexts. This is the two-stage theory of meaning which we saw at work in Tom Deidun. But ethical behaviour only makes sense within traditions of debate and discernment, and so we can only ever talk of Scripture and ethics as they are embodied in the church through liturgy, performance and testing. There is no Scripture which Christians 'use' in detachment from the church. The use of 'use' in talking of Scripture and ethics is doubtless a reflection of assumptions relating to the notion of 'applied ethics'. (I can't help also think that this inelegant verb contains an echo of the consumptive norms of modernity. Just as Christians do not 'take' time to worship but learn to dwell within time fittingly, so too with Scripture.) In the mode of thinking which makes the 'use' of Scripture intelligible, Christians are presumed to start off where everybody else starts off – in a neutral arena which is just 'there' and which presents us with 'givens'. Because it is assumed that this is where Christians start off – rather than from within an extended argument about how to follow Christ and understand Scripture faithfully – it is presumed there is a problem when Christians then move into 'Christian' mode and seek to 'use' the Bible in one 'applied' situation after another, with the implication that our understanding of those 'situations' is not already shaped by the kind of people we have become and are becoming through participation in the church.[21]

Nor can one escape the importance of discernment and formation by appealing to the use and application of seemingly naked scriptural 'rules'. Just as ethical action is only intelligible by reference to a wider realm of divine and human action, so too rules are always embedded in more comprehensive – as supplied by say, narrative – settings.[22] (Equally, in company with Brian Brock,

---

19.   William C. Spohn, 'Scripture' in Gilbert Meilaender and William Werpehowski (eds), *The Oxford Handbook of Theological Ethics* (Oxford: Oxford University Press, 2005), pp. 93–111 (104).

20.   One of the more recent examples is J. W. Rogerson, *According to the Scriptures? The Challenge of Using the Bible in Social, Moral, and Political Questions* (London: Equinox, 2007).

21.   I am indebted to Fowl and Jones, *Reading in Communion* for many of the insights here expressed.

22.   For more on these thoughts see Alasdair MacIntyre, 'Does Applied Ethics Rest on a Mistake?', *The Monist* 67 (1984), pp. 498–513, to which his answer is (unsurprisingly) – yes.

we must say that the narrative elements of the Bible *require* the non-narrative elements.[23]) Divorced from the setting of Jesus' life, the Sermon on the Mount will be read as a set of worthy, but unattainable, ideals.[24] Christians have much to learn from recent appeals to narrative in a host of fields, but we should not trade one general hermeneutics for another. What is important is not narrative in itself but the nature of the God revealed in the narratives. We are saved by God, not by narratives. Accordingly, the 'narratability' of Christian action, which is sustained by attention to the narrative of Scripture, is dependent 'on what they [the biblical narratives] tell us about God: a certain kind of existence is possible for us *because* God is gracious, and we know God to be gracious because we have learned in these narratives who God is'.[25] With this restraint upon the excesses of narrative approaches in place, we can say that moral action is intelligible not by episodic attention to isolated acts. Christian moral action makes sense rather when situated within a wider region of *narratable* divine-human activity.[26] Churches who 'bind and loose' according to Mt. 18.15-22 are not therefore 'using' Scripture: they are *participating* in an activity which renders visible the shape of God's costly forgiveness and through which, as Jesus promised, God is also acting.[27] Attempts to universalize the commandments or precepts of Scripture in abstraction from the people whose practices render them intelligible are bound to fail. To quote Yoder again,

> we cannot do ethics for everyone . . . Cross-bearing in the hope of resurrection, enemy-love as the reflection of God's love, forgiving as one has been forgiven, behavior change describable as expressing regeneration or sanctification, *do not make sense in the context of unbelief.*[28]

Focusing on isolated rules may support the idea that the moral life is a question of one decision after another, but it does little to further our understanding of how through time Scripture sustains the moral life. Scripture's

---

MacIntyre is not against rules and laws, but rather argues they are only intelligible when housed within the more comprehensive setting provided by virtues and traditions.

23. Brian Brock, *Singing the Ethos of God: On the Place of Christian Ethics in Scripture* (Grand Rapids: Eerdmans, 2007), p. 33.

24. Vigen Guroian, *Ethics after Christendom: Toward an Ecclesial Christian Ethic* (Eugene: Wipf and Stock, 2004), p. 65, admirably ties the Beatitudes to the church – which arises out of Jesus' death and resurrection – when he writes: 'We know that it is possible to live the beatitudes because the church exists.'

25. William C. Placher, 'Paul Ricoeur and Postliberal Theology: A Conflict of Interpretations?', *Modern Theology* 4 (1987), pp. 35–52 (44). Cited in L. Gregory Jones, 'Alasdair MacIntyre on Narrative, Community, and the Moral Life', *Modern Theology* 4 (1987), pp. 53–69 (59).

26. Graham Ward, 'A Christian Act: Politics and Liturgical Practice' in Rashkover and Pecknold (eds), *Liturgy, Time, and the Politics of Redemption*, pp. 29–49 (40–41).

27. John Howard Yoder, *Body Politics: Five Practices of the Christian Community Before the Watching World* (Scottdale: Herald, 2002), p. 1.

28. Yoder, *Priestly Kingdom*, p. 110 (emphasis added).

most important role is not in resolving crisis points but in training us to respond at the right time in the right way to the situations in which we find ourselves.[29]

A further problem implicit in the use of Scripture is that such projects often end up buttressing 'values' developed independently from the church and its practices.[30] This is evident starkly in 'social gospel' readings of Jesus and the Gospels which swiftly align the Gospels with talk of redistributive justice, equality and rights. Such proposals can find themselves working with models of justice of a distinctly 'extrinsic' character,[31] that is an understanding of justice developed independently from the location of scriptural reading spoken of in the previous chapter. All attempts to relate Scripture to the Christian moral life draw upon extra-biblical resources. The risk is that this is not always recognized by the church who otherwise should scrutinize whether what the world understands as freedom 'is big enough and true enough to say everything that the name of Jesus must mean'.[32] When what Christians mean by justice is filled out only by recourse to the state's redistribution of wealth or by appeal to human rights, the risk is that Scripture is being 'mined in order to prove that Christianity is up to the challenge, that is, that it is a faith that does secular justice with the best of them'.[33] One of the many problems with this is that once

---

29. See Wells, *Improvisation*, p. 77.

30. Nicholas M. Healy, 'Practices and the New Ecclesiology: Misplaced Concreteness?', *IJST* 5 (2003), pp. 287–308, points out that the term – 'practices' – is a rather slippery term. By talking of practices, I mean to refer to a series of actions (peace-making, forgiveness of sins, truth-telling) rendered visible in the life of a people brought into being by Jesus' Lordship over those forces that would estrange us from one another – violence, sin and untruth. To engage in the practices of the church is not a project of auto-generation or creativity, but participation in Christ's new creation. To identify the truth-telling of the church as a *practice* is to locate it not in a wider model of sociality, say in a rosy optimism that societies work best when they are truthful, but in the reality of the new order brought into being by the life, death and resurrection of Jesus and the sending of the Spirit. None of this is to deny that when Christians practise hospitality, they will not act out of a series of overlapping commitments, influences and motivations (*pace* Healy, 'Practices and the New Ecclesiology', pp. 291–96). But it is to say that the Christian practice of peace-making, although there will be points of convergence with secular pacifists, looks rather different in the eschatological setting provided by the death and resurrection of Jesus. I think Healy confuses the prescriptive task of Christian ethics – saying what we should strive for – with the descriptive task – identifying the conditions in which we have to work. Needless to say, Christian ethics does not view as determinative the situation in which we find ourselves.

31. Daniel M. Bell Jr., 'Jesus, the Jews, and the Politics of God's Justice', *Ex Auditu* 22 (2006), pp. 87–112 (89). At places C. S. Song's *Jesus, the Crucified People* (Minneapolis: Fortress, 1990), aligns Jesus alongside a 'liberation' which has an extrinsic character, see for example pp. 2–6.

32. John Howard Yoder, *For the Nations: Essays Public and Evangelical* (Grand Rapids: Eerdmans, 1997), p. 121.

33. Bell, 'Jesus, the Jews, and the Politics of God's Justice', p. 90. As Bell goes on to say, 'When the reading of Scripture on justice is informed not by the politics of modernity but by the tradition and practices of the church, we see that justice is inseparable from the scriptural drama of redemption, of the renewal and restoration of the communion of all in divine love in accord with the divine creative intent . . . the call to justice is the call to be joined to Christ and so to Christ's

the community of disciples and Scripture are regarded as extrinsic to justice it is not, of course, very long until both are regarded as *unnecessary* for under-standing the nature of justice. The figure of Jesus becomes a mere cipher for a 'value' – such as peace – developed independently of scriptural reading, discernment and performance. Such a move is a form of forgetting that peace is filled out by the particular shape and form of Jesus' life and teaching, for 'he is our peace' (Eph. 2.14).[34]

Such attempts to 'use' Scripture can find themselves allies of those forms of Christian participation in 'public' society which seek to translate Christian categories of justice or peace into less particular and embarrassing categories. Scripture and liturgy are seen as instrumental to projects of justice regarded as more all-embracing and universal. But the church does not need to 'use' Scrip-ture to talk about justice. In the liturgy, the church is invited to participate in the new world of the gospel; in this setting neither Scripture nor liturgy need be left behind but both must be extended out 'so that all might be gathered in the com-munion of charity that is possible in Christ'.[35] When the church gathers in worship, it makes known that it is a *gathered* community drawn from all nations (Jn 12.32). When the gathered people greet one another – perhaps with a holy kiss (1 Cor. 16.20) – the church is making known that the peace which Jesus brings is invalidated if we do not seek reconciliation from one another (Mt. 5.23–24).[36] When the church hears the Word preached, she seeks to dwell richly in the Word of Christ (Col. 3.16). And when the church receives the Eucharist, the church is receiving that which is given 'for the life of the world' (Jn 6.51). The church does not 'use' Scripture in the liturgy – she participates in it. Scripture and church are coordinated by liturgy.[37] In this register, it is plain that anxious inquiries as to how Scripture might be used in ethical debates are a symptom of the fragmentation of our moral lives.

My argument is that Scripture need not be translated and applied to isolated dilemmas but can be seen for what it is – that which shapes the church and is

---

body, the church, whose life is just insofar as its life is centered in and ordered by Jesus who is the justice of God' (100).

34. Stanley Hauerwas and William H. Willimon, *Resident Aliens: A provocative Christian assessment of culture and ministry for people who know that something is wrong* (Nashville: Abingdon, 1989), p. 38: 'Big words like "peace" and "justice," slogans the church adopts under the presumption that, even if people do not know what "Jesus Christ is Lord" means, they will know what peace and justice means, are words awaiting content. The church really does not know what these words mean apart from the life and death of Jesus of Nazareth.'

35. Daniel M. Bell, Jr, 'Deliberating: Justice and Liberation' in Stanley Hauerwas and Samuel Wells (eds), *The Blackwell Companion to Christian Ethics* (Oxford: Blackwell, 2006), pp. 182–95 (192).

36. William T. Cavanaugh, 'Discerning: Politics and Reconciliation' in Hauerwas and Wells (eds), *Blackwell Companion to Christian Ethics*, pp. 196–208.

37. Alexander Schmemann, *The Eucharist: Sacrament of the Kingdom* (trans. Paul Kachur; Crestwood: St Vladimir's Seminary Press, 2003), p. 66, states that when Scripture is not ordered to the liturgy the result is its 'decomposition'.

embedded in a region of divine-human activity through the church's life. Whereas individualist modes of reading stoke the view that ethics is concerned with crisis points in which Scripture can be enlisted and 'used', a reading shaped by the church encourages those timeful and corporate habits which sustain faithful performance of Scripture.[38] A text which is 'used' has a merely punctiliar relationship to our lives. To rehearse the concerns expressed in the previous chapter in response to John Webster's work, such episodic accounts have difficulty locating Scripture in the length of our lives. In response to those who presume that Scripture is simply 'there' waiting to be 'used' in ethical debates, the church's timeful performance is a challenge to assumptions that ethics is about making a series of 'decisions' unrelated to one another. Stanley Hauerwas, in his reaction against 'quandary ethics' provides a reminder of a further problematic assumption in talk of 'using' Scripture in ethical deliberation. Reacting against quandary ethics as a form of thinking which poses the moral life as a series of unrelated crisis decisions that have to be made, Hauerwas is instead determined to re-describe ethics as a timeful practice where the question of 'Who am I to be?' is more decisive than the question, 'What am I to do?'. Fraught questions about what we are to do are explicable only by reference to the question of who we are. More recently, Hauerwas has proposed that the metaphor of 'journeying' is a faithful way to relate the Christian life to the Gospels. Such a metaphor allows for an element of unpredictability, but it indicates also Hauerwas' move away from the voluntaristic-sounding 'who am I to be?' towards the question, 'who are we becoming?'.[39] This is a question which a decision-based ethical approach – how should I use Scripture? – is ill-equipped to answer; in this outlook our acts are all too often removed from a wider frame of intelligibility (both in terms of who we are as moral agents and the narrative of Scripture). We might say therefore that 'use' of the Bible implies what Stanley Hauerwas and Charles Pinches call a 'trip-like morality', an assumption that our moral life is explicable only by appeal to a series of unrelated decisions we make. 'Journeying' with the Bible 'implies movement from place to place – which takes time – but also *development* over time of the one who journeys'.[40]

A text like the Sermon on the Mount needs therefore to be disentangled from mistaken convictions that its use alone can help us make 'decisions'. (John Howard Yoder, as we shall see, helps us see a far broader range in which it can be located.) As argued, when Christians think that Scripture is a resource to be 'used' in ethical debates, they tend to gravitate towards the 'rules' of the Bible.

38.   Stanley Hauerwas and Samuel Wells, 'How The Church Managed Before There was Ethics' in Hauerwas and Wells (eds), *The Blackwell Companion to Christian Ethics*, pp. 39–50 (49).

39.   Katangole, *Beyond Universal Reason*, pp. 67–68.

40.   Stanley Hauerwas and Charles Pinches, *Christians Among the Virtues: Theological Conversations with Ancient and Modern Ethics* (Notre Dame: University of Notre Dame Press, 1997), p. 18.

This focus on 'rules' betrays a reliance upon preformed ethical assumptions and warrants the insight of James Gustafson that, 'how an author uses Scripture is determined to a considerable extent by how he defines the task of Christian ethics'.[41] We should therefore be rightly suspicious of those who are unwilling to explore how what is presented as being a 'biblical' ethic might just be the reflection of prevailing norms and assumptions about the nature of ethics. But what ethics 'is' is not a 'given'. That we assume 'rules' to be the ethical axis of Scripture may well just reflect modern assumptions as to the importance of rules and laws. In modernity, where we have become resigned to the 'unsettlable' nature of the common good, and have lost sight of the teleological direction of our lives,[42] rules have come to assume a necessarily important place. A reading of Scripture which is alert to the danger of 'using' it will thus be keen to place the precepts of the text within the wider narrative setting that lend them their intelligibility. Those who assume that being 'biblical' means following the rules set out in Scripture need to be reminded that such a strategy betrays that they are themselves captive to the modern pursuit of an ahistorical ethic. In the elusive question of what it is to be 'biblical', Hauerwas states that 'A "biblical ethic" will necessarily be one that portrays life as growth and development. In contrast, an emphasis on rule-determined obligations abstracted from this story makes our existence appear to be only "one damn thing after another".'[43] Figural reading's insistence that events narrated in the Bible are not unrelated to one another and not to be read as self-enclosed is mutually supportive of this insight.

To lend this point – that the Bible is not something we use but is a text profitably embedded within the length of our lives – some exegetical concreteness we can turn to Romans 6. In contrast to those who would see Romans as neatly splitting between eleven 'theological' chapters and five subsequent 'ethical' chapters, we can blur these categories by looking to Paul's teaching on baptism as intensely ethical. We might be tempted to think that Paul's ethics was the application of his beliefs, putting those beliefs to good 'use' if you like.

41. James M. Gustafson, 'The Place of Scripture in Christian Ethics: A Methodological Study' in Charles E. Curran and Richard A. McCormick (eds), *Readings in Moral Theology No. 4: The Use of the Bible in Moral Theology* (New York: Paulist, 1984), pp. 151–77 (152).

42. MacIntyre, *After Virtue*, pp. 118–19. The intention of the opening chapter of this book was precisely to locate Scripture within its appropriate teleological setting, a setting which also lends Christian ethics its intelligibility. So, Joseph Ratzinger counsels that the scriptural texts must be looked at 'in light of the total movement of history and in light of history's central event, Jesus Christ' (Ratzinger, 'Biblical Interpretation in Crisis', p. 20). To be candid, Ratzinger counsels that the church's reading of Scripture's needs to combine *both* this teleological principle and the historical principle of examining the texts in their original context. In the light of my argument in Chapter 1, I am much more circumspect about the contribution and authority of historical criticism, and would see the 'teleological' and the 'mechanical' principle as necessarily asymmetrical in relationship.

43. Hauerwas, *Peaceable Kingdom*, p. 24.

But what we see in Romans 6 is that Paul's 'ethics' are embedded already in his 'beliefs'.[44] Accordingly, Paul's preoccupation here is not what we should do, but with setting out who Christians are by pointing to the world in which they have been placed. Paul presents a participative account of the Christian life in the narrative of Jesus. Accordingly, Jesus' life, death and resurrection provides the narrative setting for understanding the Christian life:

> Do you not know that all of us who have been baptized into Christ Jesus were baptized into his death? Therefore we have been buried with him by baptism into death, so that, just as Christ was raised from the dead by the glory of the Father, so we too might walk in newness of life. (Rom. 6.3–4)

Other examples of where Paul appreciates that the story of Christ is already ethical could be cited, not least Phil. 2.5–11, verses that cannot be separated from the wider context of the whole letter.[45] This location of the Christian's life in the larger narrative provided by Jesus' life is surely a reinforcement of Alasdair MacIntyre's injunction that the question "'What am I to do?'" can only be answered by turning first to the question, "'Of what story or stories do I find myself a part?'".[46] More harrying than the question of how we are to 'use' the Bible is therefore the question, 'How am I to participate in the biblical world?'.

Once again, here is the importance of our insistent reminder about the inseparability of Scripture and the church. Talk of 'using' the Bible in ethical debates is the residue of Enlightenment-based models of morality which impede the church's necessary ministry of reorientating our desires. The church is the school where we learn to be part of God's story and are weaned off the notion that we are to be masters of a story of our own devising. The order of the relationship implicit in talk of 'using' the Bible is a reminder that all too often 'to use is to manipulate for one's own satisfactions. It is an act of domination'.[47] This was something that Karl Barth realized, who presents a variant attack on the use of Scripture and the disjuncture between theory and practice in which it is often implicated:

> When we assimilate something . . . [w]e utilise it in accordance with what we are and what we are not, with what we like and what we do not like. The Word of God, however, cannot be used along these lines . . . If the Church is the assembly of those who hear the Word of God, in the last resort this necessarily means the assembly of those who make use of it. But this, too, can mean only the assembly of those who are ready and willing that the Word of God on its part should make use of them . . . instead of our

---

44. Stanley Hauerwas, 'The Need for an Ending', *The Modern Churchman* 28 (1986), pp. 3–7 (5).
45. David G. Horrell, *Solidarity and Difference: A Contemporary Reading of Paul's Ethics* (London: T&T Clark International, 2005), pp. 206–14.
46. MacIntyre, *After Virtue*, p. 216.
47. Ward, 'A Christian Act: Politics and Liturgical Practice', p. 44.

making use of Scripture at every stage, it is Scripture itself which uses us – the *usus scripturae* in which *scriptura* is not object but subject, and the hearer and reader is not subject but object.[48]

The Bible isn't a book of rules seeking application – it is the book of the church. Nor is it a text which, independent of its interpretation, has a meaning we can 'use'. The Bible isn't a divine problem-solver. Far more decisively, as the providential strains of figural reading reinforce, Scripture is a text used by God. By participating in the life and liturgy of the church, the people of God hope that Scripture will make use of them. In thesis form, we can therefore make the following claim: *The problem with 'using' Scripture is that it bolsters a view of the text as a resource the reader can plunder when faced with ethical quandaries, rather than a text that is sustained only by its relationship to Christ and its life within the church. The reader – the moral agent – of Scripture is to be understood by reference to her relationship with Christ and her location within the church. This is who the reader is. Scripture is not something we can use, and so isolate, apart from its relationship to Christ and its location within the church. The text as Scripture is 'caught up', webbed, within this particular, non-negotiable life and setting.*

## On Reasoning with Scripture – The Witness of John Howard Yoder

We quite simply need exemplars to help us stop 'using' Scripture in Christian ethical discussions. We need people who have lived with Scripture and allowed it to infiltrate their thinking and reasoning. One such resource is the work of the Mennonite theologian and ethicist, John Howard Yoder (1927–1997). To understand John Howard Yoder's reading of Scripture is to know that there can be no talk of him 'using' Scripture, for in line with one of the main arguments of this book Yoder's reading of Scripture cannot wander far from his understanding of the nature of Scripture itself, Christ and the church. Yoder can't *use* Scripture to argue for pacifism because pacifism is not a position one can understand in isolation from the community in which scriptural reading is embedded, the church, nor is it a stance that makes sense apart from the one to whom Scripture is directed, Jesus. That Yoder does not 'use' Scripture is no doubt because he understood that there is no 'scratch' from which we can start in any debate or conversation. With Yoder, we must recognize that in our scriptural reading and reasoning we are always entering 'midstream'.[49]

---

48.   Karl Barth, *Church Dogmatics* I/2 (trans. G. T. Thomson and Harold Knight; London: T&T Clark International, 2004), pp. 737–38.

49.   John Howard Yoder, 'Against the Death Penalty' in H. Wayne House and John Howard Yoder, *The Death Penalty Debate: Two Opposing Views of Capital Punishment* (Dallas: Word, 1991), pp. 105–79 (107–08).

In this part of the chapter, I intend to trace how, with Yoder's help, we can see that a 'peace-making' (Mt. 5.9) church – which is about much more than not taking up arms – is inseparable from scriptural reading and performance. Scriptural reading and discipleship are, for Yoder, mutually informing practices. To attend to Yoder as a scriptural reasoner is to pay close attention to the interplay among the practices Yoder espouses, his scriptural reading and his theological convictions.

It is not uncommon to encounter high praise for Yoder's reading of Scripture. Duncan Forrester acclaims it as 'often fresh, imaginative, and penetrating', whilst Stanley Hauerwas writes ruefully that he wishes he 'could be as competent a scriptural reasoner as Yoder was'.[50] Although many theologians and ethicists can exert relatively little labour on the actual reading of Scripture and its claims, the same cannot be said of Yoder, onetime Professor of Theology at Notre Dame and committed pacifist. Aside from his justly influential *Politics of Jesus*, published in 1972 and lightly augmented in 1994, Yoder's considerable body of work evinces a constant, thorough attention both to Scripture and the reality of God's rule it seeks to make known.

Put simply and boldly, Yoder reads Scripture as the story of the people of God, determined that the realism of this story should enjoy a more decisive status than the realism with which Christians are urged to view their place in and responsibilities to the world. To be 'realistic' is to see how Scripture makes known the grain of the universe, how the world works. As a Christian theologian and ethicist, Yoder has no hesitation in thinking *through* and *with* Scripture, trusting in the continuity between the people of Scripture and the people of God today. Across both the Old and New Testaments, the people of God are identified as a people 'not in charge'.[51] Yoder implores that we should not see our minority status as a nasty turn of history but precisely how God would have it. So, the Old Testament recounts a people who place their trust in God. The Genesis story of Babel is read as a reminder that God is not against diversity or community-dependent language, but rather the descent into babble – the denial that one can talk across these communities. Jeremiah, an important diaspora voice for Yoder, speaks of seeking the welfare of the city in which exiles find themselves (Jer. 29.7). Such diasporic existence, which recognizes that it is for the people of God not to be in control but rather to rely upon the grace of God, remains a much more important insight than do well worn

---

50. Duncan B. Forrester, 'John Howard Yoder (1927-1997)' in John Witte Jr and Frank S. Alexander (eds), *The Teachings of Modern Christianity on Law, Politics and Human Nature*, Vol. 2 (2 vols; New York: Columbia University Press, 2006), pp. 481–500 (482); Stanley Hauerwas, 'Foreword' in Craig A. Carter, *The Politics of the Cross: The Theology and Social Ethics of John Howard Yoder* (Grand Rapids: Brazos, 2001), pp. 9–11 (10).

51. Yoder, 'On Not Being in Charge'.

emancipatory readings of the exodus.[52] Paul, armed with a gospel that he takes to the Gentiles, reveals the importance of cross-cultural communication. Yoder reminds us that the most cited Old Testament verse in the New Testament is Ps. 110.1, 'The Lord says to my lord: "Sit at my right hand, till I make your enemies your footstool"', and on this basis advances that the New Testament points to Christ's reign over the powers and principalities of the world (Phil. 2.10; Col. 2.15).[53] The New Testament reveals not just Christ's rule but also how Christians are to live as servants in the world as those who know that the cross is the key to history. Therefore, both the Old Testament (including the 'holy wars', which Yoder reads as an instance of Israel's trust in God) and the New Testament speak of a people 'not in charge', a disposition and outlook on the world central to Yoder's pacifism and his analysis of those ways of thinking which have persuaded Christians to believe participation in war to be 'responsible'. Christians are free from having to guide and direct history down the right track, for their lives are already orientated to the one decisive reality of history. Far from Scripture being a decorative addition to Yoder's work, far from piously nodding at texts he feels he ought to include, Scripture therefore plays a constitutive role for how and what Yoder thinks as a disciple who sings of 'the Resurrection of the slain Lamb'.[54]

It should be said that we would be disappointed if we turned to Yoder looking for extensive and elaborate doctrines of Scripture. I suspect that Yoder would be impatient with some of the theological clarity attempted in the first chapter of this book. Yoder does not rush to offer an a priori theory of the biblical text or of biblical authority, and he frequently expresses exasperation at evangelical approaches which variously reduced Scripture to a dull set of propositions, were distracted by issues like textual infallibility, or supposed that the meaning of Scripture was perspicuous. There is, Yoder wryly notes, a tendency for those with high views of the biblical text to have a low view of what they can learn from rereading the text.[55] The Bible for Yoder is important for the function it

---

52. John Howard Yoder, '"See How They Go with Their Face to the Sun"' in *For the Nations*, pp. 51–78; John Howard Yoder, 'Exodus and Exile: The Two Faces of Liberation' in Curran and McCormick (eds), *Readings in Moral Theology No. 4*, pp. 337–53. This involvement in the context in which Christians find themselves should tell us that there is nothing 'sectarian' about Yoder's reading of Scripture. What is more important, rather, is the *non-territorial* and vulnerable aspect of a diasporic church. See Bell, 'Jesus, the Jews, and the Politics of God's Justice', pp. 101–02, and Chris K. Huebner, *A Precarious Peace: Yoderian Explorations on Theology, Knowledge, and Identity* (Polyglossia: Radical Reformation Theologies; Waterloo: Herald, 2006), pp. 125–26.

53. John Howard Yoder, *Discipleship as Political Responsibility* (trans. Timothy J. Geddert; Scottdale: Herald, 2003), p. 19.

54. John Howard Yoder, 'Armaments and Eschatology', *SCE* 1 (1988), pp. 43–61 (58).

55. John Howard Yoder, *Christian Attitudes to War, Peace, and Revolution: A Companion to Bainton* (Elkhart: Co-Op Bookstore, 1983), p. 425.

has in churches of discernment and performance, not for its presumed textual properties. Yoder's motivations here are a combination of his well-advertised suspicion of methodology, a corresponding wariness of overwrought hermeneutical models and a misgiving that talk of hermeneutics often marks little more than the evasion of actually following Jesus in his ways of non-violence. 'The real issue is not whether Jesus can make sense in a world far from Galilee, but whether – when he meets us in our world, as he does in fact – we want to follow him.'[56] When one is rooted in a community that reads the canon as authoritative, it simply isn't helpful, in Yoder's terms, to reflect on *why* Scripture has authority.[57] Form must follow function, or as Yoder directly says, '[t]he life of the community is prior to all methodological distillations'.[58] Rather than worrying about what ethical lessons he gets *from* Scripture or fretting about the ethical models we (appropriately or not) bring *to* Scripture, Yoder's mode of reading is therefore self-confessedly modest and particular in scope, simply 'taking the texts as they stand, for what they seem to want to say, about the shape of the shared life of the first Christians, holding to a necessary minimum the concern any academic has with getting the preliminaries right'.[59]

Neither establishing with what principles to begin nor imposing an interpretative grid upon the texts, Yoder prioritizes 'the confession of rootedness in historical community'.[60] Within this setting Scripture has a specific ministry of helping the church to ascertain whether its life is faithful to its original commission.[61] Scripture is thus replete with resources for 'critique and renewal' and the primary gap between it and us is one of moral performance.[62] Yoder's positioning of Scripture as a text of remembrance, a text reminding the church constantly that we do not do what it says, is the closest he comes to offering what we might call an ontology of Scripture. This text, transmitting the church's collective memory, reaches 'back again to the origins', an event which has the capacity to reshape and guide the church's journeying.[63] Reaching back to

---

56. Yoder, *Priestly Kingdom*, p. 62.

57. John Howard Yoder, *To Hear the Word* (Eugene: Wipf and Stock, 2001), p. 77.

58. John Howard Yoder, 'Walk and Word: The Alternatives to Methodologism' in Stanley Hauerwas, Nancey Murphy and Mark Nation (eds), *Theology Without Foundations: Religious Practice and the Future of Theological Truth* (Nashville: Abingdon, 1994), pp. 77–90 (82).

59. Yoder, *Body Politics*, p. 11. In line with his hermeneutical wariness Yoder also resisted investing in any one ethical model, recognizing that the complexity of the moral life cannot be served by attention to one model alone. See Yoder, 'Walk and Word', p. 81.

60. Yoder, *Priestly Kingdom*, p. 7.

61. With this ministry in mind, Yoder often expresses appreciation for Krister Stendahl's distinction between what the Bible 'meant' and what it 'means', an upbraiding reminder that what the church thinks Scripture presently means may not accord with the text's original intent. It is not so clear to me that he needs to rely upon Stendahl's distinctions if, as he insists, the meaning of Scripture is mediated ecclesiastically. See Yoder, *Priestly Kingdom*, p. 117.

62. Yoder, *Body Politics*, p. 59.

63. Yoder, *Priestly Kingdom*, p. 70.

biblical texts is a reaching back to the foundational event that is Jesus' life and ministry. Describing reading as a 'looping back' to this foundational event reinforces that tradition and the church's reading of Scripture cannot be understood as a constant and assured growth like a tree, but rather is 'like a vine: a story of constant interruption of organic growth in favour of a pruning and a new chance for roots'.[64] In the original vision of the Anabaptists this is not, Yoder quickly emphasizes, a naïve primitivism. It is not a return to 'GO', as if we could flee from our historicity.[65] In correspondence with the thoughts articulated towards the end of Chapter 1 of this book, the movement for Yoder is not ultimately back, but forward in the light of the church's foundational narrative.[66] In this sense, Scripture 'is the collective scribal memory, the store *par excellence* of treasures old and new',[67] and the theologian's job is simply to point to new treasures which might be heard afresh in our present context (cf. Mt. 13.52).

Resisting reading the New Testament as an ethical textbook replete with isolable precepts or 'undiscussible divine commands',[68] Yoder's attention remains fixed not on Jesus' 'words without the work nor the work without the words'.[69] The New Testament shapes Christian moral action not first because we follow its various imperatives but because we heed its 'proclamation of a new social possibility of the human story'.[70] Accordingly, the burden of Yoder's attention to Jesus in *The Politics of Jesus* falls not on his teaching, but on the shape and form of Jesus' life. It is striking that Mt. 5.39 ('If anyone strikes you on the right cheek, turn the other also') is not cited once throughout *The Politics of Jesus*. Anxious to be seen as a follower of Jesus rather than of a rule, Yoder emphasizes that it is Jesus' life – as it reveals the character of God and the cosmos under God's rule – which fills in and gives structure to the Sermon on the Mount.[71] Jesus' life encloses the Sermon within 'the good news of the new world that is on the way in the power of the God who forgives and restores'.[72] One way of understanding this is to realize that bids to 'Christianise' society by applying precepts which we imagine to be universally accessible is a form

64. Yoder, *Priestly Kingdom*, p. 69.

65. Yoder, *Jewish-Christian Schism*, p. 138.

66. John Howard Yoder, 'The Hermeneutics of the Anabaptists', *The Mennonite Quarterly Review* 41 (1967), pp. 291–308 (302).

67. Yoder, *Priestly Kingdom*, p. 31.

68. Yoder, 'Walk and Word', p. 88.

69. Yoder, *Royal Priesthood*, p. 133.

70. John Howard Yoder, 'The Prophetic Task of Pastoral Ministry: The Gospels' in Earl E. Shelp and Ronald H. Sutherland (eds), *The Pastor as Prophet* (New York: Pilgrim, 1985), pp. 78–98 (84).

71. See also John Howard Yoder, 'The Political Axioms of the Sermon on the Mount' in *The Original Revolution*, pp. 34–51.

72. John Howard Yoder, 'Jesus – A Model of Radical Political Action' in David Neville and Philip Matthews (eds), *Faith and Freedom: Christian Ethics in a Pluralist Culture* (Hindmarsh: Australian Theological Forum, 2003), pp. 163–69 (164).

of forgetting that biblical precepts are intelligible only by attending to the shape and pattern of Jesus' life and the people which this particular life makes possible – the church. Looking to the Bible as a series of naked precepts risks that Puritanical model where rules are imposed on society 'independent of the faith of the persons called to respect them'.[73] Yoder's attention remains on 'the thickness of the narrative of the Gospel as a new social style'.[74] Put simply, pacifism is less a conformity to a series of precepts and more a responsive conformity to the form of Jesus' own non-violent life now lived out by the church.

Clearing some of the obstructions that lie in the way of our performance of the gospel story, Yoder identifies the heresy of Constantinianism. As *symbolized* by the conversion of Constantine, this is a mode of thinking which confuses the work of the nation with the work of the church, the inevitable result being the dilution of discipleship. Responsibility is *determined* by responsibility to the nation, not to the gospel and God's rule. The misstep, as Yoder sees it, is when the question of what Christians should do becomes conflated with the question of what the whole society should do.[75] This is the mode of thinking which displaces the realism of the scriptural story (a God who wills his followers to be not in control and who rules through the cross) with the supposed more determinative realities of the situations with which we are faced. Disciples do not need to answer the question, 'What would happen if everybody was a pacifist?', because discipleship is only intelligible from within the thickness of a people whose practices embody their belief that Christ is truly Lord. Disciples make known that history is not decisively conveyed by nations and empires but by peaceable people witnessing to the cross and its dismantling of violence. The way of thinking which Yoder identified by the name of 'Constantinianism' dulls our imaginations to the *intensification* at the heart of the Sermon on the Mount, an ethic which tells us to love our enemies and pray for those who persecute us for 'if you greet only your brothers and sisters what more are you doing than others?' (Mt. 5.47). Ethical stances that presume to be responsible for nation states determine our enemies by the flags they were born under.[76] By bidding us to love our enemies, Jesus prevents us from thinking that killing our enemy is a form of loving our neighbour.

Yoder's theology is a powerful reminder that something has gone awry if, when speaking of Christ, our attention is not directed towards the *human* Jesus of the Gospels. Equally, Yoder insists that Christology is inseparable from

---

73.   Yoder, 'Against the Death Penalty', p. 141.

74.   John Howard Yoder, 'War as a Moral Problem in the Early Church: The Historian's Hermeneutical Assumptions' in Harvey L. Dyck (ed.), *The Pacifist Impulse in Historical Perspective* (Toronto: University of Toronto Press, 1996), pp. 90–110 (95).

75.   See Yoder, *Priestly Kingdom*, pp. 135–47, and Yoder, *Original Revolution*, pp. 52–84.

76.   Yoder, *Original Revolution*, p. 41; John Howard Yoder, *He Came Preaching Peace* (Scottdale: Herald, 1985), p. 20.

discipleship, the Christian life. Yoder therefore refrains from reading the Gospel narratives as a series of metaphysical riddles. Indeed, as suggested above, Yoder would regard those who only read Scripture 'as validation for the corpus of orthodox dogma that claims to be its marrow' as misdirecting their energy and ignoring the corrective function of Scripture.[77] In *The Politics of Jesus*, Yoder reads the Bible in line with this corrective function by recovering the significance of the human Jesus of the Gospels (especially Luke) for social ethics. This, Yoder says, makes him *more*, not less, truly Chalcedonian for he is more committed to the authoritativeness and decisiveness of Jesus' humanity than is often made clear in 'orthodox' theology.[78] To be precise, it is what the human Jesus does in the course of his narratively rendered life that absorbs Yoder's interest rather than the mere incarnation, 'salvation by birth' as Yoder tartly describes this tendency. The humanity of Jesus by itself is not what saves humanity – but rather the 'encounter between God and humanity'.[79] However, as tempting as it might be to see Yoder's stated respect for Chalcedonian Christology as a mere doffing of the cap, the more pressing task is to heed Yoder's charge that it is Chalcedonian Christians as they aligned themselves with the ruling powers who ended up paying scant attention to the humanity of Jesus and the kind of life he led. Doctrine and ethics were thus separated from one another. Rendered in dogmatic terms what Yoder is reminding us is that *the same one* confessed as 'Lord' is the human Jesus of Nazareth, and it is in this context that we must pay renewed attention to what Jesus said and did.[80] Yoder's attention is firmly on *who* Jesus is and *what* he does, an attention that does not seek to detract from Jesus' divinity. As Yoder himself says,

> [t]he doctrine of the two natures of the Divine Son, enshrined in the formulae of Chalcedon, has come to be a metaphysical puzzle. Yet what these notions originally meant, and should still mean, is that God takes history so seriously that there is no more adequate definition of God's eternal purposes than in the utterly human historicity of the Jew Jesus.[81]

Yoder therefore resists reading Gospel-narrated incidents in Jesus' life such as the temptations in the wilderness, his struggle in Gethsemane or the cross as

---

77.   John Howard Yoder, *Karl Barth and the Problem of War and Other Essays on Barth* (Mark Thiessen Nation (ed.); Eugene: Cascade, 2003), p. 171.

78.   For a sympathetic account of Yoder on this question see Alain Epp Weaver, 'Missionary Christology: John Howard Yoder and the Creeds', *The Mennonite Quarterly Review* 74 (2000), pp. 423–39.

79.   John Howard Yoder, *Preface to Theology: Christology and Theological Method* (Grand Rapids: Brazos, 2002), p. 220 (both references).

80.   John Howard Yoder, 'How H. Richard Niebuhr Reasoned: A Critique of *Christ and Culture*' in *Authentic Transformation: A New Vision of Christ and Culture*, with Glen H. Staasen and D. M. Yeager (Nashville: Abingdon, 1996), pp. 31–89 (68).

81.   Yoder, 'Prophetic Task', p. 98.

foils for speculating how the divine and human natures in Christ jostle along-side one another. For Yoder, the doctrines which we use to plot the shape and saving efficacy of Jesus' life – incarnation, Jesus' sinlessness, resurrection, ascension – are filled out by attending to the historicity of Jesus.[82] The voice heard at Jesus' baptism declaring Jesus' sonship is not an ontological pro-nouncement but states clearly the commission which brands Jesus' life.[83] It is a commission which is distinctly political and will push Jesus to wrestle with exactly what kind of political action he is to embody. Throughout his life, Jesus is tempted to seize the levers of history rather than undergo the way of suffer-ing obedience to the Father. In the wilderness, Satan tempts Jesus with worldly dominion, but Jesus' resistance to the power offered him shows that the agency of the state and obedience to God cannot be merged, not even in the person of the Son.[84] In Gethsemane, Jesus is not wrestling with two wills or his fear of death, but he is tempted finally with the option of armed Zealot insurrection. However, in treading the way of the cross and resisting the opportunity to engage his enemies on their own 'terrain', Jesus ultimately denudes them of their power by placing his trust in God.[85]

Underlining themes we have seen before, Yoder insists that Phil. 2.5–11 does not primarily invite us to look at the relationship between Christ's divine and human natures. Rather than being a meditation on 'essences' and 'substances', the text points to the cross as a demonstration that Jesus is 'willing to suffer any loss or seeming defeat for the sake of obedience'.[86] The hymn is not indicating Jesus' descent from an exalted status to a humble status and then his re-ascent to the exalted status he had before. Yoder rather reads the hymn as dwelling seriously on Jesus' humanity. 'His way to be godlike was human-like.'[87] In being perfectly human, Jesus was humanity and God in perfect communion, obedient all the way to the 'concreteness' of a Roman cross where the powers were defeated.[88] Jesus did not grasp at divinity or try to wrestle free from the limitations of creatureliness, and so Jesus 'was not Lord before in the same sense that he is now Lord'.[89] In this setting, the cross is not aligned with doc-trines of propitiation but is instead 'a political alternative to both insurrection and quietism'.[90] When Jesus 'counted equality with God not a thing to be seized

82. Yoder, *Discipleship as Political Responsibility*, p. 54.

83. John Howard Yoder, *The Politics of Jesus: Vicit Agnus Noster* (Grand Rapids: Eerdmans, 1972), p. 30.

84. Yoder, *Discipleship as Political Responsibility*, p. 31.

85. Yoder, *Jewish-Christian Schism*, p. 175.

86. Yoder, *Royal Priesthood*, p. 147.

87. Yoder, *He Came Preaching Peace*, p. 91.

88. Yoder, *Politics of Jesus*, p. 162.

89. Yoder, *Preface to Theology*, p. 86.

90. Yoder, *Politics of Jesus*, p. 43. See also John Howard Yoder, 'The Way of the Peacemaker' in John A. Lapp (ed.), *Peacemakers in a Broken World* (Scottdale: Herald, 1969), pp. 111–25: 'The cross of Christ was a clear, expectable, predictable, normal result of a fact that in a world that didn't want His kind of man around He was God's kind of man, teaching God's truth and living

hold of' (Phil. 2.6, Yoder's translation), he wasn't slipping out of his divine skin but was renouncing the opportunity to direct events and move history down 'the right track' in a bid for effectiveness.[91] Christ's rule therefore breaks out of his obedience, his trust in God (itself Abrahamic in shape) and his refusal to adopt the mechanisms of the powers around him. Disciples who follow Jesus now are therefore to live similar lives which resist the lure of worldly power. Disciples have no need to rule because Christ is Lord.[92] Like Christ, they are to know what it is to be 'not in charge'. And, like the Christ of the Gospels, the faithfulness of Christians will be measured not by their effectiveness but by their patient submission.

It is usually at this point that some readers of Yoder start becoming anxious at his alleged lack of commitment to realism and ontological categories.[93] Does Yoder ensure that his account of the Christian life, reasoned in company with Scripture, is robustly located in God's eccentric action? Yoder may not often adopt the language of 'natures' in relation to Christ, but that is no indication that he is not a realist. The New Testament practices such as forgiveness and economic sharing which Yoder urges the church to embody are responses to the 'new world reality' only made possible by the life, crucifixion and resurrection of Jesus of Nazareth.[94] Discipleship is not a mere repetition of Jesus' life and is more even than a following of his example but is, in the words of one of Yoder's interpreters, 'a kind of sacramental or liturgical repetition in the very body of Christ himself'.[95] Significant here is Yoder's insistence that 2 Cor. 5.17 is not to be translated, 'If anyone is in Christ there is a whole new creature', but 'If anyone is in Christ there is *a whole new world*'.[96] Jesus' acceptance of his death on a Roman cross was more than just resigned submission, and it certainly was not an instance of misfortune. It was nothing less than 'an ontological decision, dictated by a truer picture of what the world really is'.[97] This is why discipleship is more then than merely imitation of an inspiring teacher – disciples of Jesus are working with 'the grain of the universe'.[98] Yoder is quite emphatic that the early Christians' confession of Jesus Christ as 'Lord' is a statement that is about nothing less than 'the cosmos, the way the world really is'.[99] Indeed, he even says that the confession of Jesus' Lordship is not so much

---

God's kind of life right in the middle of a society that could not stand for it. That's why He was put to death' (120).

91.  Yoder, *Politics of Jesus*, p. 242.
92.  Yoder, *Original Revolution*, p. 119.
93.  For example, A. James Reimer, 'Theological Orthodoxy and Jewish Christianity: A Personal Tribute to John Howard Yoder' in *The Wisdom of the Cross*, pp. 430–49.
94.  Yoder, *Jewish-Christian Schism*, p. 72.
95.  Huebner, *Precarious Peace*, p. 62.
96.  Yoder, *To Hear the Word*, pp. 9–27.
97.  Yoder, 'The Prophetic Task', p. 91.
98.  Yoder, 'Armaments and Eschatology', p. 58.
99.  Yoder, *Royal Priesthood*, p. 131.

a statement about Jesus' *person* as it is about the cosmos.[100] Pacifism is action grounded in the truth of the world, definitively unveiled in the life of Jesus, a Jew from Nazareth. And about the status of this person, Yoder is emphatic that, '[i]f Jesus Christ was not who historic Christianity confesses he was, *the revelation in life of a real man of the character of God himself*, then this one argument for pacifism collapses'.[101]

The cosmic understanding of Jesus' work is to a large extent resourced by Yoder's attention to the New Testament's apocalyptic literature. Yoder resists reductionist accounts which seek to locate apocalyptic texts psychologically as a response to a persecuted or marginalized status. Nor, of course, does Yoder read apocalyptic literature as a neat timetable for future events. Far better to read Revelation in line with its liturgical intentions:

> The biblical seers were not compensating for desperation – at least they did not say they were. They said they were engaging in doxology, restating in a new setting their proclamation of the resurrection. They were testifying that the powers of oppression were swallowed up in God's larger story, whereas our modern explanations try to do it the other way 'round, by subsuming God talk in our own visions of human dignity and therapy.[102]

This identification of Revelation as liturgical literature can helpfully be linked to Yoder's affirmation that worship cultivates a counter-view of what history is.[103] Singing the hymns in Revelation were, for the community that first sang them, a form of 'performative proclamation. It redefines the cosmos in a way prerequisite to the moral independence which it takes to speak truth to power and to persevere in living against the stream when no reward is in sight'.[104] Again, the biblical theme of patient acceptance of not being in charge emerges.

The apocalyptic worldview knows that the cross holds the key to the movement of history, not worldly rulers (elected or otherwise). Whilst people in positions of power justify violent actions by pointing to the results that will follow, apocalyptic people although powerless in worldly terms know that time is held sway by the cross and empty tomb. The chief value of apocalyptic literature for Yoder is that it launches an assault against dominant strains of ethical thinking which reason consequentially. In contrast to those who reason with the aid of apocalyptic literature, consequentialists assume that the result of our actions can be known. Moreover, consequentialists also often adopt the

---

100. John Howard Yoder, 'The Anabaptist Shape of Liberation' in Harry Loewen (ed.), *Why I am a Mennonite: Essays in Mennonite Identity* (Kitchener: Herald, 1988), pp. 338–48 (348).

101. Yoder, *Politics of Jesus*, p. 237.

102. John Howard Yoder, 'Ethics and Eschatology', *Ex Auditu* 6 (1990), pp. 119–28 (123).

103. Yoder, *Priestly Kingdom*, p. 43.

104. Yoder, 'Armaments and Eschatology', p. 53.

stance of those in power.[105] This is certainly not, as we have seen, the shape of Jesus' life of obedience. Like Jesus, disciples have an obedient faith that trusts in God for results. Moreover, apocalyptic people who know that the church is to mediate the truth of the Lamb that was slain are aware that '[n]onresistance is right, in the deepest sense, not because it works, but because it anticipates the triumph of the Lamb that was slain'.[106] Consequential reasoning, Yoder charges, therefore works against the grain of Scripture (and so of the cosmos). To justify violence in the name of some hoped for peace 'is to connect project and hope backwards'. Scripture rather connects project and hope in such a way that we do not justify present action on the basis of presumed consequences. Christian activity is *already* located within 'the nature of that end that we confess has been initiated in the Incarnation, Crucifixion, Resurrection, and Ascension of Jesus'.[107] Once again we see the strong realist tone to Yoder's work. It is a realism borne from attention to Scripture. People who allow their minds to be irrigated by the apocalyptic texts of Scripture are freed from having to ask such Constantinian questions as, 'What would happen if everybody did this?', knowing that history is firmly in the hands of the slain lamb. 'Worthy is the Lamb that was slaughtered to receive power and wealth and wisdom and might and honor and glory and blessing!'(Rev. 5.12)

We have seen that for Yoder peaceableness is the conformity of our lives to the nature of God. The Sermon on the Mount is to be followed not as a bold set of precepts but because Christians are people formed by a peaceable God and the practices of reconciling truth-telling. Pacifist discipleship is about much more than not taking up arms (although it is certainly that). It is fundamentally about imitating God who is 'by nature a reconciler, a maker of shalom'.[108] An indispensable means of imitating God and participating in the work of his Son is by living within a people of 'binding and loosing'. The church only has a peace to extend out into the world if it first exhibits peace in its own life. Yoder places great significance upon the following injunction of Mt. 18.15-18:

> If another member of the church sins against you, go and point out the fault when the two of you are alone. If the member listens to you, you have regained that one. But if you are not listened to, take one or two others with you, so that every word may be confirmed by the evidence of two or three witnesses. If the member refuses to listen to them, tell it to the church . . . Truly, I tell you, whatever you bind on earth will be bound in heaven and whatever you loose on earth will be loosed in heaven.

105. Yoder, 'Ethics and Eschatology', p. 122.

106. Yoder, *Original Revolution*, p. 61.

107. John Howard Yoder, '*The Challenge of Peace*: A Historic Peace Perspective' in Charles J. Reid Jr (ed.), *Peace in a Nuclear Age: The Bishops' Pastoral Letter in Perspective* (Washington: Catholic University of America Press, 1986), pp. 273–90 (287 – both quotes).

108. Yoder, *He Came Preaching Peace*, p. 34.

As Yoder recognizes, the church's actions of sin-naming and reconciliation represent a participation in the work of God. 'Whatever you bind on earth will be bound in heaven' (Mt. 18.18).[109] The process of sin-naming before one another is not a punitive practice but restorative, and it is carried out in the midst of a people who love and trust one another. It arises therefore not from an *imposition* of moral standards, but from the church's collective moral discernment. The text realizes that conflict is not only inevitable but 'socially useful', especially when it is allowed to expand into the way of public reconciliation.[110] The peace of the gospel therefore meets the inevitable human predilection towards conflict by offering practices of 'truth-finding and community-building'.[111] In a world of truth-evasion and violence, Christians seek not to control the world but offer only their own visible performance of truth-telling.

Reading Yoder is a form of relearning what we think is important in relating Scripture to ethics. For Yoder church and Scripture are 'fundamentally interdependent'.[112] Scripture, for Yoder, is to be read within a specific region, the people of God who live vulnerably now, and in the patient hope that the powers have been defeated. Unlike Tom Deidun, with whom this chapter started out on its way, Yoder does not fret about how to relate Scripture to ethics. More important than worrying what theory we are to bring to the text is the confession that there 'is simply no place to start thinking prior to being engaged in a tradition'.[113] Yet, Yoder's mode of scriptural reasoning, in which Scripture is integrated into his thinking, should not be seen as a form of scriptural silencing, for always Scripture is to remain a treasury with riches to interrupt us and set us refreshed on our way again.

## The Patience of God's People

It hardly needs said that in matters of ethics, the church has always disagreed and continues to disagree about the contribution and meaning of Scripture. That the unity of the church is not necessarily based on agreement is a reminder that the church is an extended argument about how to follow Christ and understand Scripture faithfully (the two being inseparable). If this is accurate then it is appropriate to ask what kind of virtues are needed to sustain such an argument. This part of the chapter therefore takes its rise from a haunting claim by Stanley Hauerwas that, '[t]he question of the moral significance of Scripture . . . turns out to be a question about what kind of community the church must be to be able to make the narratives of scripture central for

---

109.   Yoder, *Body Politics*, p. 3.
110.   Yoder, *Body Politics*, p. 8.
111.   Yoder, *Body Politics*, p. 13.
112.   Huebner, *Precarious Peace*, p. 62.
113.   Hauerwas, *Better Hope*, p. 131.

its life'.[114] Specifically, I will suggest that the virtue the church needs most when it is reading Scripture – and disagreeing about its meaning – is patience.[115] One topic most recently conflicting the church is, of course, homosexuality. But rather than pose yet another argument about what Scripture does or does not say about homosexual behaviour (a debate which has occupied an inordinate amount of the church's recent energies and attention), I want instead to ask the following: what kind of people must the church be to disagree about Scripture and yet remain in communion? And, how does the virtue of patience sustain our vocation of reading Scripture? Maintaining the right order is important here. First, we must chart the theological context of patience – the world in which readers of Scripture have been placed. Then, only from within this setting, we must sketch something of the patience Christians can now embody in their reading of Scripture.

The first-steps to understanding patience are recalling why Christians are apocalyptic people, and so patient people. Apocalyptic people are patient because they trust that God in Christ has done all that needs to be done in raising Christ from the dead. We have time to disagree because time is not strictly 'ours', but is gifted to us and is that space in which we may grow together in love. An eschatological orientation to the completeness of what God has accomplished in Christ allows us to engage vulnerably with one another knowing that to attain our identity, hidden for now in Christ, 'waiting and patience are needful, that we may fulfil that which we have begun to be, and may receive that which we believe and hope for, according to God's own showing'.[116] Patient Christians resist taking an epic perspective above time and conflict, adopting instead a dramatic perspective within time. Trusting that our salvation is complete, we do not yet know precisely *how* it is complete.[117] Hoping 'for what we do not see, we wait . . . with patience' (Rom. 8.25), knowing that such patience is working now with 'the grain of the universe'.[118] Patience is there-fore, as Donald Wood notes, informed by a robust teleology.[119] Patience is a Christian virtue that is only sustained by being embedded within what God has done – and the patience he has shown – in Jesus Christ. Patience is first seen in

---

114. Hauerwas, *Community of Character*, p. 68.

115. W. Jay Wood, *Epistemology: Becoming Intellectually Virtuous* (Contours of Christian Philosophy; Downers Grove: InterVarsity Press, 1998), p. 45, describes virtues as 'dispositional properties, along with the concerns and capacities for judgment and action that constitute them . . . deeply embedded parts of character that readily dispose us to feel, to think and to act in morally appropriate ways as our changing circumstances require'. Cited in Treier, *Virtue and the Voice of God*, p. 168.

116. Cyprian, 'Treatise IX: On the Advantage of Patience', § 13, in *Ante-Nicene Fathers*, Vol. V (Alexander Roberts and James Donaldson (eds); trans. Ernest Wallis; 10 vols; Peabody: Hendrickson, 1995), pp. 484–91 (487).

117. Healy, *Church, World and the Christian Life*.

118. Yoder, 'Armaments and Eschatology', p. 58.

119. Wood, *Barth's Theology of Interpretation*, p. 7.

the shape of Jesus' life, he who lives under time, and then anchored in the world by the risen Jesus' mastery over all time. 'I am the first and the last . . . I was dead, and see, I am alive for ever and ever' (Rev. 1.17-18). As such, patience is responsive to time in the light of Christ.

Just as readers of Scripture are patient in the wake of God's revelation in Christ, so too patient reading takes its rise from a clear grasp of Scripture's commissioned ministry – its role as an instrument of Christ – in the church. There is nothing new about the church disagreeing about Scripture. Indeed, the church has always disagreed about Scripture in some way. The issue we need to relearn is rather how the church is to endure one another patiently. That we have forgotten how to do this marks our neglect of Scripture's ministry. Scripture is, as Augustine pointed out, given so that the church may grow closer to one another in communion. Fellow interpreters must not therefore vaunt their interpretation over that of other interpreters but instead seek to build up the community. Speaking specifically about the variety of interpretations that can be held in relation to the creation account in Genesis Augustine states:

> See now how stupid it is, among so large a mass of entirely correct interpretations which can be elicited from those words, rashly to assert that a particular one has the best claim to be Moses' view, and by destructive disputes to offend against charity itself, *which is the principle of everything he said in the texts we are attempting to expound*.[120]

In other words, attention to the church as a community in possession of readerly virtues can never be decoupled from attention to the ministry of Scripture – which is not to foster division, but to bind the church together as the body of Christ.

Patience allows the church to endure with one another when it disagrees, providing the habits of receptivity and vulnerability 'required to keep the debate alive'[121]. The patient person is willing to be receptive to the action of God in unexpected places and people and as such is willing to yield control.[122] Once again, rendered in the specific terms theological ethics requires, Christians are patient not because this is a virtue that flows naturally from their life together, but because 'patience is God's nature' and because God has made the

---

120. Augustine, *Confessions* XII.xxv.35 (trans. Henry Chadwick; Oxford World's Classics; Oxford: Oxford University Press, 1998), p. 265 (emphasis added). See Pamela Bright, 'St Augustine' in Justin S. Holcomb (ed.), *Christian Theologies of Scripture: A Comparative Introduction* (New York: New York University Press, 2006), pp. 39–59 (48–49) for these insights.

121. Huebner, *Precarious Peace*, p. 130.

122. See Philip D. Kenneson, *Life on the Vine: Cultivating the Fruit of the Spirit in Christian Community* (Downers Grove: InterVarsity Press, 1999), p. 109. See also Charles Mathewes, *A Theology of Public Life* (Cambridge Studies in Christian Doctrine, 17; Cambridge: Cambridge University Press, 2007), pp. 11–12.

church one (Jn 17.20-23).[123] The virtue of patience is *first* a description of who God is and how he acts.[124] Accordingly, patience is not grounded in a sentimental optimism. Rather, it is grounded in a conviction that God in Christ Jesus has done all that was needed to be done to enable us to seek to live in unity. Appropriately, Cyprian was keen to assert that patience is intelligible only as an imitation of God:

> From Him patience begins; from Him its glory and its dignity take their rise. The origin and greatness of patience proceed from God as its author. Man ought to love the thing which is dear to God; the good which the Divine Majesty loves, it commends. If God is our Lord and Father, let us imitate the patience of our Lord.[125]

Just as Christ lived patiently – living timefully as a human who lived, grew, suffered and was killed – so too Christians are required to learn how to live faithfully in time.[126] And just as Jesus suffered patiently, trusting in God, so too Christian patience is evidence that we trust 'God with the church's life itself'.[127] Patience is the name of the virtue which rises up from this trust. Scripture always has more work to do within the church, which means that an impatient reader will be a reader who thinks they have nothing to learn from rereading the text in the company of new readers.[128] The question – 'Do we as a reading community have the appropriate skills to read Scripture?' – must not crowd out the more basic question, 'What is God doing with Scripture?'. The Christian virtue of patience is therefore sustained by continued (re)learning of God's providential ordering of the world, the church and Scripture.[129] If providence

---

123. Tertullian, 'Of Patience', § 3, in *Ante-Nicene Fathers*, Vol. III (Alexander Roberts and James Donaldson (eds); trans. S. Thelwall; 10 vols; Peabody: Hendrickson, 1995), pp. 707–17 (708). Rachel Muers, 'Silence and the Patience of God', *Modern Theology* 17 (2001), pp. 85–98 (86–87), helpfully charts three movements of God in relation to time: he *gives* it so that the world may in freedom come to know him, he *endures* it in his Son and he *fixes* time within an eschatological horizon.

124. James F. Kay, *Preaching and Theology* (Preaching and Its Partners; St Louis: Chalice Press, 2007), p. 37.

125. Cyprian, 'On the Advantage of Patience', § 3, in *Ante-Nicene Fathers*, Vol. 3, p. 484.

126. Radner, *Hope Among the Fragments*, p. 120, 'the history of the Church, which is the history of the Lord writ small and long, proclaims: It is for the sake of charity that we suffer our disagreements . . . The irony of Christian patience is that it is an eternal hastening into the midst of this story, rather than one that hurries to break out of it.' For patience as a virtue learned in the footsteps of Jesus' patient submission to the Father see W. H. Vanstone, *The Stature of Waiting* (London: Darton, Longman, and Todd, 1982).

127. Radner, *Hope Among the Fragments*, p. 192.

128. Ellen F. Davis, 'The Soil That Is Scripture' in William P. Brown (ed.), *Engaging Biblical Authority: Perspectives on the Bible as Scripture* (Louisville: Westminster John Knox, 2007), pp. 36–44 (42).

129. See Charles T. Mathewes, 'Faith, Hope, and Agony: Christian Political Participation Beyond Liberalism', *Annual of the Society of Christian Ethics* 21 (2001), pp. 125–50: 'the lesson

assures us that time is shot through with the promises of God, patience is the corresponding action on our part.[130]

With the right theological attention, the receptive and vulnerable shape of patient reading is therefore placed in its appropriate setting. Only because we know that God has given us all the time we need, and only because the unity of the church is something given to us, can we say with Chris K. Huebner that patience as a practice unfolds:

> in fragments and ad hoc alliances, slowly proceeding through the hard work of an open conversation whose parameters cannot be defined prior to a concrete encounter. It seeks to hear all the relevant voices in a conversation and resists the violent tendency to silence anyone by virtue of the way the debate is constructed in advance of actual engagement . . . .In short, this theological inquiry lingers timefully and patiently, resisting the temptation to self-absolutization.[131]

In other words, the unity of the church requires us not to draw borders around what or who will be listened to. Unity is not to be found by hasty exclusion but through vulnerable encounters. As those who are willing to be vulnerable patient readers expose themselves to others who have encountered Scripture differently. Once again, it is important to be theologically specific here. Readers of Scripture are disciples responsive to the life, death and resurrection of Jesus Christ. Such disciples are peaceable people who engage in practices of attention – sin-naming, truth-telling, service to one another – and, as such, *they are formed* to be patient people in correspondence to the patience of God. Patience is something *learned* by participating in the liturgy in repeated actions like the remembrance of prayer, listening to Scripture and following the movement of the sermon.[132] In other words, just as we have seen that the Christian life (not least pacifism) is about much more than following a set of rules but is embedded in a series of practices and commitments which are mutually supportive of scriptural reading, so too the patience that accompanies Christian scriptural reading is an insistence that discipleship implicates us in 'a different way' of reading.[133] What it is to be a 'good' scriptural reader is inseparable

---

of providence is not that history can be finally solved, like a cryptogram, but that it must be endured . . . appreciation of Providence teaches one to remain humble and open to God's new thing, not to get too comfortable in any worldly dispensation, because we remain aware of the distance separating it from our ultimate home' (139).

130. Karl Barth, *Church Dogmatics* III/4 (trans. A. T. Mackay, T. H. L. Parker, H. Knight, H. A. Kennedy, and J. Marks; London: T&T Clark International, 2004), p. 517. Cited in Bader-Saye, 'Figuring Time'.

131. Huebner, *Precarious Peace*, p. 45.

132. Samuel Wells, 'How Common Worship Forms Local Character', *SCE* 15 (2002), pp. 66–74; Oliver O'Donovan, *Liturgy and Ethics* (Grove Ethical Studies; Bramcote: Grove Books, 1993), p. 8.

133. Huebner, *Precarious Peace*, p. 99. A theological focus on the practices of peaceableness (sharing the peace, celebrating the Eucharist, refusing to take up arms) rejects the artificial and

from our formation as disciples. If scriptural reading and discipleship are mutually sustaining activities, one should expect pacifism to be correlative with being patient readers of Scripture.[134] Christians are patient readers of Scripture not as an implication of what they believe, but because the very shape of their beliefs and practices forms them to be patient.[135] Those beliefs include an attention to providence, a trust in faithfulness rather than effectiveness and a knowledge that God would have us not in charge. We saw such pacifist practices in Yoder's reading of Matthew 18 – a church of peacemakers is not somehow miraculously free of conflict but is more ready to recognize and name sin as sin, to live with disagreement and to seek reconciliation. *How* the church reads is therefore a deeply political question, inseparable from watching its life together.

How then are patient readers to understand the nature of Christian unity? Certainly, this unity is both a christological and an ecclesiological imperative. 'I ask . . . that they may all be one. As you, Father, are in me and I am in you . . . so that the world may believe that you have sent me' (Jn 17.20–21). In our reading of Scripture, we are expected to fully explore the unity in which the church has been placed. Just as Yoder reminds us that peace is not the absence of conflict but the channelling of conflict towards reconciliation, so too the church's unity will not be based on lazy agreement, but fundamentally grows out of *disagreement*. A church that thinks unity is based on agreement is likely to reach a crisis point when disagreements naturally occur and is liable to split. To be in unity is therefore to know how, in the light of the gospel, to disagree. After all, working 'together when we agree is not yet the gospel'.[136] An understanding of church unity based on the peace-making practices of Matthew 18 recognizes that 'the functional meaning of church unity is not that people agree and, therefore, work together but that where they disagree they recognize the need to talk together with a view to reconciliation'.[137] There is a unity that emerges from the inevitability of disagreement, tracks down the common ground which makes communication possible and works through points of disagreement with the help of the practices of the gospel. To suppose that unity is *not* the work of the gospel but is rather the basis of our agreeing

---

imposed separation of thought from action, and sees 'in a practice a form of cooperative and meaningful human endeavor in which the two are inextricably entwined': Craig R. Dykstra and Dorothy C. Bass, 'A Theological Understanding of Christian Practices' in Miroslav Volf and Dorothy C. Bass (eds), *Practicing Theology: Beliefs and Practices in Christian Life* (Grand Rapids: Eerdmans, 2002), pp. 13–32 (21).

134. For the links between pacifism and patience see Scott Bader-Saye, *Following Jesus in a Culture of Fear* (Christian Practice of Everyday Series; Grand Rapids: Brazos, 2007), pp. 128–29.

135. Cf. Stanley Hauerwas, 'Pacifism: Some Philosophical Considerations', *Faith and Philosophy* 2 (1985), pp. 99–104 (100).

136. John Howard Yoder, 'On Christian Unity: The Way from Below', *Pro Ecclesia* 9 (2000), pp. 165–83 (177).

137. Yoder, *Royal Priesthood*, p. 292.

with one another 'is the sociological form of works religion, namely the understanding that the reality of the gospel is the product of human performance'.[138]

Difference, in this setting, is not unexamined. The church is not, Yoder is keen to insist, a mirror of the pluralism with which it is surrounded, a mode of living which is merely 'diversity without unity, variation without asking the truth question, work at cross purposes without accountable discipline'.[139] Patience is not an apathetic lurch into sheer diversity. Rather, the church's arguments about the significance of the Jesus story take place in a context of '*constrained* disagreement'.[140] The church does not need to model the undemanding pluralism of a society that lacks an eschatological orientation. Patience can, of course, become deformed. It can collapse into a form of resigned apathy, an idle hunch that all we have is our disagreement. Patience is not however about the hypostatizing of our disagreements, but about the nature and persistence of our attention to one another, and our determination to endure with one another. Patience, not arising from a resignation to interminable difference, is sustained by an eschatological hope that our disagreement is contained within a larger story which will ultimately heal our differences, that in the company of the Spirit and in the context of the church's unity there is much to learn from Christians who read differently 'even if I cannot yet see how'.[141] Patient reading of Scripture is an eschatological virtue.

Despite all this, it is important to speak of that moment when communication will cease, for 'if the notion of fidelity is not to fade into a fog where nothing is verifiable, the notion of infidelity as a real possibility must continue to be operational'.[142] As Rowan Williams reminds us, living with disagreement is not a polite way of avoiding the need to recognize when and where a decisive break in the community is required. There *are* limits to disagreement and the church must be alert to the point at which the shared language becomes too meagre to sustain collective ethical discernment. But that point cannot be reached or articulated – if it is – *before* Christians have undertaken together a long process of attentiveness to those with whom they disagree, where

> we watch to see if our partners take the same kind of *time*, sense that they are under the same kind of judgement or scrutiny, approach the issue with the same attempt to be dispossessed by the truth they are engaging with.[143]

---

138. Yoder, *Royal Priesthood*, p. 292.

139. Yoder, *Royal Priesthood*, p. 293.

140. The phrase belongs to Alasdair MacIntyre, *Three Rival Versions of Moral Enquiry: Encyclopaedia, Genealogy, and Tradition* (London: Duckworth, 1990), p. 231. It is used in the sense I am deploying it in Joel James Shuman, *The Body of Compassion: Ethics, Medicine and the Church* (Radical Traditions; Boulder: Westview Press, 1999), p. 111.

141. O'Donovan, *Church in Crisis*, p. 33.

142. Yoder, *Priestly Kingdom*, p. 67.

143. Rowan Williams, 'Making Moral Decisions' in Robin Gill (ed.), *The Cambridge Companion to Christian Ethics* (Cambridge: Cambridge University Press, 2001), pp. 3–15 (11, emphasis added).

This section began with Hauerwas' claim that '[t]he question of the moral significance of Scripture . . . turns out to be a question about what kind of community the church must be to be able to make the narratives of scripture central for its life'.[144] My response was to point to the importance of learning to be patient readers of Scripture, for patience is above all responsive to what God in Jesus Christ has completed and so sees time as it now is: caught in the hope of the resurrection. Patience therefore allows us to endure the tensiveness of Christian life together, a difficulty that comes to the fore when reading Scripture. In an account which brings together time and community, Jean Vanier ends up making an eloquent plea for the kind of patience only the gospel can provide:

> Individual growth toward love and wisdom is slow. A community's growth is even slower. Members of a community have to be great friends of time. They have to learn that many things will resolve themselves if they are given enough time. It can be a great mistake to want, in the name of clarity and truth, to push things too quickly to a resolution. Some people enjoy confrontation and highlighting divisions. This is not always healthy. It is better to be a friend of time. But clearly too, people should not pretend that problems don't exist by refusing to listen to the rumblings of discontent; they must be aware of the tensions.[145]

## Conclusion

This chapter has placed considerable emphasis on the role of the church in ethical performance and discernment. In making such an emphasis, we should remind ourselves of what was advanced in the previous chapter – appeals to the church and to divine agency should not be seen as competitors for our attention. One way to ensure that attention to the church does not degenerate into optimistic appeals for human sociality is to recall that at the centre of the church's moral discernment is the activity of the Holy Spirit.[146]

From this focus on the church emerge the arguments of this chapter: we need to quit talk of 'using' the Bible, we need to be trained to reason with Scripture and we need to know how to disagree about Scripture. Attempts to 'use' the Bible assume that the nature of 'ethics' is something stable for which the Bible can be enlisted. Ethics, as we have seen, is not some autonomous realm, but is always webbed within a series of theological commitments, recognized or not. Moreover, the argument that we do not 'use' the Bible is in effect a reminder that there is no such thing as *sola Scriptura*, a theme which I will expand in the next chapter. The solution to our divisions is less likely to

---

144. Hauerwas, *Community of Character*, p. 68.
145. Jean Vanier, *Community and Growth* (trans. Ann Shearer; London: Darton, Longman and Todd, 1979), p. 80. Cited in Shuman, *Body of Compassion*, p. 145.
146. Yoder, *Royal Priesthood*, p. 139.

be found in isolated portions of Scripture and more likely to be found in the interpretative virtue that is patience, which is a recognition of the sheer 'difficulty of belonging to the Church' and, we should say, of reasoning with Scripture.[147]

147.   Williams, *On Christian Theology*, p. 58.

## Chapter 3

## SCRIPTURE AND DOCTRINE OR, THERE'S NO SUCH THING AS *SOLA SCRIPTURA* AND IT'S A GOOD THING TOO[1]

*From his fullness we have all received, grace upon grace*

(Jn 1.16)

*The duty of every good interpreter is to contemplate not the words, but the sense of the words.*[2]

## *Introduction: The Responsibilities of Talking about Christ*

Having advanced a theological proposal in relation to how Scripture relates to ethical discernment, I turn now to examine the relationship between Scripture and doctrine. This order is a quite deliberate reminder that the treatment of ethics *after* we've sorted out our theology is only a convention, and one that has often let us forget that ethics is *already* theological.[3]

We can orientate ourselves to the task of relating doctrinal thinking to scriptural reading by posing the question: what are the responsibilities of talking about Christ? Two responsibilities would seem to immediately suggest themselves. The first responsibility of talk about Christ can be laid out with drastic simplicity: all talk of Christ is sustained first and last by its attention to the scriptural text. Such is the responsibility that I seek to rise to in this chapter. It is a responsibility I will now expand upon.

---

1.  With apologies to Stanley Fish. I am obviously mimicking his *There's No Such Thing as Free Speech, and It's a Good Thing Too* (New York: Oxford University Press, 1994).

2.  Thomas Aquinas, *S. Thomae Aquinatis Super Evangelium S. Matthaei lectura* 27, no 2321 (Raphaelis Cai (ed.); Marietti: Turin, 1951), p. 358. Cited and translated in Ratzinger, 'Biblical Interpretation in Crisis', p. 21.

3.  Note the order of McClendon's, *Systematic Theology* where Volume 1 – 'Ethics' – was placed before Volume 2 – 'Doctrine'. What we deem to be 'ethics' should stand '*at the beginning* of Christian theological reflection': Hauerwas, *Peaceable Kingdom*, p. 16 (emphasis original).

The prime responsibility of Christology is not first to be original[4] but faithfully to read the 'divine address' that is Scripture.[5] In order to fulfil this task, theology does of course need resources other than Scripture. This is to recognize with Robert Jenson that if we think *sola Scriptura* means understanding Scripture '"apart from creed, teaching office, or authoritative liturgy"' then we are resting on an 'oxymoron' (think of the obvious contradiction of the church that says it has no creed but the Bible).[6] If the first responsibility of talking about Christ is to evince an attention to Scripture, we need to be more precise about the nature of doctrine and its relationship to Scripture.

Calvin himself, to alight upon a theologian firmly associated with a *sola Scriptura* approach, was keenly aware that theology always needed to deploy extra-canonical words and resources. That we use words and concepts not found in Scripture itself – in a bid to help us understand this same text – is not a sign that we have departed from the fabric of Scripture. Writing against his opponents Calvin writes that if

> they call a foreign word one that cannot be shown to stand written syllable by syllable in Scripture, they are indeed imposing upon us an unjust law which condemns all interpretation not patched together out of the fabric of Scripture . . . [i]f anyone, then, finds fault with the novelty of the words [Calvin is talking of such words as 'Trinity' and 'Persons'] does he not deserve to be judged as bearing the light of truth unworthily, since he is finding fault with what renders the truth plain and clear.[7]

When Calvin's counsel is not heeded, *sola Scriptura* often mutates into biblical scholarship alone. Understanding the Bible in this way of thinking is wholly defined by reference to its (often putative) context of production. It is as if we are reading a text that has had no impact, a text without any subsequent readers. Writing more than 50 years ago G. E. Wright's diagnosis (not espousal) of this mindset common among 'biblical Christians' drawn to biblical scholarship is still remarkably apposite:

> When one has the Bible, what need is there for subtleties and sophistries of theology? In evangelical Christianity, the Bible is typically read with scant regard for the long and intricate dialogue with the Bible that is the history of Christian theology. Many (most?) Protestant Biblical scholars are attracted to the field in the first place by an evangelical

---

4.  It is the task of theology not first to be 'creative', but 'faithful'. Being a faithful reader of Scripture is to read it with the aim of saying something for the life of the church today. Stanley Hauerwas and William Willimon put it even more strongly: 'theology cannot help but be unfaithful if it is "creative"': 'Why *Resident Aliens* Struck a Chord' in Stanley Hauerwas, *In Good Company: The Church as Polis* (Notre Dame: University of Notre Dame Press, 1995), pp. 51–63 (53).

5.  John Webster, 'Jesus Christ' in Timothy Larsen and Daniel J. Treier (eds), *The Cambridge Companion to Evangelical Theology* (Cambridge: Cambridge University Press, 2007), pp. 51–63 (61).

6.  Jenson, *Systematic Theology*, Vol. 1, p. 28.

7.  Calvin, *Institutes*, I.xiii.3, p. 124.

piety of this kind, and – whatever else is abandoned under the notoriously destructive impact of the so-called "historical-critical method" – the abstraction of the biblical texts from their theological *Wirkungsgeschichte* is tenaciously maintained.[8]

Such endeavours help identify historical-criticism, the engine of much biblical scholarship, as the modern attempt to '"start over" in a manner that left behind the gifts of the past'.[9] Accordingly, historical criticism is notoriously restricted in *what* history it is interested in. Fundamentalism and historical criticism both presume that the church and the church's teaching is an obstacle, not an aid, to reading Scripture well.

For the purposes of this chapter talk of Christ is, determinedly, not just a matter of exegesis alone and nor is it an attempt to manoeuvre ourselves behind the text: it is a dogmatic expansion on *who* Jesus of Nazareth is in relation to the triune God and *what* the saving significance of his work is in relation to humanity and the world. But every such dogmatic expansion has the responsibility of demonstrating that it is rooted in the reading of Scripture as a text constituted by its testimony to Christ. This is to say that doctrine is not an imposition upon the texts but a leading out from the texts. Or better, it is a leading out that is always ready and able to turn back to the texts themselves. For, in regard to the Gospels, doctrine is not an improvement upon the narratives themselves, but it is only an attempt to turn our attention to the one who is spoken of. The testing ground for doctrine – talk about God dispossessed by its object of enquiry – is not the academic conference circuit but the church's reading and proclamation of Scripture. Theology, insofar as it is nourished by attention to Scripture, turns to Scripture not once, as though 'juicing an orange',[10] but again and again. The point of the orange juicing metaphor of W. T. Dickens is that the purpose of Scripture is not to lead us to doctrine as if it was there that our task was finished, but the purpose of Scripture, of which doctrine is an auxiliary, is to lead us to Christ. And in leading us to Christ our language is to be continually interrogated as to its faithfulness. So we can say also that scriptural reading becomes disordered if it is carried out as an exercise in *proving* doctrine. Doctrine and Scripture are vitally related, mutually informing, although (crucially) not the same. To say anything otherwise is to confuse our reading of the text with the text itself and so confine Scripture within our present understanding.

In the course of this chapter, I will rise to the responsibility of reading Scripture by paying particular attention to John's Gospel, keeping company with a variety of theologians to help me understand the sense of the words, or 'the

8.    G. E. Wright, *God Who Acts: Biblical Theology as Recital* (London: SCM, 1952), p. 110. Cited in Michael S. Horton, *Covenant and Eschatology: The Divine Drama* (Louisville: Westminster John Knox, 2002), p. 221.

9.    Hauerwas, *Performing the Faith*, p. 147.

10.    W. T. Dickens, 'Hans Urs von Balthasar' in Holcomb (ed.), *Christian Theologies of Scripture*, pp. 202–19 (205).

way the words go'.[11] And although the company we keep is a reminder that it is always fool-hardy to think that all we need is Scripture, the reading of John's Gospel and the cluster of resources I will draw from (Edward Irving, Karl Barth and Hans Urs von Balthasar among them) has one target in mind: that we, as readers of Scripture, may be drawn anew to the shock of the Gospels, and so to the One who speaks and acts in unbroken unity with the will of God (Jn 4.34; 5.30; 8.29; 15.10). In this regard, Robert Jenson binds the office of christological thinking to the Gospel narratives in an admirably concise manner, '[w]hat Christology is – or ought to be – about is the Jesus who appears in the Gospels, as he is in fact the Son of God as he was accused of claiming to be'.[12]

If the first responsibility of all Christology is to the scriptural witness, a duty for which doctrine is an aid, a second and further responsibility is to the main-tenance of a healthy interaction between Jesus' person and work, or to what Balthasar would understand as the creative tension between Jesus' *being* (that which he has always been) and his *becoming* (his mission).[13] What Jesus does is reciprocal with who he is and, likewise, there can be no detached considera-tion of who Jesus is without attention to the specific life he reveals and enacts. Tenaciously maintaining the interdependence between Jesus' person and work secures Jesus as both the subject and the object of his life, death and resurrec-tion.[14] On the consequences of neglecting the inseparable connection between what Jesus does and who he is, Robert Jenson states darkly that 'Philip Melanchton's maxim that to know God is to know his benefits can hold only where the identity of the God to be known is antecedently secure. In modern context, it is plainly false and has been a disaster for the church.'[15] Asking *who* Christ is involves us in equal measure attending to *what* he does for us – a lesson we can learn by patient reading of John's Gospel. *Not* asking these two

---

11.   David S. Yeago, 'The New Testament and the Nicene Dogma: A Contribution to the Recovery of Theological Exegesis', *Pro Ecclesia* 3 (1994), pp. 152–64 (161).

12.   Jenson, *Systematic Theology*, Vol. 1, p. 134. See Jn 5.18: 'For this reason the Jews were seeking all the more to kill him, because he was not only breaking the sabbath, but was also calling God his own Father, thereby making himself equal to God.'

13.   Hans Urs von Balthasar, *The Glory of the Lord: A Theological Aesthetics*, Vol. 1 (trans. Erasmo Leiva-Herikakis; 7 vols; Edinburgh: T&T Clark, 1982), pgs 469–72, 668–69 emphasizes the unique concordance that the Fourth Gospel presents between Jesus' person and his work (what Balthasar calls Jesus' 'mission'). Jesus raises Lazarus from the dead because he *is* resurrection (Jn 11.25), he heals the blind because he *is* light (Jn 8.12), he feeds people with bread because he *is* the bread of life (Jn 6.35), he cleanses his disciples by bathing their feet in water because he *is* the living water of God (Jn 4.13; 7.37). So closely does Balthasar keep together Jesus' person and work that he can say Jesus *is* his mission.

14.   This is the very strong emphasis of Bruce L. McCormack, 'The Ontological Presupposi-tions of Barth's Doctrine of Atonement' in Charles E. Hill and Frank A. James III (eds), *The Glory of the Atonement: Biblical, Historical and Practical Perspectives* (Downers Grove: InterVarsity Press, 2004), pp. 346–66.

15.   Jenson, *Systematic Theology*, Vol. 1, p. 51 n.68.

questions together risks allowing salvation to become extrinsic to the particularity of Jesus' divine-human action. Jesus comes to represent a 'value' (self-sacrifice, trust in God, patience) which he confirms and we could just as well know without the cross.[16] But to the reader of John's Gospel, it is plain that to abide in the benefits of Jesus is to be drawn into the company of the triune God (Jn 16.14–15), and so one can only know the identity of God by attending both to what Jesus does and who he is. 'He who has seen me has seen the Father' (Jn 14.9).

The nature of the two christological responsibilities outlined – to Scripture and to the integrity between Jesus' person and work – can be clarified by turning to some recent works in Christology. While there is much to learn from these works ultimately, in my opinion, they do not consistently keep their eye on the two responsibilities I have set out.

Robert Sherman's *King, Priest and Prophet: A Trinitarian Theology of Atonement* enthusiastically adopts Christ's threefold office as priest, king and prophet as a template for theological exegesis. Sherman maintains an impressive level of fidelity to the first of our stated christological responsibilities: a lively conversation is maintained throughout with the scriptural deposit. Indeed, he is as attentive to the biblical *text* as he is to Jesus' *work* as narrated by Scripture. Nevertheless, despite eloquent pleas to the contrary, Sherman's treatment of Jesus is ultimately not bound closely enough to ontological considerations of Jesus' ministry and humanity. The implication of this is that Sherman cannot demonstrate with enough persistence that Jesus' *particular* work and ministry as priest, prophet and king is salvific precisely because the work and words of Jesus Christ as priest, king and prophet are ontologically bound up with who Jesus eternally is in relation to his Father.[17] This may seem an odd claim to make given that Sherman wants to keep the work of the Son bound up within the trinitarian relations, but there is little explicit consideration of the reciprocal relationship between who Jesus eternally is in the triune relations and what Jesus reveals in his ministry as priest, king and prophet. If all Christology is reflection on eternal states of being made present, real and temporal in Jesus of Nazareth, then ontological considerations are necessary at every stage of theological thinking, and not just something to be inserted at the beginning as they are in Sherman's work. Balthasar, whose own work is committed both to Scripture and to the union between Jesus' person and work, advises those

16.  David S. Yeago, 'Crucified Also for Us under Pontius Pilate: Six Propositions on the Preaching of the Cross' in Christopher R. Seitz (ed.), *Nicene Christianity: The Future for a New Ecumenism* (Grand Rapids: Brazos, 2001), pp. 87–105 (89–91).

17.  One of the few explicit concessions that Sherman makes to ontological considerations is towards the beginning of his book where he outlines his theological underpinnings, 'we know God by what he does for us in his saving acts, and what he does reveals what he is – and this is not just "for us" or merely in our experience of him, but as he is in himself': Robert Sherman, *King, Priest and Prophet: A Trinitarian Theology of Atonement* (Theology for the Twenty-First Century; New York: T&T Clark International, 2004), p. 61; see also pgs. 160, 172 n.2, 195.

pondering the figure of Christ that attention should be fixed on the movement of the eternal into our time:

> Jesus *became* what he already was, both before the world's foundation [cf. Jn 17.5] and during his earthly ministry: this must be taken with absolute seriousness by every Christology . . . [a] dynamic Christology must not be sundered from its ontological counterpart.[18]

Sherman's relative ontological reserve may not be unrelated to his candid investment in narrative readings of Scripture, a mode of reading which in some guises *can* end up sidelining ontological considerations.[19] (Robert Jenson's *Systematic Theology*, for example, is a work that rests very heavily on the importance of the scriptural narratives but never to the exclusion of ontological questions.) Hans Frei, writing about Barth's understanding of the relationship between the Gospel narratives and the doctrine of the Incarnation, states that '[t]he meaning of the doctrine is the story; not: the meaning of the story is the doctrine'.[20] We certainly cannot understand Christ other than through narrative and, to a lesser extent, doctrine, but both the story and doctrine are derivative upon Christ. Narrative is important, but it is not sufficient. Thus Christ's work as king, priest and prophet needs to be grounded in the extra-textual labour of articulating who Christ is in the purposes of God if we are to wrestle with John's riddling claim that through the words and acts of Jesus God himself is revealed, 'the word that you hear is not mine, but is from the Father who sent me' (Jn 14.24), or, even more startlingly, '[w]hoever sees me sees him who sent me' (Jn 12.45). In Jesus of Nazareth the veil over eternity has been lifted, and in Jesus' person a radical co-presence of time and eternity is to be seen: 'Before Abraham was, I am' (Jn 8.58). The 'real' Jesus is the one who existed before the foundation of the world. A theological reading of John through the *triplex munus* tradition cannot rely on narrative alone and requires a quite specific and dogmatic attention to the person of Christ, a realization that *what* Jesus enacts and says only makes sense set alongside an equally insistent attention to *who* he is, 'the works that the Father has given me to complete, the very works that I am doing, testify on my behalf that the Father has sent me' (Jn 5.36). Indeed, the Fourth Gospel maintains a very tight identity between who Jesus is – the Son sent by his Father – and the work he has been commanded (Jn 10.18; 14.31) to complete by his Father, 'The works that I do in my Father's name testify to me . . . The Father and I are one' (Jn 10.25, 30).

---

18.   Hans Urs von Balthasar, *Mysterium Paschale: The Mystery of Easter* (trans. Aidan Nichols; Edinburgh: T&T Clark, 1990), pp. 207–08.

19.   James Fodor, 'Postliberal Theology' in David F. Ford (ed.) with Rachel Muers, *The Modern Theologians: An Introduction to Christian Theology since 1918* (Oxford: Blackwell, 3rd edn, 2005), pp. 229–48 (237–41).

20.   Hans W. Frei, *Types of Christian Theology* (George Hunsinger and William C. Placher (eds); New Haven: Yale University Press, 1992), p. 90.

One recent christological essay which *has* maintained a suitably tight relationship between Jesus' person and work, but has neglected to show how such insights must arise (in some way) from scriptural reading, is Kathryn Tanner's *Jesus, Humanity and Trinity: A Brief Systematic Theology*. Tanner presents an impressive perspective on Christ's identity, demonstrating the indissoluble union between *who* Jesus is as the second person of the Trinity made flesh and the saving effects of *what* he does. The cross, for example, is primarily saving because of who died on the cross, and who assumed our death. Shying away from forensic or penal understandings of the atonement, for Tanner it is attention to the ultimate reality of Christ's person that helps us understand the effectiveness of Christ's work. In her own words, the cross saves because 'sin and death have been assumed by the One, the Word, who cannot be conquered by them'.[21] Tanner proceeds to link her penetrating Alexandrian presentation of Christ's person to contemporary ethical, political and eschatological considerations. But in a book richly conversant with ancient and modern Christology, it is deeply frustrating that Tanner is reluctant to enter into dialogue with the very source of christological thinking: Scripture and the New Testament in particular. Such an omission would be less troubling were it not that all of the patristic writers Tanner draws inspiration from, whilst they drew upon appropriate philosophical resources of their day, bent their minds and writing to the startling reality of the scriptural revelation.[22] Writing before Tanner's book was published Francis Watson stated presciently as follows:

> The christologies of Athanasius and of Schleiermacher are not autonomous productions springing from abstract theological premises, but are shaped and permeated by their authors' reading of the biblical texts. A dialogue with such christologies that is not at the same time and explicitly a dialogue about biblical interpretation will be seriously flawed.[23]

The ultimate point of continuity between ourselves and Gregory of Nyssa or Maximus the Confessor is not that we instinctively draw upon the same conceptual or philosophical tools of dogmatic clarification – plainly we don't – but that we are reading the same scriptural deposit, and through that reading our task is to make Christ more clearly known. Christology, both then and now, is a lens cleaning exercise that we may read the Gospel narratives more clearly,

---

21. Kathryn Tanner, *Jesus, Humanity and the Trinity: A Brief Systematic Theology* (Current Issues in Theology; Edinburgh: T&T Clark, 2001), p. 29.

22. Jaroslav Pelikan, '"Council or Father or Scripture": The Concept of Authority in the Theology of Maximus the Confessor' in David Neiman and Margaret Schatkin (eds), *The Heritage of the Early Church* (Orientalia Christiana Analecta, 195; Rome: Pont. Institutum Studiorum Orientalum, 1973), pp. 277–88. See also Willie James Jennings, 'Undoing our Abandonment: Reading Scripture through the Sinlessness of Jesus', *Ex Auditu* 14 (1998), pp. 85–96 (87–88).

23. Francis Watson, 'The Scope of Hermeneutics' in Colin E. Gunton (ed.), *The Cambridge Companion to Christian Doctrine* (Cambridge: Cambridge University Press, 1997), pp. 65–80 (74).

and incumbent upon all Christology is that it roots itself in the fertile ground of Scripture. Tanner's scriptural reticence suggests that the departmental divisions of the Theology Faculty absolve the theologian of the need to attend to Scripture herself. What is lost here is not, please take note, an intramural opportunity to show how theologians may learn from biblical scholarship (or vice-versa), but a wider demonstration of how doctrine and Scripture relate one to the other. 'The task of exegesis is far too important to be devolved upon biblical technicians.'[24] Readers of Tanner's book are left in their own time to establish how what she says has anything to do with Scripture, or worse are left with the idea that the doctrine of the Incarnation could have a life of itself apart from Scripture. What Tanner therefore invites her readers to forget is that doctrine is a set of lenses with which and through which we may more clearly read Scripture.

Robert Sherman's and Kathryn Tanner's essays should not be regarded as isolated examples. Both are running along well-worn christological tracks. In advancing a narrative justification for reading the New Testament's presentation of Christ through the threefold office, Sherman keeps company with figures like George Stroup, who invests a similar optimism in the potential of narrative theology.[25] Sherman's work is also nourished to some extent by the overworked, and wholly constructed, opposition between ontological and functional modes of christological thinking. A corresponding enthusiasm for Scripture, for Jesus' threefold office, and a marked ontological reserve in relation to Christ's person is evidenced by Michael Horton's *Lord and Servant: A Covenant Christology*.[26] Frustrated by what he regards as the Apollinarian tendencies of theologians like Robert Jenson, Horton advocates the incarnation as 'the proper covenantal conversation: the Lord speaking, and the servant answering back to God's glory'.[27] In this setting, reconciliation 'is a matter of restoring the right relationships rather than overcoming conditions of ontological finitude'.[28] But we cannot, I repeat, suppose that to concentrate on Jesus' work is to remove ourselves from ontological implications: involving ourselves in questions about Jesus' work is to confront issues surrounding Jesus' identity for the two are mutually dependent. Only consideration of who Jesus is can nourish fidelity to what he does and likewise what Jesus does reveals his identity.

---

24. Webster, *Word and Church*, p. 110.
25. George W. Stroup, *Jesus Christ for Today* (Philadelphia: Westminster, 1982), pp. 88–106. Note the comments in relation to Calvin's deployment of narrative and God's covenant history in Stephen Edmondson, *Calvin's Christology* (Cambridge: Cambridge University Press, 2004), pp. 223–26. Calvin is, of course, widely regarded as the most substantial thinkers on Christ's *triplex munus*.
26. Michael S. Horton, *Lord and Servant: A Covenant Christology* (Louisville: Westminster John Knox, 2005), pp. 159–270.
27. Horton, *Lord and Servant*, p. 162.
28. Horton, *Lord and Servant*, p. 179.

[T]he words that you gave to me I have given to them . . . I came from you . . . I made your name known to them, and I will make it known, so that the love with which you have loved me may be in them, and I in them (Jn 17.8, 26)

We might suppose that Scripture can be kept separate from questions of ontology, but if the claims of John are contemplated and meditated on, it will not be long before we will be moved 'to give some account of how these things can be conceived to be'.[29] Contrary to the implications Horton risks courting Jesus' obedience is of saving value, not because it is the fruit and activity of Christ's humanity alone, nor indeed of the Word alone: rather the *subject* of Christ's obedience is the divine-human unity. We cannot therefore work through the Gospels apportioning certain activities of Jesus to his divine nature, and others to his human nature. Were we to do this, the single work of Christ as the work of a single subject would be fatally undermined.[30] It is not the Logos alone who saves us – otherwise God could have saved us by a means that was far less costly than his enfleshment in our world. Nor is it Christ's human nature that saves us – otherwise the obedience of Christ could only be of subjective and exemplary value, and not objective. At all times, what saves humanity is the divine-human person. The implication of this is that ontological considerations are inescapable for theologically engaged readers of Scripture.

Tanner's work, on the other hand, runs along the tracks of a Christology robustly confident that Chalcedonian frames of reference can speak to contemporary sensibilities and concerns. Such thinking sits very comfortably alongside, and indeed is partly inspired by, the christological vision of Thomas F. Torrance for whom 'reconciliation is not something added to hypostatic union so much as the hypostatic union itself at work in expiation and atonement'.[31] Throughout his work, Torrance maintained an inseparable relationship between Christ's person and work and so salvation is consistently a profoundly ontological event.[32] Like Tanner, however, Torrance's writing is frustratingly reticent when it comes to Scripture (although Torrance is more attentive to Israel than Tanner). Such observations could also be made for other equally robust neo-Chalcedonian thinkers. As Niall Coll notes in his study of

29.  Colin E. Gunton, *Yesterday and Today: A Study of Continuities in Christology* (London: Darton, Longman and Todd, 1983), p. 126.

30.  McCormack, 'The Ontological Presuppositions of Barth's Doctrine of the Atonement', pp. 354–55.

31.  Thomas F. Torrance, 'The Atonement and the Oneness of the Church', *SJT* 7 (1954), pp. 245–69 (247).

32.  Thomas F. Torrance, *Preaching Christ Today: The Gospel and Scientific Thinking* (Grand Rapids: Eerdmans, 1994), p. 27; *The Trinitarian Faith: The Evangelical Theology of the Ancient Catholic Church* (Edinburgh: T & T Clark, 1988), p. 158; 'Cheap and Costly Grace' in *God and Rationality* (London: Oxford University Press, 1971), pp. 56–85 (64).

twentieth-century Anglican Christologies, Eric Mascall's Christology was notably restrained exegetically.[33]

From this excursion into some recent christological trends, let us return to the twin responsibilities of christological thinking with which this chapter started. *Doctrinal talk of Christ must expose itself to the reading of Scripture and remain alert to the vital and dynamic relationship between Jesus' person and work.* Overworked and partly imagined oppositions between functional Christologies and ontological Christologies, between Christologies 'from above' or 'from below', between 'Logos Christologies' and 'Spirit Christologies', between biblical Christologies and so-called 'Hellenised' Christologies are better retired rather than put to service yet once more.[34] In line with the strains of the opening chapter, reading of Scripture attentive to the actions of which it is part will find little room for such divisions. Christology needs to be seen and practised as an engagement with the implications of the way the story goes in the Gospels, an entry into the *Sache* of the texts. There is nothing new about all this of course. Maximus the Confessor, Edward Irving and Hans Urs von Balthasar – to cite three thinkers from very different periods of history – all demonstrate Christologies undeniably responsive to the scriptural deposit and to the specific life therein narrated. A Christology attentive to the Johannine text is therefore best conceived, to deploy the felicitous phrase of Mark McIntosh, 'from within'.[35] Christology is a pursuit in manoeuvring our minds (and wills) into the sphere of our specific object of attention, nothing less than a seeking of that sense of astonishment and controversy which, throughout the Fourth Gospel, accompanies Christ's revelation.

My intention now is to sketch a Christology responsive to and grounded in reading the Fourth Gospel. It is worth setting out what I seek to do – and not do – here. This chapter is not primarily a contribution to Johannine theology, a project which might imply that understanding the author's historical intention or meaning is my preoccupation. Stephen Fowl's claim, one with which I concur, that '[a]ny attempt to tie a single stable account of meaning to authorial intention will put Christians in an awkward relationship to the OT',[36] is a reminder that all theological interpretation of Scripture is unlikely to proceed

---

33.  Niall Coll, *Christ in Eternity and Time: Modern Anglican Perspectives* (Dublin: Four Courts Press, 2001), pp. 55–90.

34.  See Nicholas Lash, 'Up and Down in Christology' in Stephen Sykes and Derek Holmes (eds), *New Studies in Theology* 1 (London: Duckworth, 1980), pp. 31–46.

35.  Mark A. McIntosh, *Christology from Within: Spirituality and the Incarnation in Hans Urs von Balthasar* (Studies in Spirituality and Theology, 3; Notre Dame: University of Notre Dame Press, 1996).

36.  Stephen E. Fowl, 'The Role of Authorial Intention in the Theological Interpretation of Scripture' in Joel B. Green and Max Turner (eds), *Between Two Horizons: Spanning New Testament Studies and Systematic Theology* (Grand Rapids: Eerdmans, 2000), pp. 71–87 (80). Fowl draws upon the earlier arguments of Stout, 'What is the Meaning of a Text?'. See the helpful discussion of Fowl's stance on authorial intention in D. Christopher Spinks, *The Bible and the Crisis*

very far if a recovered authorial intention is seen as a baseline for interpretation beyond which one cannot legitimately proceed. Not assuming responsibility for unfolding the intentions or thoughts of the Fourth's Gospel's author, this chapter is not an instance of biblical theology, insofar as that is often understood.[37] When I refer to 'John' in this chapter, I am in no sense confusing my reading of the text with what a retrieval of the author's intentions and 'meaning' might look like. Theological interpretation of Scripture has a host of authorities to which it must attend – the way the words go, their wider canonical context, Scripture's location in the purposes of God and the life of the church – all quite distinct from a putative, reconstructed authorial intention.[38] Correspondingly, it is necessary to think through and with those theological resources that act as an 'interpretive tool, a guide to grasping the force and implications of the gospel story'.[39] In this register, I am free from worrying whether my account in this chapter is 'anachronistic' (a charge betraying a host of assumptions about time of which theological interpretation should be wary) because the aim of this chapter is to follow the forward momentum of the text, using doctrine as an aid to releasing the text's pressure (an image picked up from Forsyth). We might say therefore that how far we find doctrine to be a fitting exegesis of Scripture is determined by the extent to which we have allowed Scripture to press in on us.[40] Or, to deploy the insight of Paul Ricoeur, in reading John it is my intention 'to follow its movement from sense to reference: from what it says, to what it talks about'.[41] Scripture is ostensive – it refers to Christ. Reading Scripture theologically is to read Scripture attentive to this 'ever-greater' dimension of its referent (Jn 1.50; 4.11f; 5.20, 36; 8.53; 14.12, 28) and so to read Scripture seized of Jesus' promise that the Spirit will guide us 'into all the truth' (Jn 16.13).[42] In this chapter, I clearly say *more* than the author of the Fourth Gospel says, although I hope not to say more than is warranted by the pressure of the text.

---

*of Meaning: Debates on the Theological Interpretation of Scripture* (T&T Clark Theology; London: T&T Clark, 2007), pp. 41–67.

37. R. R. Reno, 'Biblical Theology and Theological Exegesis' in Craig G. Bartholomew, Mary Healy, Karl Möller and Robin Parry (eds), *Out of Egypt: Biblical Theology and Biblical Interpretation* (Scripture and Hermeneutics Series, 5; Bletchley: Paternoster, 2004), pp. 385–408 draws out the differences between the two, arguing that theological exegesis stays closer to the text.

38. So also Treier, *Virtue and the Voice of God*, p. 151.

39. Yeago, 'Crucified Also for Us under Pontius Pilate', p. 92.

40. See Thomas F. Torrance, *Reality and Evangelical Theology: The Realism of Christian Revelation* (Downers Grove: InterVarsity Press, 1999), p. 113, who writes that the *homoousion* is not the fruit of human creativity but 'a truth which forced itself upon the understanding of the church as it allowed the biblical witness to imprint its own conceptual pattern upon its mind'.

41. Paul Ricoeur, *Interpretation Theory: Discourse and the Surplus of Meaning* (Fort Worth: Texas Christian University Press, 1976), pp. 87–88. See also Kevin J. Vanhoozer, 'Discourse on Matter: Hermeneutics and the "Miracle" of Understanding', *IJST* 7 (2005), pp. 5–37 (34).

42. Cf. Hans Urs von Balthasar, *Theo-Drama: Theological Dramatic Theory*, Vol. II (trans. Graham Harrison; 5 vols; San Francisco: Ignatius, 1990), pp. 128–29.

There are patently many objections that could be made against the reading that follows, from biblical studies, systematic theology and hermeneutics, and some of these I will acknowledge and respond to along the way. But, lest this essay become an overly anxious exercise in justifying the bond between Scripture and doctrine, it is necessary to let my actual reading of John act as my apologetics. As we turn now in earnest to John's Gospel it is helpful to take with us some advice of Barth's:

> When we come to the Bible with our questions – How shall I think of God and the universe? How arrive at the divine? How present myself? – it answers us, as it were, 'My dear sir, these are *your* problems: you must not ask me! . . . If you do not care to enter upon *my* questions, you may, to be sure, find in me all sorts of arguments and quasi-arguments for one or another standpoint, but you will not then find what is really here.[43]

## Incarnation and the Gospel of John

We can inch our way towards understanding the Jesus of the Fourth Gospel by approaching him from two directions: Jesus as the eternal Son in the world and Jesus as the obedient Son in the world. As will become obvious both these approaches to Jesus are porous to one another.

### Jesus the Eternal Son in the World

'What is really here', the encounter at the centre of John's Gospel, is that Jesus does not become the Son of God, but he *is* the eternal Son of God enfleshed, revealing and enacting the work of the Son within the reality of our world. In the life of Jesus of Nazareth, the eternal love of the Father for the Son and of the Son for the Father are lodged in the world's time. Only around this concrete reality can John's Gospel be understood coherently: Jesus' life of obedience to his Father and his ministry of love to those whom the Father has given him is the mediation to the world of the mutual love between the Father and the Son.[44] A string of verses is the source for such a dogmatic sounding beginning. 'I glorified you on earth by finishing the work that you gave me to do. So now, Father, glorify me in your own presence with the glory that I had in your presence before the world existed' (Jn 17.4–5). 'As the Father has loved me, so I have loved you' (Jn 15.9). 'Having loved his own who were in the world he loved them to the end' (Jn 13.1). 'The Father loves the Son and has placed all

---

43. Barth, *The Word of God and the Word of Man*, pp. 42–43 (emphasis original).
44. See also Jenson, *Systematic Theology*, Vol. 1, p. 93, who says of John's Gospel: 'this Gospel explicitly recounts the simultaneous and identical course of Jesus' life in Israel with his disciples and his life with the Father as the Son. So read, this Gospel has been a chief New Testament inspiration of developed trinitarian doctrine. Read otherwise, it always resists coherent interpretation.'

things in his hands' (Jn 3.35). 'I made your name known to them, and I will make it known, so that the love with which you have loved me may be in them, and I in them' (Jn 17.26). 'I do as the Father has commanded me, so that the world may know that I love the Father' (Jn 14.31). We can say in response to these verses that the appearance of the Son is the good news that the triune God 'does not allow His history to be His and ours ours, but causes them to take place as a common history'.[45]

In four words to which all our talk of Christ is but a footnote, the prologue unmistakably identifies the eternal Word with the startling reality of a particular enfleshed human being: 'the Word became flesh' (Jn 1.14a). The same Word who, we had earlier been told, was involved in the creation of the world, and who 'was' God (Jn 1.1–2) has been personally present in our flesh.[46] The 'Word' of Jn 1.1–2 is clearly to be understood around Jn 1.14. God, who spoke the world into being, is now to be heard, not through a prophet like Moses (Jn 1.17) but through the one in whom 'human and divine speaking become one'.[47] 'The words that I say to you I do not speak on my own . . . Believe me that I am in the Father and the Father is in me' (Jn 14.10–11). The entire Gospel is therefore framed by the two realities which John presents incontestably together and alongside one another: the eternity of the creating Word and the sheer particularity and time of the one who is Jesus of Nazareth. The one who is plainly known as 'Jesus son of Joseph from Nazareth' (Jn 1.45) is the same one who acknowledges that his Father loved him 'before the foundation of the world' (Jn 17.24) and who even in the world '*sees* what the Father is doing' (Jn 5.19). Not only is the love that extends out to us in the Son, in which we are to abide (Jn 15.9), the love that has eternally flowed between Father and Son but more even than this the love now made visible in Jesus of Nazareth (Jn 13.34) is the love of the one through whom all things came into being (Jn 1.3). As the Scottish theologian of the nineteenth century, Edward Irving, appreciated, the Son's eternal origins are a rich source of pastoral comfort:

> What . . . an exalted birthplace and most noble stock doth it give to every creature, to me, to you, dear brethren, to think that we were seen of a long time, yea from the beginning of days, yea from all eternity . . . and were loved and beloved of the Father

45.   Karl Barth, *Church Dogmatics* IV/1 (trans. G. W. Bromiley; London: T&T Clark International, 2004), p. 7.

46.   Along with William S. Kurz, 'Beyond Historical Criticism: Reading John's Prologue as Catholics' in Luke T. Johnson and William S. Kurz, *The Future of Catholic Biblical Scholarship: A Constructive Conversation* (Grand Rapids: Eerdmans, 2002), pp. 159–81 (170) the anarthrous *theos* in Jn 1.1 is best translated as 'the Word was God' rather than 'divine was the Word', it not being uncommon for predicates in Greek to lack a definite article. What this verse points to is a distinction yet a unity between the Word and the one Jesus called 'my Father'. See Karl Barth, *Witness to the Word: A Commentary on John 1* (trans. Geoffrey W. Bromiley; Grand Rapids: Eerdmans, 1986), p. 22.

47.   Oliver Davies, 'Cosmic Speech and the Liturgy of Silence' in Rashkover and Pecknold (eds), *Liturgy, Time, and the Politics of Redemption*, pp. 215–26 (223).

before all time, as a part – an essential part – of His own dear Son . . . It lifts my ignoble
being into a high nobility, it linketh my solitary and divided substance into high
alliance . . . how comforteth it my soul to know that the Son Himself . . . should bring
us back again into that most sure and perfect blessedness which He had, and which in
Him we had, before the world was![48]

The meeting of time and eternity in the person of Jesus Christ is therefore
'what is really here' in the Fourth Gospel. As the decisive entry of eternity into
our time, Jesus can look both forward to his betrayal, death on the cross (Jn 2.4;
3.14–15) and resurrection (Jn 2.19) and backwards to what he saw and heard
in his pre-existent state (Jn 3.32; 8.26, 38, 40; 15.15). The Johannine Christ is
the one who, although he comes after John the Baptist nonetheless precedes
him (Jn 1.15, 30) for he was in the presence of God 'before the world existed'
(Jn 17.5) and his glory was seen by Isaiah (Jn 12.41). Even more incredibly, the
Johannine Jesus says, 'Before Abraham was, I am' (Jn 8.58). The God we see
in the Word made flesh is a God who, far from fleeing from time, 'is *more*
temporal than we are, who is ahead of us, and behind us, before us and after
us'.[49] Jesus' pre-existent status is a reminder that his coming is no random
occurrence, for he is the one who was, and is and is to come, the one whom
Moses himself wrote about (Jn 5.46). But, alongside his pre-existent status,
Jesus is, in the persistent refrain of John, the one who has been 'sent' (the
phrase 'he who sent me' is found some thirty times in John) and he has been
sent to fulfil a particular mission in our time, 'I declare to the world what I have
heard from him' (Jn 8.26). As one who has been sent, Jesus' life is constantly
lived under the pressure of 'the hour' (Jn 2.4; 7.6, 8, 30; 8.20; 13.1; 17.1), a
reality to which he himself must be reconciled, 'what should I say – "Father,
save me from this hour"? No, it is for this reason that I have come to this hour'
(Jn 12.27). Jesus' earthly life and person is bound on both its sides (its beginning and its end) by the eternal volition of the triune fellowship, so that we can
say with P. T. Forsyth that Jesus' human ministry 'was . . . the obverse of a
heavenly eternal deed'.[50] The victory of this entry of eternity into our time is of
course made known fully in the resurrection, the decisive validation of Jesus'
teaching and mission: 'Jesus answered them, 'Destroy this temple, and in three
days I will raise it up.' . . . After he was raised from the dead, his disciples
remembered that he had said this; they believed the scripture and the word that
Jesus had spoken' (Jn 2.19, 22).

Living out a life in which time and eternity decisively meet, Jesus secures by
what he does the eternal love of God for the world (Jn 3.16): 'having loved his
own who were in the world, he loved them to the end' (Jn 13.1). Jesus' love is

---

48. Cited in *Edward Irving: The Trinitarian Face of God* (Graham W. P. McFarlane (ed.);
The Devotional Library; Edinburgh: Saint Andrew's Press, 1996), pp. 27–28.
49. Yoder, *Preface to Theology*, p. 276 (emphasis added).
50. Forsyth, *Person and Place of Jesus Christ*, p. 271.

no fickle emotion, but is the fullness (Jn 1.16) of God's love in our world. The love which is made manifest in the time of Jesus' ministry is, Calvin reminds us, a love which is 'constant and eternal' and which even death could not 'quench'.[51] The love manifest in Jesus' life, of which there is none greater (Jn 15.13), *is* the love of the Father for the world at the same time as it is the Son's love for the Father returned in his completed work.[52]

Jn 1.14 is also a reminder that throughout our contemplation of the figure of Christ in the Fourth Gospel, we are required to emphasize neither the divinity proper to the Word at the expense of Jesus' humanity nor vice-versa, but determinedly both at the same time. 'We do not divide', Cyril of Alexandria counsels, 'the evangelical narratives of our Lord among . . . two subjects . . . [O]ne must attribute all the narratives in the Gospels strictly to one subject, to the *Logos*' one hypostasis become flesh.'[53] The reason why it is important to look to Jesus as the Word made flesh with equal emphasis on both the Word and the flesh is that Jesus Christ breaks the boundaries of all that we previously knew of humanity and divinity. Christ takes our humanity into the life of God (Jn 10.10), and God is seen in our world (Jn 14.9). As far as possible, we must not import what we imagine humanity and divinity to be into our reading of the Gospels, but let our understanding of God and of humanity flow from the claims and implications of the Gospels themselves. William Jennings warns us against contemporary repetitions of Nestorius' error who, in his anxiety to keep the divine and human natures of Christ apart and differentiated, read Scripture in a mode where

> [w]ho God is and what it means to be human are less established by the gospel story and more affirmed by it . . . a Nestorius-like reading of the text takes away all the surprises. It reduces divinity and humanity to exactly what we already assume about humanity and divinity.[54]

Reading the Gospels with surprise is determined to follow the way the words go. The same Gospel that can apparently scale the heights of Christology has no hesitation in emphasizing the sheer ordinariness of 'the man called Jesus' (Jn 9.11), a permanent reminder that the task of Christology is 'to think together without loss to either side and without indulging in premature appeals to paradox the temporal and the eternal as they are made known in . . . Jesus of Nazareth'.[55] Theological readings of John's Gospel need not worry whether it

---

51. *Comm. Jn 13.1.*

52. Hans Urs von Balthasar, *You Have Words of Eternal Life: Scripture Meditations* (trans. Dennis Martin; San Francisco: Ignatius, 2004), p. 190.

53. Cyril of Alexandria, 'Third Letter to Nestorius', cited in Jenson, *Systematic Theology*, Vol. 1, p. 129 n. 18.

54. Jennings, 'Undoing Our Abandonment', p. 90.

55. Gunton, *Yesterday and Today*, p. 206.

is better to think 'from above' or 'from below'; it is best to begin from *within* the astonishing implications of Jn 1.14 as these are enacted in Jesus' life:

> the starting point of Paul and John was *Christ*, a divine being. Then they said that the *Logos* become (*sic*) flesh. But perhaps because they had to speak so *strongly*, their thesis was overlooked and people only heard their starting point . . . [m]istakes arise when only a *part* of a sentence is heard.[56]

Put in other words, our attention must be to the Word and flesh together, not in isolation. In this single and particular person God has pitched his being in our midst, assuming human being into the being of the Word and so healing humanity from within rather than 'over our heads'.[57] Jesus of Nazareth is not therefore solely human, nor is he solely divine: he is *concurrently* divine and human in the one person, and he brings what is human and what is divine into a renewed and healing communion. In the movement of the incarnation, the Word made flesh is in no way swamped by the reality of flesh. The Word can never cease being what it is and the act of incarnation is the expansion of the Word outwards in freedom to assume and indwell what it was not before. With attention to both sides of Jn 1.14, Jesus can therefore be seen as who John persistently claims him to be: the true revelation and presence of God himself (Jn 1.18; 2.21; 4.26; 6.46; 8.26; 12.45; 14.9), the reconciliation *to God* offered on our behalf (Jn 17.19), the Lamb of God whose 'food is to do the will of him who sent me and to complete his work' (Jn 4.34), the true light of the world (Jn 8.12) and he who lives a life that can only be 'completed' on the cross (Jn 19.30).

Attentive reading of Jn 1.14 is therefore indispensable to understanding the Fourth Gospel's *narration* of a redeeming *life* through which God is revealed and the 'fullness' of his grace imparted to the children of God (Jn 1.16). Hasty readings of the Fourth Gospel – usually ones that read Jn 1.14 one-sidedly – can encourage an essentialist Christology, as if all the Son of God had to do was to slip on some flesh and carry out a charade of a life so as to redeem us. Not for the first time in this chapter however we need to confront the concerns of those anxious that an overemphasis on Jesus' eternal origins is likely to swamp his humanity and so threaten a 'realistic' Christology.[58] Is the Logos

---

56. John D. Godsey, *Karl Barth's Table-Talk* (*SJT* Occasional Papers, 10; Edinburgh: Oliver and Boyd, 1963), p. 63.

57. Thomas F. Torrance, *The Mediation of Christ* (Didsbury Lectures; Exeter: Paternoster, 1983), p. 90.

58. Christology – the claim that God moved through the world in Jesus of Nazareth – necessarily does not have, as its first preoccupation, the attempt to be 'realistic'. See Cyril of Alexandria, *On the Unity of Christ* (trans. John Anthony McGuckin; Crestwood: St Vladimir's Seminary Press, 1995), p. 61: 'the mystery of Christ runs the risk of being disbelieved precisely because it is so incredibly wonderful. For God was in humanity. He who was above all creation was in our human condition.' By 'realistic', I intend to point to Christ as the decisive meeting of divinity and our

Christology of John's Gospel amenable to portraying a human Jesus? Can one speak, like John, of Jesus as the eternal Son of God and leave intact a human figure we can recognize? Does the eternal Son submerge the historicity of his mission? John Macquarrie, for instance, is worried that if

> the directive principle in Jesus Christ was not human but divine, then to some extent his whole story becomes a sham. His resistance to temptation, his courage in the face of suffering, his obedience even to the cross, those things which evoke our deepest responses, are all the work of God in disguise.[59]

So too, Colin Gunton has expressed concern that if Jesus' humanity is subordinated to the Word, and therefore the will of God, there is the corresponding 'threat of a swallowing up of the humanity in the divine action', and of a human life so devoid of real human decisions that it is best understood as operating on 'automatic pilot'.[60]

Once again, some counsel from Karl Barth funds an initial response to these fears: 'Christology has to consider and to state who Jesus Christ is, who in revelation exercises God's power over man'.[61] Who is it that exercises God's power over humanity in the Fourth Gospel? An answer can be sketched by wrestling with the obedience of Jesus neither from above, nor from below, but from 'within'. It is to that task that I now turn.

### Jesus the Obedient Son in the World

The Jesus who emerges from the Fourth Gospel is not some ready-made saviour, but the eternal Son of God enfleshed and saturated with a sense of his mission, the works he has to *do* and *accomplish* in order to glorify and make known the one who sent him (John 17). 'Christ was neither a thinker before a problem nor a poet before a dream, but a doer before a task.'[62] And the task that Jesus had to complete was to go the way of the cross after which, through the resurrection, humanity would be given life abundantly. 'I came that they may have life and have it abundantly' (Jn 10.10). Only after his work of life, death and resurrection was accomplished would Jesus' body become the locus of God's vivifying presence (Jn 2.19–21) and would he bestow upon us the life-giving Spirit (Jn 6.63; 7.37–39). Jesus speaks further of this work he must

---

humanity, so that we are able to say that our humanity has been transformed as a result of this encounter. It is the nature and extent of Christ's contact with our humanity that is then at stake in a theological reading of John's Gospel.

59. John Macquarrie, *Christology Revisited* (London: SCM, 1998), p. 53.

60. Colin Gunton, *Christ and Creation* (Didsbury Lectures; Carlisle: Paternoster, 1992), pp. 48–49.

61. Barth, *Church Dogmatics* I/2, p. 125.

62. P. T. Forsyth, 'A Rallying Ground for the Free Churches' in *Gospel and Authority*, pp. 95–117 (102). See also Forsyth, *Cruciality of the Cross*, p. 12: 'Even in John, Jesus is not a disguised God urging people to pierce His veil; He is there to do a work that only His death could do'.

accomplish when he states that 'unless a grain of wheat falls into the earth and dies, it remains just a single grain; but if it dies, it bears much fruit' (Jn 12.24). Jesus, the one who *is* the 'the resurrection and the life' (Jn 11.25), *must die* before new life can sprout because only at his death is his life opened up for all. This is the work he must 'complete' (Jn 4.34; 5.36). In the context of this lonely work, Jesus prays to the Father towards the end of his ministry, 'I glorified you on earth by finishing the work you gave me to do' (Jn 17.4). It is only on the cross, the hour which Jesus' entire life has been moving towards, the taking up of the command which he has followed through to the end (Jn 10.18; 15.10), and the cup which he consents to receive from the Father (Jn 18.11), that he can say 'it is finished' (Jn 19.30). For it is on the cross that the ultimate reality of Jesus' life is revealed: 'when you have lifted up the Son of Man, then you will know that I am and that I do nothing of myself' (Jn 8.28). Here on the sheer contingency of a Roman cross is hoisted the one without whom not one thing would have come into being (Jn 1.3). Or, to put this last sentence in the starkness of the Fourth Gospel's language: 'He was in the world, and the world came into being through him; yet the world did not know him' (Jn 1.10).

Attention to the particular mission-saturated figure of the Fourth Gospel narrative is the start of a response to suggestions that the Johannine Jesus is little more than a puppet whose strings are pulled by God or, as Ernst Käsemann enthusiastically charged, 'God striding the earth'.[63] Those who accuse John of presenting 'a god who dips into history but scarcely touches it' have a tendency to operate with dualist conceptions of God abstracted from God's own act of self-revelation.[64] Accusations of doceticism hurled in John's direction are too hasty in applying versions of divinity and humanity worked out in isolation from each other, and too slow in attending to the particularity of the way Jesus' story goes. To be sure, we must be careful here not to *impose* on the Fourth Gospel a two-natures Christology, as if the text somehow needed our help. More urgent is to fall under the text's weight, what it wills to make known: the decisive confrontation of two realities alongside one another. As a human Jesus obeys the will of God and as the Son he acts in utter freedom because he is truly the loving Son of the Father. If we are resolved to not separate these two

---

63. Ernst Käsemann, *The Testament of Jesus: A Study of the Gospel of John in the Light of Chapter 17* (trans. Gerhard Krodel; London: SCM, 1968), p. 9. It is not hard to find New Testament scholars fundamentally agreeing with Käsemann's thesis: for example, J. A. du Rand, 'The Characterization of Jesus as Depicted in the Narrative of the Fourth Gospel', *Neotestamentica* 19 (1985), pp. 18–36 (29–30). See, in critical response to Käsemann, Marianne M. Thompson, *The Humanity of Jesus* (Philadelphia: Fortress, 1988); Günther Bornkamm, 'Towards the Interpretation of John's Gospel: A Discussion of *The Testament of Jesus*' in John Ashton (ed.), *The Interpretation of John* (trans. John Ashton; London: SPCK, 1986), pp. 79–98; Leon Morris, 'The Jesus of Saint John' in Robert A. Guelich (ed.), *Unity and Diversity in New Testament Theology* (Grand Rapids: Eerdmans, 1978), pp. 37–53.

64. Eric Lane Titus, 'The Fourth Gospel and the Historical Jesus' in F. F. Trotter (ed.), *Jesus and the Historian: Written in Honor of Ernest Cadman Colwell* (Philadelphia: Westminster, 1968), pp. 98–113 (104).

movements, the life of Jesus of Nazareth can be apprehended as 'all that is human opening out into the divine, and, at the same time, all that is divine entering into the human'.[65] In this way we should read together such verses as Jn 4.34, 'My food is to do the will of him who sent me and to complete his work' or Jn 15.10, 'I have kept my Father's commandments and abide in his love'. The narrative – and its implications – invites us into the truth uttered by the creeds. 'What His manhood is, and therefore true manhood, we cannot read into Him from elsewhere, but must be told by Him',[66] or in the language of the Fourth Gospel itself, 'The true light, which enlightens everyone, was coming into the world' (Jn 1.9). Robert Jenson is surely right to remind us that the correct starting point for talk of Christ is 'the concrete fact of the protagonist of the Gospels',[67] and not the riddling talk of 'natures', concepts which should properly be regarded only as secondary tools to help us read the Gospel claims more keenly.

The Christ event in the Fourth Gospel is that Jesus is one whose own 'volitional foundation [is] in the heavens'.[68] Jesus' mission executed in our time is an outworking of his eternal, filial status, a reality impressed upon us strongly when Jn 17.4–5 is read with equal attention to *both* its sides. Jesus' work is truly completed on earth, and so in our time, but the glory now manifest in the world has its origins in eternity: 'I glorified you on earth by finishing the work that you gave me to do. So now, Father, glorify me in your own presence with the glory that I had in your presence before the world existed.' In the light of Jesus' filial obedience it is more helpful therefore not to speak of John as presenting a Logos-Christology but a resolutely Father-Son Christology. The obedience which the Son enacts is not an achievement of Jesus' titanic human effort alone. Nor is it a punctiliar bursting into the world of the Son's eternal obedience to the Father, once revealed and then retracted. The nature of Christ's victory is rather the overcoming of the world (Jn 16.33) by enacting in time and in the fleshly life of a human the eternal relation between the Father and the Son. In line with the patience we emphasized in the previous chapter, Jesus therefore lives under and in time, waiting for the 'hour' (Jn 2.4; 4.21, 23; 5.25, 2; 13.1). Jesus, being the Word made flesh, could have bypassed the vicissitudes of time and graduated immediately to his glorified state 'but such a thing', Cyril of Alexandria rightly warns us,

> would have smacked of wonder-working, and would have been out of key with the plan
> of the economy . . . he allowed the limitations of the manhood to have dominion over
> himself. This was so arranged as part of his 'likeness to us', for we advance to greater
> things little by little.[69]

65. Hans Urs von Balthasar, *Prayer* (trans. A. V. Littledale; London: SPCK, 1973), p. 132.
66. Barth, *Church Dogmatics* IV/1, p. 131.
67. Robert W. Jenson, 'For Us. . . . He Was Made Man' in Seitz (ed.), *Nicene Christianity*, pp. 75–85 (82).
68. Forsyth, *Person and Place of Christ*, p. 282.
69. Cyril of Alexandria, *On the Unity of Christ*, p. 110.

Jesus' action of washing the disciples' feet (Jn 13.1–11) therefore reveals that which is true of Jesus' whole life under time, namely 'the strange and rare paradox of Lordship in servant's form and divine glory in human abasement'.[70] In this setting, we need be less nervous about verses like Jn 8.28, 13.16, 14.24 and 17.5 which point to Jesus' servant-like role or so-called 'subordinate' status in relation to the Father.

A clear strand running throughout John presents Jesus as a Son in direct command of a ministry directed towards the glorification of his Father. Jesus is no 'vacuum, the mere place where God lives and does his work as another and a stranger'.[71] The cross is not same fate which happens *to* Jesus – it is an offering of obedience presented *by* the Son to the Father 'so that the world may know I love the Father' (Jn 14.31). Jesus speaks of his active role in sacrificing his own life (Jn 10.17–18), in raising people from the dead (Jn 6.40, 54), in glorification (Jn 7.18; 13.31),[72] in sending the Spirit (Jn 15.26; 16.7) and even in raising himself from the dead (Jn 2.19). Jesus Christ, in the direction which John pushes us towards, is not divine and human in antithesis to each other, but in resolute conjunction and his mission is to make known and convey the life of God by setting down his own life voluntarily, 'I lay down my life for the sheep' (Jn 10.15). Only in *this* way is Jesus' life 'God's will in action'.[73] So too a sense of what W. F. Lofthouse (to whom we shall return) calls Jesus' 'startling independence' is conveyed by Jn 17.19:[74] 'for their sakes I sanctify myself, so that they also may be sanctified in truth'. The direction of Jesus' ministry is therefore real and not inevitable, dynamic and not static:

> *I* lay down my life in order to take it up again. No one takes it from me, but *I* lay it down of my accord. *I* have power to lay it down, and *I* have power to take it up again. *I* have received this command from my Father (Jn 10.17–18).[75]

Commenting directly on this proclamation of Jesus Edward Irving had this to say:

> In these words Christ asserteth three things: first, that no one whatsoever, man or angel, had power to take His life from Him; the second, that it was by himself laid down; and the third, that this was done by the commandment of the Father. These three things

---

70. Cyril of Alexandria, *On the Unity of Christ*, p. 101. See also Jenson, *Systematic Theology*, Vol. 1, p. 109.

71. Karl Barth, *Church Dogmatics* III/2 (trans. Harold Knight *et al.*; London: T&T Clark International, 2004), p. 64.

72. Barth, *Church Dogmatics* III/2, p. 65.

73. Forsyth, 'Revelation and the Person of Christ', p. 120.

74. W. F. Lofthouse, *The Father and the Son: A Study in Johannine Thought* (London: SCM, 1934), p. 41.

75. Marianne M. Thompson, *The God of the Gospel of John* (Grand Rapids: Eerdmans, 2001), p. 95.

concur in His act of dying: a commandment of the Father, His own free will to obey that commandment, and His total independence of any third power or influence. Every act of His life was of the same kind; done of the free will, without constraint, in obedience to the absolute will of the Father.[76]

The 'I' who speaks in these Johannine verses, the 'I' who makes known the Son's obedience to his Father, is the unique and unrepeatable figure that is the Word made flesh, with emphasis unequivocally on both the Word *and* the flesh. The two are not operating in parallel fashion, but concurrently. Edward Irving is worth quoting again:

The person, the *I* who speaketh, acteth, suffereth in Christ is not the Divine nature, nor yet is it the human nature alone; but it is the Divine nature having passed into the human nature, and therein effecting its will and purpose of acting or of suffering. I totally reject . . . the language of those divines who say, 'Now the Divine nature acteth, now the human nature acteth'; language which I hold to be essentially Nestorian.[77]

The life of Jesus, a life filled full with purposive resolve, comes to its climax with Jesus' arrest, the point at which his obedience breaks out in the glory of the revelation of Jesus' eternal name: 'I am' (Jn 18.5). Yet interestingly, Jesus' active obedience leads him to being acted upon. The truth of Jesus – and indeed of God – is seen in his act of freely handing himself over to what the hour now demands. 'He who has seen me has seen the Father' (Jn 14.9), or in the words of V. H. Vanstone who applies these words to Jesus' arrest, 'Jesus, in handing Himself over, in passing of His own will from action to passion, enacts and discloses that which, at the deepest level, is distinctive of divinity, distinctive of God.'[78] Yet, at this theophanic moment it is the soldiers who have come *to do to Jesus* the will of his enemies who collapse to the ground in fear (Jn 18.6). Jesus enacts in the Kidron valley garden the truth underpinning his work and mission: that God so loved the world he *gave* his only Son.

The obedience of the Son to the Father is therefore purposive and patient – active, yet willing to wait and willing to suffer. The perspective which must shape our reading of the Fourth Gospel's witness is that Christ's victory – his overcoming – is his eternal relation to the Father not in quiescent repose but in lively action.[79] To be sure, the obedience shown by Jesus is not that with which Jesus *attains* unity with his Father, rather the work which is completed through his obedience is the 'continuous expression of that unity'.[80]

---

76. Edward Irving, *The Collected Writings of Edward Irving*, Vol. V (G. Carlyle (ed.); 5 vols; London: Alexander Strahan, 1865), pp. 148–49.

77. Irving, *Collected Writings of Edward Irving*, Vol. V, p. 134. Cited in Colin E. Gunton, 'Two Dogmas Revisited: Edward Irving's Christology', *SJT* 41 (1988), pp. 359–76 (364).

78. Vanstone, *Stature of Waiting*, p. 89.

79. Forsyth, 'Revelation and the Person of Christ', p. 126.

80. Forsyth, 'Revelation and the Person of Christ', p. 125.

To cursory readers of John's Gospel, the obedience of the Johannine Jesus (Jn 4.34; 5.30; 6.38; 8.29, 55; 9.31; 14.31; 15.10; 17.4; 18.11) can seem like the obedience of a porcelain figurine. Can we really say that in Jesus' obedience we are to see one whose life is an authentic encounter of God with humanity and of humanity with God? If the obedience of Jesus of Nazareth is the enactment in our time of the love and obedience that eternally inheres between the Father and the Son could Jesus have realistically disobeyed? Is Jesus' life not like a loaded dice, destined always to land the right way up? What kind of freedom does the eternal Son have?

The first response to these concerns must be that the obedience of the Son was an obedience truly carried out in our time and in a human: only as such can it touch us and be truly redemptive. The logic of the entirety of Jn 1.14 compels us to take with full seriousness the absolute concurrence of our time with the eternal Father-Son relationship. As Karl Barth writes:

> the time of Jesus is also a time like all other times . . . it occurred once and once for all . . . it had beginning, duration and end . . . [o]nly a docetic attitude to Jesus can deny that His being in time also means what being in time means for us all. Our recognition of His true humanity depends on an acceptance of this proposition. Even the recognition of His true deity, implying as it does the identity between His time and God's, does not rule out this simple meaning of His being in time. On the contrary, it includes it.[81]

The perfect coincidence between the eternal mandate of God and Jesus' freely offered obedience (Jn 10.18) is a real occurrence *within* our time. It is because of this real encounter that the cross, this handing over which is Jesus' hour, is 'the supremely authoritative moment in human history'.[82]

A second response to fears about Jesus' obedience takes its inspiration from Hans Urs von Balthasar. Jesus, when he is obedient to the Father, is acting in deepest correspondence with who he is, and so it is when he is obedient that he is most free. The command which Jesus states he 'has received from my Father' (Jn 10.18) is no external imposition but is in accord with his status as the loving Son: 'I always do what is pleasing to him' (Jn 8.29) or, in the context of his farewell discourses, 'I do as the Father has commanded me, so that the world may know that I love the Father' (Jn 14.31). Balthasar posits an analogy of the possessed artist as a way of understanding the nature of Jesus' freedom. In the same way that '[t]he artist is never more free than when . . . he is, as it were, "possessed" by the true "idea" . . . and follows its sovereign commands', so too, 'when Jesus lays hold of his mission and fashions it, he is not obeying

81.   Barth, *Church Dogmatics* III/2, p. 463. Cited in Richard Roberts, 'Karl Barth's Doctrine of Time: Its Nature and Implications' in *A Theology on its Way: Essays on Karl Barth* (Edinburgh: T&T Clark, 1991), pp. 1–58 (51).

82.   Donald M. MacKinnon, *Borderlands of Theology and Other Essays* (George W. Roberts and Donovan E. Smucker (eds); London: Lutterworth, 1968), p. 81.

some alien power . . . [i]t is precisely in embracing his Father's will that Jesus discovers his own, most profound identity as the eternal Son'.[83] The identity of Jesus, the one who is in ceaseless prayer with God (Jn 11.42), who dwells continually in the presence of God (Jn 8.29), who hears God (Jn 5.30) and who sees God (Jn 5.19), is therefore inseparable from his divine commission: 'I came that they may have life, and have it abundantly' (Jn 10.10). Jesus' dwelling in his Father (Jn 14.10) 'neither infringes, nor violates, nor overwhelms him in his personal will, but leads his own being to its full realisation' as the Son.[84]

The Sonship revealed in the Fourth Gospel is therefore a call to pay attention to this very specific life: Jesus 'proving himself on earth the very thing that he was in heaven; that is, a continuous perfect act of filial love'.[85] Attention, as always, must be riveted to both sides of the equation: the Son reveals his eternal, filial obedience on earth and in a human, Jesus of Nazareth. Forsyth, adopting the language of Heb. 5.8, helpfully reminds us that Jesus *learned* obedience, 'but he did not learn *to obey*'.[86] This would seem to do justice to the dual attention that must be paid to Jesus' eternal subsistence with his Father and the temporal execution of his Sonship. The life of Jesus is not the vertical imposition of the eternal Father-Son relationship but the horizontal 'translation' of this relationship.[87] The seemingly impossible intersection of the eternal and temporal can be seen if we pay close attention to Jn 6.38. The verse begins with a reference to the Son's coming from the time and space of eternity, ends by referring to the will of the one who has sent him and has at its centre a clear reference to an independent will: 'I have come down from heaven, not to do my own will, but the will of him who sent me'. No verse could more aptly reveal the reconciling movement of Jesus' ministry: the complete concert of the human will with the divine will, Jesus' saving will to obey the will of the Father.[88] It is notable that this verse begins with a reference to Jesus' coming 'down from heaven' but immediately adds, somewhat unexpectedly (at least for hasty readers of John), that this one who has come down from heaven has his own will which he is bending to the will of his Father. Jn 5.30 is equally significant here: 'I seek to do not my own will but the will of him who sent me'. Jesus' life is the concurrence of the vertical will of the Father to give his Son

83. Hans Urs von Balthasar, *Theo-Drama: Theological Dramatic Theory*, Vol. V (trans. Graham Harrison; 5 vols; San Francisco: Ignatius, 1992), pp. 198–200. The obedience of Jesus, guided and inspired by the Holy Spirit, is a crucial theme in Balthasar's Christology: see John Saward, *The Mysteries of March: Hans Urs von Balthasar on the Incarnation and Easter* (Washington: Catholic University of America Press, 1990), pp. 21–27.

84. Balthasar, *Prayer*, pp. 150–51.

85. Austin Farrer, *The Brink of Mystery* (Charles C. Conti (ed.); London: SPCK, 1976), p. 20.

86. Forsyth, 'Revelation and the Person of Christ', p. 125 (emphasis added).

87. Hans Urs von Balthasar, *A Theology of History* (no translator cited; London: Sheed and Ward, 1964), p. 27.

88. See Gunton, *Yesterday and Today*, pp. 91–92.

for the life of the world (Jn 3.16) with the horizontal enactment of this will by Jesus: 'I lay down my life in order to take it up again' (Jn 10.17).[89]

This reading of Jn 6.38 and the narrative of John as a whole can be consolidated by recalling, with the help of Stanley Hauerwas and Charles Pinches, that obedience always implies a relationship and thus two wills. Obedience 'requires that the one who obeys must perceive his will as potentially at odds with the will of his lord . . . [t]he wills need not *actually* be at odds, just potentially'.[90] Jesus' obedience flows from a relationship with the Father where 'the Son has come to share entirely in the purpose of the Father; he knows his mind and conforms to it willingly'.[91] In this setting we might prefer to see Jesus' life as a constant prayer in action (Jn 11.42).[92] Even, indeed especially, in the Fourth Gospel Jesus' obedience is neither imposed nor is it automatic: instead it is something that really *happens* in the life of a human conforming the direction of his life to the mission which he has been sent to complete: 'Now my soul is troubled. And what should I say – "Father, save me from this hour"? No, it is for this reason that I have come to this hour' (Jn 12.27). In this verse, we are reminded yet again that Jesus' life has a *purpose* which cannot just be announced but must be accomplished ('for this reason . . . '). Jesus must live out his unity with the Father in a timely fashion ('I have come to this hour . . . ').

If some find it difficult to accept the humanity of John's Jesus another strand of Johannine interpretation reveals a preference for interpreting the obedience of the Johannine Jesus as an instance of moral heroism. For example, Jesus' uniqueness, according to John A. T. Robinson, is morally, rather than ontologically, grounded.[93] There are a number of problems with approaches like Robinson's and others like W. F. Lofthouse which cast Jesus' obedience as the summit of human striving.[94] Here, it is important to attend to the human Jesus of the Fourth Gospel with as much theological clarity as we can muster. For if the union between Jesus and God gets stuck on the moral plane then it is difficult to articulate how Jesus' obedience has more saving relevance than that of any other holy person. Why, after all, should Jesus' obedience be more saving than that of any other martyr? Jesus' obedience is saving not because he is *more* obedient than us, nor because he provides an example of obedience worthy of imitation (though both of these statements are true in themselves), but because his obedience decisively spans both divinity and humanity, and it is only this reality that overcomes the world (Jn 16.33). Treatments of Jesus'

---

89. Balthasar's reading of the Fourth Gospel in his *Theo-Drama* evidently lie behind the thoughts being articulated here.

90. Hauerwas and Pinches, *Christians Among the Virtues*, pp. 142–43.

91. Hauerwas and Pinches, *Christians Among the Virtues*, p. 147.

92. P. T. Forsyth, *The Soul of Prayer* (Biblical and Theological Classics Library; Carlisle: Paternoster, 1998), p. 60.

93. John A. T. Robinson, *The Priority of John* (J. F. Coakley (ed.); London: SCM, 1985), p. 178.

94. See Lofthouse, *The Father and the Son*, pp. 115–18 for Jesus as the apex of humanity.

obedience exiled from ontological considerations leave themselves exposed to accusations of Pelagian grasps of Jesus' work.[95] Only an insistence upon the ontological union protects Jesus' vicarious obedience as saving precisely because it is an act within God at the same time as it is an act within humanity. We must recall the interpretative tool that is the insistence that Jesus does 'divine things in a human way' and 'human things in a divine way'.[96] A concentration on Jesus' work of obedience in deliberate abstraction from Jesus' person loses sight of precisely why Jesus' faithful obedience is saving.[97] A moral perspective on Jesus' obedience can only ripple the surface of our humanity and our relationship with God. Jesus 'is God and humanity in perfect relationship with one another',[98] both the truth of the eternal Son's filial existence and the truth of our humanity unmasked: 'the true light, which enlightens everyone, was coming into the world' (Jn 1.9).

It is plain that for readers of John's Gospel it is tempting to deflect the pressure of the text. The teaching of Jesus and what he makes visible is hard to accept (Jn 6.60). With one eye fixed firmly on the liberal theology in which he had been schooled, Forsyth urged the church of his day not to regard Jesus 'as one of us' and so 'a rival', but instead 'God's gift of grace to us'.[99] To put it simply, our starting point is *not* unity with the Father, Jesus' is. Some struggles with the Johannine Jesus demonstrate an unwillingness to confront the one who, at the same time that he must endure the struggles common to humanity, must also be the one who singularly overcomes the world (Jn 16.33). The primary offence of Christ was and is not his brotherly sympathy with our human struggles. Jesus is more than sympathetic to our plight; he *is himself* constitutive of a new reality. Or, in Johannine terms, Jesus *is* the light of the world (Jn 8.12). Jesus' obedience cannot therefore be placed on the same plane as ours, no matter how relevant this might appear to make him to our needs. What we 'need' is to shed 'the jealous complaint that He has an advantage' and recognize instead that Jesus' singular obedience is what makes our subsequent obedience possible.[100] Jesus' life and work therefore reveals more than a principle – for example, that it is important to be obedient to the Father – but it *enacts* the filial obedience between the Father and Son, lodging it in our world of sin and disarray and so enabling (through the Spirit) our subsequent obedience. In terms which P. T. Forsyth would recognize, Jesus' obedience is more than a highpoint in the evolution of human achieving; it is the victorious

---

95. James B. Torrance, 'The Priesthood of Jesus' in T. H. L. Parker (ed.), *Essays in Christology for Karl Barth* (London: Lutterworth, 1956), pp. 155–73 (158).

96. Yeago, 'Crucified Also For Us under Pontius Pilate', p. 92.

97. Torrance, *Mediation of Christ*, p. 92.

98. Jonathan R. Wilson, *God So Loved the World: A Christology for Disciples* (Grand Rapids: Baker Academic, 2001), p. 74.

99. Forsyth, 'Revelation and the Person of Christ', p. 129.

100. Forsyth, 'Revelation and the Person of Christ', p. 128.

act of God in Christ which 'overcomes the world' (Jn 16.33).[101] In our desire to secure Jesus' solidarity with humanity, grip must not be lost on Jesus' distinctiveness, for the work accomplished by Jesus is only possible and only effective for us because he and the Father are 'one' (Jn 10.30). The scandal of the gospel – and what leads to Jesus' death – is precisely this identity between Jesus and God. Jesus is 'full of grace and truth' (Jn 1.16) only because of this saving identity. This is the radical reality of the Word made flesh:

> He has not merely healed me, in passing, of an old trouble, but has given me eternal life . . . He has made a moral change in me, which, for years and years, has worked outwards from the very core of my moral self, and subdued everything else to its obedience . . . It is not merely that he spoke to me of God or God's doings, but in him God directly spoke to me; and more, he did in me, and for me, the thing that only God's real presence could do.[102]

But, if we are to dwell a little longer in the mystery of the gospel revelation, as soon as this note is sounded, we need to rebalance our emphasis by insisting that Jesus' true humanity – and so the truth of our humanity – is revealed in his obedience.[103] This is to be reminded of the misstep that is presuming that '"*our*" humanity could be the criterion by which to judge the incarnation of God'.[104] It is precisely by attending to his filial obedience – where to some readers of John Jesus seems to be *most* removed from us – that we must begin working out what it means to say with Thomas Torrance that 'no Gospel more than the Fourth Gospel stresses the humanity of Jesus so much'.[105] Here we can return to the Prologue. If Jesus' life establishes 'what it is to be God and what it is to be creature',[106] the one in whom the truth of who we are can now be found, then this is because *he* is the one in whom all things were created (Jn 1.3). The Word and the flesh are not to be understood as competitors for our attention, but in perfect conjunction.

As true man Jesus becomes himself 'the covenant partner God has summoned Israel to be',[107] in whom those who are not part of Israel are privileged now to indwell. Jesus reveals true humanity, living out an obedient life proper

---

101.   See Forsyth, *Cruciality of the Cross*, pp. 63–64.

102.   P. T. Forsyth, 'The Distinctive Thing in Christian Experience' in *Gospel and Authority*, pp. 54–74 (64).

103.   Here is where Forsyth's characteristic antinomies are less helpful. See for example, Forsyth, *Cruciality of the Cross*, p. 27, 'He [Jesus] was God doing the very best for man, and not man doing the very best before God'.

104.   Aaron Riches, 'After Chalcedon: The Oneness of Christ and the Dyothelite Mediation of his Theandric Unity', *Modern Theology* 24 (2008), pp. 199–224 (201, emphasis added).

105.   Thomas F. Torrance, *Space, Time and Resurrection* (Edinburgh: T&T Clark, 1998), p. 169.

106.   Robert W. Jenson, 'The Strange New World of the Bible' in Root and Buckley (eds), *Sharper Than a Two-Edged Sword*, pp. 22–31 (29).

107.   Yeago, 'Crucified Also for Us under Pontius Pilate', p. 98.

to the second Adam, and so we can say that 'God became man that man might become more truly human'.[108] It is surely worth noticing that the culmination of Jesus' obedient life – his hoisting on a cross – marks the time when he 'will draw all people to myself' (Jn 12.32). (Also of note here is how Jesus' hour is seemingly precipitated by the message that some Greeks wished to meet him [Jn. 12.20–27].) It is therefore a mistake to regard Jesus as less 'realistically' human the more obedient he is to God, as if our 'humanity' is marked by striking free from God. That Jesus is commandeered by his Sonship – the relationship with his Father that is eternal in its origins yet one that is temporally lived out and performed – is no reason for finding the humanity of Jesus somehow unconvincing, in a similar (not parallel) way that Christians are no less human the more they walk by grace. It is important here not to import into our model of obedience assumptions which would see freedom as self-creation or models of freedom which would see humanity and divinity as essentially competitive in their relationship to one another.[109] Jesus' freedom is certainly not a freedom of self-creation. Rather, Jesus reveals the truth of humanity in the shape of his obedience, and returns the obedience he has lived out and completed in the time of a human life back to the Father. Jesus' whole life is therefore a priestly offering of obedience: 'I glorified you on earth by finishing the work you gave me to do' (Jn 17.4).[110] Jesus lives in ceaseless fellowship with his Father and is a 'true man' because he completes the will of the Father.[111] 'My food is to do the will of him who sent me and to complete his work' (Jn 4.34). The remarkable obedience which runs throughout the whole course of the Johannine Jesus' life is not an argument that Jesus' humanity is inauthentic or unrealistic. On, the contrary, it is a revelation that Christ is for us the 'true man' needed in order that *we* may enter into renewed fellowship with the Father. Calvin himself realized that as equally as we needed to stress the divinity of Jesus so too an emphasis on Jesus' humanity was essential:

> [t]he second requirement of our reconciliation with God was this: that man, who by his disobedience had become lost, should by way of remedy counter it with obedience . . . Accordingly, our Lord came forth as true man and took the person and the name of Adam in order to take Adam's place in obeying the Father . . . In short, since neither as God alone could he feel death, nor as man alone could he overcome it, he coupled human nature with divine that to atone for sin he might submit the weakness of the one

108. Riches, 'After Chalcedon', p. 202.

109. John Webster, 'Evangelical Freedom' in Catherine Sider Hamilton (ed.), *The Homosexuality Debate: Faith Seeking Understanding* (Toronto: Anglican Book Centre, 2003), pp. 109–23. In the language of John's Gospel it is through discipleship that we come to know the truth that will make us free (Jn 8.31–32).

110. Jesus' priestly obedience is a popular Reformed motif: see Horton, *Lord and Servant*, p. 226; James B. Torrance, *Worship, Community and the Triune God of Grace* (Downers Grove: Inter Varsity Press, 1996), p. 48; Gunton, *Christ and Creation*, pp. 56–57.

111. Calvin, *Institutes* II.xii.3, p. 466.

to death; and that, wrestling with death by the power of the other nature, he might win victory for us.[112]

With attention to Jn 1.14's claim that 'the Word became flesh', and with a corresponding willingness to attend to the divinity and humanity of Jesus together, we can hear Jesus' words with renewed force: 'Those who abide in me and I in them bear much fruit, because apart from me you can do nothing' (Jn 15.5).

## Conclusion

Some notes on the meditations of this chapter can be offered in conclusion.

1. There can, quite simply, be no understanding of the Gospel narratives without explanation. The scriptural narratives are inseparable from the need to explain what is indicated by them. Theological exegesis is motivated by the cheerful confidence that the church's teachings – doctrine – can help us follow the way the words go in the Gospels.
2. It has been this chapter's intention to have followed the way the words go in John's Gospel. The mystery for the theologically engaged reader of John is how we may speak of Christ achieving something in time which he already had – unity with the Father. When Rowan Williams writes that 'Jesus . . . is so related to the eternal relation of the Son to the Father that his human life is the embodiment in time of that eternal relation' we can read this as a fitting summary of the Fourth Gospel.[113] To have truly overcome the world Jesus must have achieved something in time that was a genuinely dramatic happening. But equally, to be saving Jesus must have revealed in time that which is rooted in the deepest recesses of eternity. This chapter has endeavoured not to resolve this mystery but to dwell in it, plumbing its depths, and approaching the figure of Jesus from numerous directions.
3. Doctrine and Scripture must be seen to be mutually informing – but they are not the same. Theological exegesis would do well to heed Oliver O'Donovan's counsel: 'The text and my reading of the text are two things, not one, and the first is the judge of the second.'[114] Accordingly, theological exegesis ends with the humble act of picking up Scripture and reading once again. 'In the beginning was the Word. . . .'

---

112. Calvin, *Institutes* II.xii.3, p. 466. See Horton, *Lord and Servant*, p. 220–32.
113. Rowan Williams, 'The Unity of the Church and the Unity of the Bible: An Analogy', *Internationale Kirkliche Zeitschrift* 91 (2001), pp. 5–21 (10).
114. O'Donovan, *Church in Crisis*, p. 80.

# Chapter 4

## PREACHING AND SCRIPTURE

### Introduction

Week in, week out, the church preaches.[1] Such a practice – preaching – makes known the church's willingness to be transformed by the gospel, a gospel, P. T. Forsyth has reminded us, enshrined in Scripture. Worship and liturgy are therefore Scripture's native habitat. 'Scripture is most at home when reverently and receptively read, spoken and heard within Christian assemblies constituted by prayer, praise and proclamation.'[2] As a practice, preaching is always rooted in the reading of Scripture, and so to think about preaching is to be implicated in thinking about Scripture (and vice-versa). In line with this book's determination to begin always in the middle, preaching is most faithfully understood as an embedded practice, initiated and generated by the summoning presence of the risen Jesus, grounded in the reading of Scripture and fixed firmly within the church. By its very nature, preaching is ecclesial – it is inescapably a communal practice in which both speaker and hearers are implicated.[3] Preaching is a practice, porous to Scripture, in which the church seeks faithfully 'to enter more fully into the receptivity and responsiveness, to others and to God, that characterize Christ and all who share in the new creation'.[4] In a book seeking to understand Scripture from within the church's practices and convictions – and so recover an understanding of what Scripture is by attending to the various actions of which it is part – an inquiry into the nature of preaching is clearly necessary. Daring to think *theologically* about preaching is an attempt to release

---

1. I use the collective term – 'the church' – advisedly. The reason why the lectionary is important is that it is one more reminder of the company which preachers keep; it is not individuals who preach, but the church.

2. Michael Pasquarello III, *Christian Preaching: A Trinitarian Theology of Proclamation* (Grand Rapids: Baker Academic, 2006), p. 136.

3. Alasdair MacIntyre's emphasis on the collective nature of practices in *After Virtue* is an important influence here. See also Brad J. Kallenberg, 'The Master Argument of MacIntyre's *After Virtue*' in Nancey Murphy, Brad J. Kallenberg and Mark Theissen Nation (eds), *Virtues and Practices in the Christian Tradition: Christian Ethics after MacIntyre* (Harrisburg: Trinity Press International, 1997), pp. 7–29: 'to participate in the community is to participate in practices because communal life is the point at which the practices intersect' (22).

4. Dykstra and Bass, 'A Theological Understanding of Christian Practices', p. 28.

the pressures on preachers to be 'relevant', to be 'effective' or to 'bridge' through hermeneutical agility the gap between our world and the world of Scripture. In response to these exigencies, which presume variously that the real world is not the biblical world or that there is not a figural pattern to history, the church points first to the sheer presence of the risen Lord and then to its own life as a people formed and transformed by what they hear. On these realities need the preacher's gaze fall, for Christ risen and present with his people is all that the preacher needs to resource her vocation.[5]

Attempts to understand preaching theologically trace an answer to the question: what is a sermon? The inquiries of this chapter into the nature of preaching are therefore deeply ontological. This is no trespass onto alien territory. The declaration of the 1566 Second Helvetic Confession that 'the preaching of the Word of God is the Word of God' is nothing if it is not an ontological statement.[6] By reflecting on what preaching *is*, I am aware that a wide variety of articles and books stand ready to tell us what preaching is not. Preaching is *not* conciliatory, *not* the words of humans about matters broadly religious, *not* a form of therapy or self-help to meet our perceived 'needs',[7] *not* apologetic, *not* a monologue, *not* an opportunity for sharing religious experience, and so on. An even more daunting variety of literature advertises itself on the basis of counselling us *how* to structure our sermons as rhetorically effective forms of communication, not a few of them with the implicit aim of helping us 'to translate and render Christianity useful, appealing, relevant, and entertaining on terms dictated by a consumerist culture'.[8] To allay any potential objections or concerns in the light of what I will say at points within this chapter defining what a sermon is not and setting out suggestions for sermon preparation are both important tasks. We need to mark out the boundaries of the sermonic form and identify what lies inside and outside of these boundaries. The church is making the most extraordinary of claims when it preaches – that in the words of humans God's Word is to be heard – and part of our commitment to this unique mode of speaking must be a demarcation of what preaching is not. (Sometimes, saying what preaching is *not* may indeed be easier than saying

---

5.   Cf. Wells, *God's Companions*, who displays a similar confidence in relation to Christian ethics.

6.   Kay, *Preaching and Theology*, pp. 18–22, reminds us that the Helvetic Confession does *not* say that preaching *is* the Word of God, but that 'The Preaching of the Word of God is the Word of God'.

7.   See, for example, L. Gregory Jones, 'The Psychological Captivity of the Church in the United States' in Carl E. Braaten and Robert W. Jenson (eds), *Either/Or: The Gospel or Neopaganism* (Grand Rapids: Eerdmans, 1995), pp. 97–112, and D. Stephen Long, 'God is Not Nice' in D. Brent Laytham (ed.), *God is Not . . .* (Grand Rapids: Brazos, 2004), pp. 39–54. The sociological discussion of North American Presbyterian and Baptist preaching on the Prodigal Son in Marsha G. Witten, *All is Forgiven: The Secular Message in American Protestantism* (Princeton: Princeton University Press, 1993), pp. 130–32 is also very helpful.

8.   Pasquarello, *Christian Preaching*, p. 166. Pasquarello is critical of such approaches.

what preaching is.) It is also quite proper to articulate how sermons might be structured, composed and delivered. Preaching is no act of magic and preachers speak as sinful creatures from within the world, not as angels from heaven. As preachers communicate in human words, it is right to consider how the words we select might best be fashioned and directed to the desired end of all preaching, namely that the gospel be extended into the church for the life of the world. As John Wright states, in a formulation that also tells us what preaching is not, rhetoric 'is necessary, but not an end unto itself. Rhetorical engagement must serve the difference found in the gospel, not naming what is already present in the individual's experience'.[9]

The negative tasks of setting out what preaching should *not* be and the rhetorical interests of homiletics therefore play important roles in Christian thinking on preaching. But, and herein is the central concern of this chapter, *these tasks are subsidiary to the positive location of preaching within the economy of salvation and the life of the people sustained by scriptural reading and performance.* Just as curriculum divisions within theology departments and seminaries have inhibited theological understanding of Scripture, so too there is a pronounced tendency for much homiletical literature to be built on weak or questionable theological foundations.[10] The curricular divisions of the modern seminary tempt us to suppose that how we structure sermons – the illustrations we use, the attempts to bridge the so-called gap between the biblical world and our world, the 'points' we make – is a theologically neutral matter. But technique, far from being a theology-free zone, is in fact shot through with theological implications and assumptions.[11] What we think of as a matter for something called 'practical theology' is ensnared in a host of (often unexamined) theological convictions. To allay the risk of divorcing preaching from theological questions, rhetorical and communicative considerations need to be ordered to those permanently 'relevant' categories that will inform us about the nature and ministry of preaching – the role of revelation, the self-proclamation of the risen and ascended Jesus and the church. Understanding what preaching 'is' through these categories is an effort in 'understanding how God's revelation makes preaching possible, necessary, and effective'.[12]

To inquire into the nature of preaching is to be implicated in the most harrying of pursuits. The source of this harassment is not the usual launching pad for many fraught sermons – how do I make this text relevant? – but attention

---

9.    John W. Wright, *Telling God's Story: Narrative Preaching for Christian Formation* (Downers Grove: IVP Academic, 2007), p. 153.

10.    This is a point demonstrated in Campbell, *Preaching Jesus*, who exposes convincingly the correlationist tendency evident in much 'narrative preaching'. See also Pasquarello, *Christian Preaching*.

11.    Paul C. McGlasson, *Invitation to Dogmatic Theology: A Canonical Approach* (Grand Rapids: Brazos, 2006), p. 174.

12.    Richard Lischer, 'Resurrection and Rhetoric' in Carl E. Braaten and Robert W. Jenson (eds), *Marks of the Body of Christ* (Grand Rapids: Eerdmans, 1999), pp. 13–24 (15).

to the astonishing claim: God speaks! The Word of God, as the Israelites recognized when they protested to Moses, is a thing of terror: 'You speak to us, and we will listen; but do not let God speak to us, or we will die' (Exod. 20.19). 'The preaching of the Word of God *is* the Word of God . . . ,' a radical identification which should both cheer and startle preachers.[13] Karl Barth is therefore correct to recognize that the urgent question is 'not How *does* one do it? but How *can* one do it?'[14] In drastic summary, my response is that preaching can be done insofar as the preacher views herself as a servant of Jesus' active self-proclamation through the Spirit. In the presence of the one who is risen – and so indestructibly with us – preaching is the echo of Jesus' words to his disciples, 'Take courage, I have overcome the world' (Jn 16.33). Moreover, preaching can be done because the preacher stands not alone in her undertaking, but is surrounded by the church. A theological account of preaching makes sense in *this* quite specific context. Starting from this location presents us with a host of questions that we might not otherwise have encountered. How is the speaking of the preacher distinct from other discourses of the church? What are the implications of Jesus' luminous presence for our methods of communication? How do we account for the sheer humanity of preaching, which either fails to manifest Jesus' presence or is plain sinful? What is the role of grace in boring out our ears? How does the church sustain and make intelligible the practice of preaching? This chapter, written with the Fourth Gospel laid out on the desk,[15] is an attempt to provide some answers to these questions. In allowing our answers to these questions to be funded by reading John's Gospel, this chapter therefore seeks to consolidate Scripture's indispensable role in theological thinking.

An initial response to the question of what preaching is can take its orientation from John Calvin's location of preaching, particularly as it can be discerned from his commentary on the Fourth Gospel. From there this chapter will proceed to embed preaching within Christ's ascended presence, the Spirit's activity, the hearing of the church and the life of the church.

## *A Brief Sketch: Calvin*

John Calvin, a zealous and committed preacher,[16] regarded preaching as an instrument that makes present the very power of God himself. In an arresting

---

13.  William H. Willimon, *Conversations with Barth on Preaching* (Nashville: Abingdon, 2006), p. 127.

14.  Karl Barth, 'The Need and Promise of Christian Preaching' in *The Word of God and the Word of Man* (trans. Douglas Horton; New York: Harper and Row, 1957), pp. 97–135 (103).

15.  I am therefore heeding Lischer, 'Resurrection and Rhetoric', p. 14, 'The New Testament . . . offers no explanation or rules for preaching, but only the affirmation of a mystery in which we are privileged to participate.'

16.  Dawn DeVries, 'Calvin's Preaching' in Donald K. McKim (ed.), *The Cambridge Companion to John Calvin* (Cambridge: Cambridge University Press, 2004), pp. 106–24, states that during the course of Calvin's 25 year Geneva ministry he preached more than 2000 times (106).

interpretation of Jn 3.14 – 'just as Moses lifted up the serpent in the wilderness, so must the Son of Man be lifted up' – Calvin saw the evangelist's typological reading of Num. 21.8 not as a reference to Jesus' 'lifting up' on the cross, as the vast bulk of tradition had previously understood it (with the support of Jn 12.32-33), but as a proleptic reference to Jesus being raised aloft in the preaching and teaching of the church 'like a standard which all would look at . . . that whosoever looks upon Him by faith will receive salvation'.[17]

A number of themes distinct to Calvin emerge from his exegesis of this verse. Preaching for Calvin is that which renders Jesus sacramentally present and visible, at least for those to whom the Spirit has given eyes to see this 'secret' sight.[18] For those endowed with perceptive 'eyes of faith' Christ is 'present with us so often as He calls us to the hope of salvation by the preaching of the Gospel'.[19] This presence in the proclaimed Word is made possible by the Holy Spirit.[20] Preaching is therefore more than an opportunity for teaching. Surprisingly, Karl Rahner's theological account of preaching translates Calvin's thought here fittingly. Preaching is 'not just the hearing of a statement about something, but the reception of the reality itself about which the audible statement is made'.[21] Christ, put simply, is present in our preaching. He is both subject and object who ultimately renders preaching effective. It is also worth noting here the precise role Calvin gives to the sensory realm: it is neither through the crafted images of the church's sculptors nor through the raising of the host that we will catch a sight of Jesus, but through obedient hearing.[22] Our eyes need not rove around the various images the church thrusts before our eyes, but to the one image seen through what is heard in preaching (Gal. 3.1).[23] Calvin therefore gives preaching an appropriately high status within God's economy of salvation:

> It is true that even in the cross He triumphed magnificently over Satan before God and the angels, blotting out the handwriting of sin and cancelling the condemnation of

---

17. *Comm. Jn. 3.14.* For discussion of Calvin's bold reading of this verse, see Dawn DeVries, *Jesus Christ in the Preaching of Calvin and Schleiermacher* (Louisville: Westminster John Knox, 1996), pp. 16–17.

18. *Comm. Jn. 14.19.* See Philip W. Butin, *Reformed Ecclesiology: Trinitarian Grace According to Calvin* (Studies in Reformed Theology and History; Princeton: Princeton Theological Seminary, 1994), who emphasizes very strongly the trinitarian nature of Calvin's theology of worship.

19. *Comm. Jn. 8.56; Comm. Jn. 7.33.*

20. *Comm. Jn. 14.26.* See John H. Leith, 'Calvin's Doctrine of the Proclamation of the Word and Its Significance for Today' in Timothy George (ed.), *John Calvin and the Church: A Prism for Reform* (Louisville: Westminster John Knox, 1990), pp. 206–29 (210–12).

21. Karl Rahner, 'The Word and the Eucharist' in *Theological Investigations*, Vol. IV (trans. Kevin Smyth; 23 vols; London: Darton, Longman and Todd, 1974), pp. 253–86 (262).

22. Perhaps because he has invested his energies in articulating a theology of sound these *visual* aspects of preaching are left unexplored in Stephen Webb's discussion of Calvin's theology of preaching in his *The Divine Voice: Christian Proclamation and the Theology of Sound* (Grand Rapids: Brazos, 2004), pp. 150–57.

23. Calvin, *Institutes*, I.xi.7, p. 107.

death. But it was only after the Gospel had been preached that this triumph began to be apparent to men.[24]

This statement is an extension of Calvin's more terse statement that 'if the gospel be not preached Jesus Christ is, as it were, buried'.[25] Only as Jesus is present to us in preaching is his salvation continually made available to us. Preaching on Jn 1.1–5 Calvin therefore states that 'when the gospel is proclaimed to us, it is a manifestation of Jesus Christ'.[26] This focus on the power of preaching was a function of Calvin's determination to position preaching firmly within God's covenantal history with Israel and the church. Preaching is God drawing into his company those who would otherwise be estranged from his presence. As a prophet Jesus came not just therefore to teach and mediate what would otherwise lie hidden in the bosom of God but also to embrace the church within his ministry. As the one sent by Jesus, the preacher now shares in Christ's own ministry. Calvin's comments on Jn 20.21 ('As the Father has sent me, so I send you') are instructive in this regard:

> hitherto he [Jesus] has discharged the office of Teacher, but now [that] he has finished His course he commits it to them [the disciples]. He means that the Father made Him a teacher of the Church on condition that He should for a time go before the rest but afterwards should substitute in His place those who would make good His absence . . . He commends them to succeed to the same test, which He had received from the Father, lays upon them the same part, and bestows on them the same authority.[27]

Preaching is a power of salvation ultimately because it is an extension of Jesus' own ministry, a ministry that is itself fixed within God's covenant with Israel and the nations. The preaching of the Word is in deepest unity with the Word that spoke creation into being, which the prophets declared, and that became flesh and dwelt among us.

As suggested at the beginning of this chapter, it is tempting to respond to Calvin's robust grasp of the Word of God by concentrating on what preaching should *not* be. Equally, for the preacher faced with empty pews it is easy to think that the most urgent task is to craft 'relevant' sermons that might draw more people towards the church. More pressing however than either of these tasks is to articulate, in company with Scripture and keen readers of it like Calvin, what preaching *is* as a human (and hence profoundly fallible) act

---

24.　*Comm. Jn. 8.28.*

25.　John Calvin, *The Mystery of Godliness and Other Sermons* (Grand Rapids: Eerdmans, 1950), p. 25. Cited in Thomas J. Davis, 'Preaching and Presence: Constructing Calvin's Homiletical Legacy' in David Foxgrover (ed.), *The Legacy of John Calvin* (Grand Rapids: Calvin Studies Society, 2000), pp. 84–111 (91).

26.　John Calvin, *Sermons on the Saving Work of Christ* (trans. Leroy Nixon; Welwyn: Evangelical Press, 1980), p. 14. Cited in Davis, 'Preaching and Presence', p. 102 n. 57.

27.　*Comm. Jn. 20.21.*

annexed by God so that the school of faith might be built up. We have seen with Calvin's help that preaching is heard, comes with power, is enlivened by the Holy Spirit and takes place in the company of the church. We may expand these clues as to how preaching 'works' by following the implications of four claims: If we speak the Word of God it is only because God is already present to us in his risen and ascended son, Jesus. If we hear the Word of God it is only because, through the Holy Spirit, we are first drawn into the triune conversation. Preaching dares to 'hear' what God makes known to us in his Son. And through time, preaching builds up the church as a people who bear witness to the truth of Jesus' Lordship.

### *The Power of Preaching is the Presence of the Ascended Christ*

Theological accounts of preaching begin with the recognition that it 'is primarily a receptive activity'.[28] As such all theological accounts of preaching are deductions from the self-sufficient reality that is the primary confession of the church: Jesus is present as crucified, risen and ascended. Preaching is a communicative act ignited by the knowledge which the risen and glorified Jesus imparts. 'His disciples did not understand these things at first; but when Jesus was glorified, then they remembered that these things had been written of him and had been done to him' (Jn 12.16). Preaching is closely allied to revelation – we can after all only speak about God because God has spoken *first* – and revelation is never very far away from God's determination to be permanently present with us: 'The light shines in the darkness and the darkness did not overcome it' (Jn 1.5).

That Jesus Christ lives (and so is present with us now) is, as Barth says, both 'the simplest and the most difficult Christological statement'.[29] Preaching is only possible because of God's self-communication and his indestructible desire to be present with us (Jn 14.3). Jesus lives as the one who died, rose and has ascended, or as John abbreviates all this, Jesus lives as the glorified one. This revelatory presence is determinative for thinking through what it is to preach.[30] What preaching is, how preaching is affective, our approach to sermons as vehicles of communication, the status of Scripture in preaching are all avenues of inquiry capable of being answered through attention to the church's Easter Day confession: He is risen indeed. Located within this setting preaching is, as it were, a resolutely 'present tense activity'. There is less need to be harried by the gap between the biblical world and our world, if we attend to the reality that in his church Christ already meets us. Therefore the 'true crisis

---

28.  Pasquarello, *Christian Preaching*, p. 129.

29.  Karl Barth, *Church Dogmatics* IV/3.1 (trans G. W. Bromiley; London: T&T Clark International, 2004), p. 39.

30.  I am indebted to Webster, 'Resurrection and Scripture', for many insights of this part of the chapter.

is created by the fact that Jesus Christ is indeed present, that the voice of the living Lord does indeed declare himself.'[31] The preacher is one who has been sent and commissioned to attest to this astounding reality of Jesus' aliveness, 'he who receives any one who I send receives me, and he who receives me receives him who sent me' (Jn 13.20).[32] The preacher is sent and so speaks with authority.[33] Preachers are, with the aid of the Spirit, agents of Christ's abiding presence in the world. The risen one who startled Mary to faith through his voice (Jn 20.16), who distributed and declared his peace among the fearful disciples (Jn 20.19, 21), who breathed on them the Holy Spirit (Jn 20.22) and who is present with them before they even know it (Jn 20.14; 21.4), speaks to us still through the Holy Spirit, 'My sheep hear my voice. I know them, and they follow me' (Jn 10.27), for the Spirit takes us into the depth of all that Jesus has said and declares to us what he continues to hear (Jn 14.26; 16.13).

Preaching is an activity that occurs from within the paradoxical shape of Jesus' presence: his absence *is* his presence.[34] Of all four Gospels, the Fourth Gospel is most clearly imbued with a sense of Jesus' presence predicated on the necessity of his absence. Throughout the farewell discourses Jesus counsels his disciples that he must leave the world and go to the Father (Jn 13.1, 3; 14.28; 16.17, 28; 17.13). 'I am no longer in the world,' Jesus curiously prays to God in the midst of his high-priestly prayer *before* his death (Jn 17.11). In line with this, Jesus tells his disciples that 'it is to your advantage that I go away, for if I do not go away, the Advocate will not come to you' (Jn 16.7). Again, the risen Jesus tells his disciples that he cannot be held onto, for he must ascend to the state which will draw us into the mutual life between the Father and the

---

31.   McGlasson, *Invitation to Dogmatic Theology*, p. 147.

32.   To be sure, the preacher preaches as a delegate of the church, and not as a freelancing individual. As Lesslie Newbigin, *The Household of God: Lectures on the Nature of the Church* (London: SCM, 1953), rightly points out in the context of commenting on Jn 13.20, Jesus is present *as* the church and 'in His people, His apostolic fellowship' (52). The church is apostolic when it preaches. I do, however, have some concerns about taking the image of being 'sent' too far. The preacher is not as divorced from the form and substance of the message as Søren Kierkegaard states in an essay setting out the differences between a genius and an apostle. An apostle possesses the knowledge that '[t]he doctrine communicated to him is not a task which he is given to ponder over, it is not given him for his own sake, he is, on the contrary, on a mission and has to proclaim the doctrine and use authority. Just as a man, sent into the town with a letter, has nothing to do with its contents, but has only to deliver it; just as a minister who is sent to a foreign court is not responsible for the content of the message, but has only to convey it correctly; so, too, an Apostle has really only to be faithful in his service, and to carry out his task.' (Søren Kierkegaard, 'Of the Difference between a Genius and an Apostle' in *The Present Age* [trans. Alexander Dru; London: Fontana Library, 1962], pp. 101–27 [124]). Surely we need to speak of the preacher's *participation* in her message?

33.   Günther Dehn, *Man and Revelation* (London: Hodder and Stoughton, 1936), p. 172.

34.   Matt Jenson, 'Real Presence: Contemporaneity in Bonhoeffer's *Christology*', *SJT* 58 (2005), pp. 143–60 (157–58).

Son. The good news the risen Jesus asks Mary to proclaim is not even indeed that he has risen, but that 'I am ascending to my Father and your Father, to my God and to your God' (Jn 20.17).[35] In the context of Jesus' status as crucified, risen and ascended five implications for considering the office of preaching immediately suggest themselves.

First, Jesus does not rise from the dead so that he can resume the earthly life and teaching that had been interrupted by his death on a Roman cross. Jesus' words from that cross – 'it is finished' (Jn 19.30) – must be taken in all their finality. Rather, Jesus rises and ascends to a new stage in his ministry and to the place from where he will govern through the Spirit.

Second, Jesus is the active agent of his presence. Preaching does not render him present. Like Scripture, preaching is an instrument of his presence. The Johannine resurrection appearance stories make it abundantly clear that Jesus maintains a lordly control over when, and to whom, he is present.[36] As Barth would emphasize, that preaching 'works', or that Jesus is present, always remains a miracle – a sheer act of grace.

Third, in ascending to the Father Jesus ascends to where, as the Johannine Jesus consistently claims, he has previously come *from* (Jn 3.13; 6.62; 17.5). But crucially he returns from where he has descended with a bloodied, wounded body and lodges this historical humanity within the life of the triune God.[37] Jesus' ascension is as bodily as his resurrection, which means that everything achieved and revealed through his teaching in his bodily life has risen and ascended with him. It is notable that when the risen and now ascended Jesus encounters the disciples in the locked room he appears in his bodily, wounded state (Jn 20.27). The ascension is no escape from Jesus' earthly ministry; the ascension marks, rather, the perduring status of Jesus' earthly ministry and his installation as the Lord of time.

> Just because it is the historical and risen Jesus who is ascended, what Jesus says to us, the Jesus whom we meet and hear through the witness of the Gospels, is identical with the eternal Word and Being of God himself.[38]

---

35. Andrew T. Lincoln, '"I Am the Resurrection and the Life": The Resurrection Message of the Fourth Gospel' in Richard N. Longenecker (ed.), *Life in the Face of Death: The Resurrection Message of the New Testament* (Grand Rapids: Eerdmans, 1998), pp. 122–44 (130–31).

36. See Willimon, *Conversations with Barth*, p. 39 for the link between John 20–21 and preaching.

37. Karl Barth, *Dogmatics in Outline* (trans. G. T. Thomson; New York: Harper and Row, 1959), p. 125.

38. Torrance, *Space, Time and Resurrection*, p. 133. As Torrance notes later on in this same book (pp. 169–70) the Fourth Gospel lays especial emphasis on the coherence between the earthly ministry of Jesus and his state of resurrection. The ascension does not therefore obliterate history but invests it with eternal significance.

But, likewise, if our preaching is to be ruled by the one who has ascended there is no other way for us to go other than 'round by Nazareth'.[39] At the ascension, Jesus' kingly, priestly and prophetic offices converge gloriously: it is as the one who has been 'lifted up' (Jn 3.14; 8.28; 12.32, 34) and who has consistently spoken the words which God has given him (Jn 17.14) that he rises to be with the Father. That these words of Jesus are raised into eternal fellowship with God the Father and anchored within this company is one way of understanding the elevated manner in which John seems to understand the very words of Jesus themselves, 'on the last day the very word that I have spoken will serve as a judge' (Jn 12.48). The ascension secures the desire we see in the earthly Jesus to be present with us and to speak to us. Jesus' ascension – his continuing incarnation – therefore calls our attention not just to the liturgical potential of his eternal priesthood,[40] but equally his continuing office as prophet. In returning to the Father, Jesus doesn't shed his flesh and resume his eternal Sonship where he had left it, but he ascends to the Father in his body as the one who was sent to speak the words of God to the world. Recourse to some words from Ephesians suggest themselves here: 'He came and proclaimed peace to you who were far off and peace to those who were near' (Eph. 2.17).

Fourth, Jesus' absence allows his presence through the Spirit and this presence with us, the church, is dependent upon his 'going away' (Jn 14.28). It is only with Jesus' absence that the disciples are drawn more deeply into the meaning of Jesus' earthly life, 'you do not know now what I am doing, but later you will understand' (Jn 13.7). In preaching, Jesus is not spatially, but relationally, present with us through the Spirit. The author of Ephesians neatly condenses all that the Fourth Gospel says about the descent and ascent of Jesus and its significance for the region of preaching when he writes, '[h]e who descended is the same one who ascended far above all the heavens, so that he might fill all things' (Eph. 4.10).[41] Jesus 'fills all things' – including our preaching – not because he is a presence diffused everywhere (for example, like a fragrance) but because he 'is everywhere accessible' through the Spirit which binds his history with ours.[42]

Fifth, Jesus' departure from the world names the time of the church as the time to proclaim the news that Jesus' Father and Jesus' God is now our Father and our God (Jn 20.17). Preaching, the churchly practice that takes place in the time between Jesus' fleshly ascension and his fleshly return, is founded in a

---

39.   Forsyth, *Positive Preaching*, p. 16.

40.   This continuing work of Christ is emphasized very strongly in the work of Thomas F. Torrance and James B. Torrance. For a powerful synthesis of their work (and numerous other rich insights) see Gerrit Scott Dawson, *Jesus Ascended: The Meaning of Christ's Continuing Incarnation* (London: T&T Clark International, 2004).

41.   Cf. Webster, 'Resurrection and Scripture', p. 138.

42.   Douglas Farrow, *Ascension and Ecclesia: On the Significance of the Doctrine of the Ascension for Ecclesiology and Christian Cosmology* (Grand Rapids: Eerdmans, 1999), p. 178.

specific commission and is fixed in a specific moment of salvation history. T. F. Torrance is worth citing here:

> The ascension means that Jesus has withdrawn Himself from history in order to allow the world time for repentance . . . [t]hat is the time in which the Church exists and carries out its mission, within the succession of history where there is time between revelation and decision, time between decision and act, time between the present and future. It is time where the present age is already interpenetrated by the age to come, but it is the time when the new age and all its final glory are held in eschatological reserve, in order to leave room to preach the Gospel and give mankind opportunity to meet with God, to repent, and believe the Gospel.[43]

Preaching is here located in the patience of God, that the world might come to hear and know the gospel. I would only nuance this to add that there is an important difference between preaching *in* the church and preaching *to* the world, namely preaching in the context of worship and preaching in the context of mission. The church can only witness to the world insofar as it has a proper and distinct understanding of preaching as worship and as a sacramental agent of edification that over time, as the Word that dwells in us richly, builds up the people of God.[44] To deploy Johannine terms, there is a balance to be struck between the Petrine commission to tend Jesus' lambs (Jn 21.15) and the outward movement and witness to the world which is also present in the Fourth Gospel (Jn 17.21). In the time announced by the ascension, the preacher confronts the church and the world with a decisiveness and authority rooted in Jesus' earthly sending, 'just as you sent me into the world, so too I have sent them into the world' (Jn 17.18). Yet, precisely as 'apostles' preachers are servants of Jesus' own summoning presence. If we take seriously the unity with which the Fourth Gospel views Jesus' death, resurrection and ascension as an act of glorification then we need not fear reading Jn 12.32 – 'I, when I am lifted up from the earth will draw all people to myself' – as a reference to Jesus' ascended state. The preacher is an agent of Jesus' will to draw all people to himself. As Peter of Blois preached on Jesus' statement in Jn 12.32:

> He descended in order to ascend, and in order to draw us with Him as he ascended. 'When I shall have been lifted up from the earth, I will draw all people to myself.' God is infinite and He can neither increase nor ascend. Therefore in order that He might increase, He became a little lower than the angels . . . we are to rejoice especially in His

---

43. Thomas F. Torrance, *Royal Priesthood: A Theology of Ordained Ministry* (Edinburgh: T&T Clark, 2nd edn, 1993), pp. 59–60. This theme is also emphasized throughout Barth's *Church Dogmatics*: see Andrew Burgess, *The Ascension in Karl Barth* (Barth Studies; Aldershot: Ashgate, 2004), pp. 53–73.
44. For this distinction see Forsyth, *Positive Preaching*, pp. 53–55.

ascension by which the way of life has been opened for us . . . in order that we might
go whither our Head has preceded, that the Head may not be without His members.[45]

The presence of the ascended Jesus in the preaching of the church rivets our
attention on Jesus as the preceding reality who wills not to be without his
'members'. The words of the ascended Jesus continue to divide (Jn 10.19), are
installed as a judging force (Jn 12.48) and continually purify (Jn 15.3). Within
this economy preaching is speech set aside by God and sanctified by the Spirit
'through which the risen and ascended Lord rules'.[46]

At this point of the discussion, lest it appear that I am drifting into blueprint
theologies of preaching, it will be helpful to take a brief look at an actual sermon on John framed around the present and interrogating reality of Jesus. In a
sermon before his Safenwil congregation in the early 1920s, Karl Barth turned
his attention to the discourse between Jesus and Nicodemus in Jn 3.1–10. Barth
begins by reflecting that religious dialogues between humans are often crafted
so as to maintain a safe distance between the interlocutors. In religious conversation we want to understand each other, but always only just enough to keep
us on opposing sides. Nicodemus comes with exactly this determination in
mind: to engage Jesus in a religious conversation, but not to be drawn into the
actual substance of Jesus' claims. Respectful of Jesus' status as a religious
teacher, Nicodemus begins politely and formally, 'Rabbi, we know that you are
a teacher who has come from God' (Jn 3.2). Jesus' response, 'Very truly, I tell
you, no one can see the kingdom of God without being born from above' (Jn
3.3), indicates that it is not his aim to be involved in a polite conversation about
religious matters. It is not any part of Jesus' intentions to talk to us 'from bank
to bank' or 'from mount to mount'.[47] Jesus appears singularly uninterested in
conversing in any conventional way and is intent on confronting Nicodemus
with a situation which will force him to come to a decision. What Nicodemus
is confronted with is therefore quite different from what he had sought in seeking out Jesus, 'there is to be no carefully moderated talk from shore to shore,
in which each will carefully maintain his own opinions. Nicodemus suddenly
found himself in the middle of the stream. The ground was taken from under
his feet.'[48]

Jesus' cryptic response to Nicodemus' approach ('without being born from
above . . .', Jn 3.3) refutes Nicodemus' attempt to understand Jesus and his
significance. Jesus doesn't react to Nicodemus' seemingly benign approach

45. Peter of Blois, *Sermo 23* (*Patrologia Latina* 207.627–30). Cited and translated in J. G.
Davies, *He Ascended Into Heaven: A Study in the History of Doctrine* (London: Lutterworth,
1958), p. 164.

46. Torrance, *Space, Time and Resurrection*, p. 121.

47. Karl Barth, 'Jesus and Nicodemus' in *Come Holy Spirit* (trans. George W. Richards, Elmer
G. Homrighausen and Karl J. Ernst; Edinburgh: T&T Clark, 1934), pp. 101–11 (104). See also the
discussion of this sermon in Robert W. Duke, *The Sermon as God's Word: Theologies for Preaching* (Nashville: Abingdon, 1980), pp. 14–29.

48. Barth, 'Jesus and Nicodemus', p. 103.

with words of rejoicing or tender warmth. On the contrary, barely has Nicodemus
spoken before Jesus has slain him with his word for 'instead of meeting Him
half way, He cut off his words before he had really begun to speak. Instead of
answering his question, He put to him an enormously difficult new question'.[49]
Jesus has no time for well-meaning religious chatter: he confronts us directly
with *his* claim. As with Nicodemus, Jesus wills that we might be dragged from
our short-sightedness to grasp a vision of God as *he* directs.

Barth's sermon reinforces a number of important homiletic implications of
Jesus' ascended presence. The most important homiletic gift preachers can
have is humility. If the context for preaching is the ascended presence of
God in Jesus Christ, then it will be impossible to think of preaching as an
opportunity to 'summon God before our minds to make him a matter for clever
discourse, but the opposite: the holy God shows himself and summons us
before him to give account of our thinking'.[50] This is in accordance with the
Jesus that impels Barth's sermon on the Nicodemus discourse – if Jesus is
present with us, he is only elusively present to us, at his will and not ours.[51]
Jesus' enigmatic response to Nicodemus is replayed in a host of other Johannine encounters where Jesus accosts his hearers with the sheer strangeness of
his message.

If Jesus is present with us then his identity is not something lost in the passing of time, nor is the 'relevance' of his speaking something to be recovered
through our historical and hermeneutical dexterity. Jesus is not someone
slipping further and further into the past. Jesus doesn't have to be made our
contemporary. The ascended Jesus makes us his contemporaries.[52] He is alive,
and as the Fourth Gospel makes clear, he is alive precisely as the historical
figure who died on a Roman cross (Jn 20.25–27). In this sense, Jesus' resurrection appearances to his disciples represent not a new coming, but are better
viewed as the revelation that the life he led and the ministry he fulfilled in
Galilee and Jerusalem is indestructible. This is what Mary is startled to see in
the garden: not that with Jesus' resurrection there is another coming, but that
the risen one speaking to her *is* the same one who spoke to her previously. The
harassment preachers feel in the light of hermeneutical worries of *how* Jesus
is to be communicated or made present in the life of his or her congregation
can be eased by attention to the acting agent of revelation, 'I have called you
friends, because I have made known to you everything that I have heard
from my Father. You did not choose me but I chose you' (Jn 15.15–16).[53]

---

49. Barth, 'Jesus and Nicodemus', p. 107.

50. John Webster, *Holiness* (London: SCM, 2003), p. 15.

51. Cf. Mark W. G. Stibbe, 'The Elusive Christ: A New Reading of the Fourth Gospel', *JSNT*
44 (1991), pp. 19–37.

52. Barth, *Church Dogmatics* III/2, p. 467.

53. Karl Barth, *Homiletics* (trans. George W. Bromiley and Donald E. Daniels; Louisville:
Westminster John Knox, 1991), p. 53, states starkly that the 'real need is not so much to get to the
people as to come from Christ'.

In the context of the one 'who is living and at large, not dead and confined to the tomb, one who is present and able to act',[54] the texts of Scripture are not commodities to be traded in the market hall of 'relevance' but are agents of Jesus continuing presence with us through the Spirit.

The school of preaching is the active, present voice of Jesus: his promise that he is with us is the fluency the preacher craves as she walks up the stairs of the pulpit. For the preacher, Jesus simply is not 'a past reality which we summon into our presence. He *is* and is present'.[55] If Jesus Christ is present in our preaching it will not be down to the skill of our analogies or the bridges we have built from 'his' world to our world: it will be because he has acted through the Spirit to be present to us as the 'light of the world' (Jn 8.12). The preacher does not himself birth or construct Jesus' presence: 'servants are not greater than their master, nor are messengers greater than the one who sent them' (Jn 13.16).[56] The witness is not greater than that which to which the witness points. The relationship between Jesus and proclamation is more one-way than two-way and the present Christ 'wants' to be proclaimed, 'As the Father has sent me, so I send you' (Jn 20.21).[57] Preaching as witness and testimony points to he who is present, he who makes the words of the preacher a local vehicle of his presence. Although I have some hesitations about his episodic strains, William Willimon puts it well when he writes: 'Jesus Christ *is* and remains God's Word as the incarnation of the Son of God. Scripture and preaching are human realities that, by the grace of God, *become* God's Word as the Incarnate Word enters them into the event of revelation.'[58] In John Webster's drastic summary therefore the preacher accosted by the presence of the ascended Jesus will order her homiletics to the reality that Jesus simply 'is not Lord if he is not the agent of his own becoming known'.[59] The risen Jesus who calls Mary to faith with the simple call of her name (Jn 20.16) reveals a freedom to reveal congruent with the Son's obedience to the Father, 'I have made your name known to those whom you gave me from the world. They were yours, and you gave them to me' (Jn 17.6).

---

54.   David S. Yeago, 'The Bible' in James J. Buckley and David S. Yeago (eds), *Knowing the Triune God: The Work of the Spirit in the Practices of the Church* (Grand Rapids: Eerdmans, 2001), pp. 49–93 (55).

55.   John Webster, 'Prolegomena to Christology: Four Theses' in *Confessing God: Essays in Christian Dogmatics II* (London: T&T Clark International, 2005), pp. 131–49 (131, emphasis added).

56.   Dietrich Bonhoeffer, *Christ the Center* (trans. Edwin H. Robertson; New York: Harper & Row, 1978), p. 51.

57.   For the presence of Christ in the work of the 'sent' disciples see Raymond Brown, *The Gospel According to St. John*, Vol. 2 (Anchor Bible; 2 vols; London: Geoffrey Chapman, 1966), p. 1036.

58.   Willimon, *Conversations with Barth*, p. 230.

59.   Webster, 'Prolegomena to Christology', p. 135.

Preaching in the presence of the risen Christ therefore has enormous potential for reordering what we might think are the chief hermeneutical burdens of preaching. We should not allow a methodologically conceived problem of a gap between the biblical world and our world cloud the truth that Christ spans all time.[60] Sermon preparation that begins with an attention to the startling presence of Jesus is bound to reshape the homiletical inquiries structured around the hermeneutical need to cross over from the world of the biblical text to the world of the church.[61] T. F. Torrance, on the sheer aliveness of the risen Jesus, is worth quoting at some length here. The resurrection is a happening that

> does not slip away from us, but keeps pace with us and outruns us as we tumble down in decay and lapse into death and the dust of past history and even comes to meet us out of the future . . . He is not dead but alive, more real than any of us. Hence he does not need to be made real for us, because he does not decay or become fixed in the past. He lives on in the present as real live continuous happening, encountering us here and now in the present and waiting for us in the future.[62]

One preacher who precisely realized the importance of Jesus' antecedent presence to the integrity of preaching was Dietrich Bonhoeffer. Lecturing to a small group of ordinands from the Confessing Church in the illegal seminary of Finkenwalde, Bonhoeffer emphasized to a quite remarkable degree the identity between the present Christ and the proclaimed Christ.[63] Not only is the proclaimed word rooted in the incarnation-event, but 'the proclaimed word *is* the incarnate Christ himself'.[64] This proclaimed one is not a past, but a present figure and the proclaimed Word is none other than 'Christ himself walking through his congregation as the Word'.[65] Jesus is the agent of his own presence – he is not rendered present through the accomplishments or insights of the preacher. The preacher is rather the vehicle for Jesus' desire to be present among believers: he has his own 'momentum' and 'self-movement',[66] and these qualities are known in the 'magnetic relationship' between the Word's desire to be present and the hearing congregation.[67] The homiletic implications of Bonhoeffer's emphasis on the desire of the Word to be present are clear.

60. Barth, *Church Dogmatics* IV/1, pp. 288–89.

61. For example, Stephen Farris, *Preaching that Matters: The Bible and Our Lives* (Louisville: Westminster John Knox, 1998).

62. Torrance, *Space, Time and Resurrection*, p. 89.

63. See Frits de Lange, *Waiting for the Word: Dietrich Bonhoeffer on Speaking about God* (trans. Martin N. Walton; Grand Rapids: Eerdmans, 2000), pp. 87–119.

64. Dietrich Bonhoeffer, *Worldly Preaching: Lectures on Homiletics* (trans. Clyde E. Fant; New York: Crossroad, 1991), p. 101 (emphasis added).

65. Bonhoeffer, *Worldly Preaching*, p. 101.

66. Bonhoeffer, *Worldly Preaching*, p. 102.

67. Bonhoeffer, *Worldly Preaching*, p. 112.

Attention will be focused on the composition of sermons which clear space for Jesus Christ as the Lord of time to be made known.

What then, we could legitimately ask, is the place of rhetorical and communication aids in preaching? If Jesus is his own radiant communication what role is there for the preacher to presume that she is communicating?[68] How are we to understand preaching as something that happens *in time* – a necessary feature that I emphasize later in this chapter? Certainly, the concern has often been expressed that some attempts to offer a theology of preaching, like that of Dietrich Ritschl, emphasize so heavily the risen Jesus as the subject of the preaching act that little space seems to be left either for the active role of the preacher or the listening congregation. In response to his own inquiry into who is responsible for proclamation, Ritschl emphasizes again and again that a sermon is 'an act of God the Father in Jesus Christ through the Holy Spirit'.[69] True, but the power of God's acting happens through and with our human words and acts, and in this sense a theology of preaching has nothing invested in denying the creatureliness of preaching and the preacher. Theological accounts of preaching must be aware of the lure of 'homiletical Docetism' as vigorously as it must defend itself against accounts that would *presume* God's sanctifying presence.[70] It is to sinful preachers that God has promised the ability to preach his Word, through our human words and in our time. The miracle of preaching – the reason why week after week we prick up our ears to listen to preachers – is that preaching is both the words of humans speaking in all their frailty *and* the promise that the church has not been abandoned to its own devices (Jn 14.18). Proper attention to the living Jesus Christ will not work to remove this offence, but will keep this tension alive. Because we must be committed to preaching as a form of human speaking attention to the form of sermons can be justified on theological grounds. Nor is there any question of a lack of preparation when preaching.

Nevertheless, questions of sermon technique, communication and construction need to be allied much more closely to theological considerations than is the norm. From within this setting rhetorical tools will be accorded a secondary, not primary role. Paul himself points to the primary reality of God's power working through his rhetorical inadequacies, 'I did not come proclaiming the mystery of God to you in lofty words or wisdom. For I decided to know nothing among you except Jesus Christ, and him crucified' (1 Cor. 2.1–2).[71] When our

---

68.  For the vexed recent history between rhetoric and theological accounts of the preaching-act see Thomas G. Long, 'And How Shall They Hear? The Listener in Contemporary Preaching' in Gail R. O'Day and Thomas G. Long (eds), *Listening to the Word: Studies in Honor of Fred B. Craddock* (Nashville: Abingdon, 1993), pp. 167–88 and James F. Kay, 'Reorientation: Homiletics as Theologically Authorized Rhetoric', *Princeton Seminary Bulletin* 24 (2003), pp. 16–35.

69.  Dietrich Ritschl, *A Theology of Proclamation* (Richmond: John Knox, 1963), p. 45.

70.  André Resner, *Preacher and Cross: Person and Message in Theology and Rhetoric* (Grand Rapids: Eerdmans, 1999), p. 62.

71.  Lischer, 'Resurrection and Rhetoric', p. 15.

faltering ability to speak of God and the risen Jesus' desire to be known meet this is always due to the initiative of God. Preaching is not an opportunity for exhibitionist artistry, but rather unites 'the two poles that are to be brought together: the Lord who gives himself and the community that hungers for him'.[72] There is an equal danger of paying excessive attention to the action of God in preaching to the exclusion of our human role as there is of concentrating on the human crafting of proclamation to the exclusion of Jesus' permanent eloquence. The commission of the preacher is to speak, and she must speak in the words of the world, but the preacher's prime responsibility is to make known that her words represent 'treasure in clay jars, so that it may be made clear that this extraordinary power belongs to God and does not come from us' (2 Cor 4.7). Note here, if we may extend Paul's metaphor, that our language is a receptacle and vehicle of Jesus' presence, something that is to be shattered and broken if it is to let the power of the treasure it carries to be released.

If we speak the Word of God it is only because God is already present to us in his risen and ascended son, Jesus.

## Preaching and the Spirit

Sermons preached by a lover and venerator of Jesus can impress us for long; but they do not regenerate till the Word is taken out of the preacher's lips and spoken by a present Spirit, through whom he is far more than Christ's lover . . . but an apostle.[73]

We have seen that Jesus must rise and ascend because it is precisely as the crucified-risen one that he broadcasts abroad knowledge of himself and it is from his ascended state that 'the Advocate comes, whom I will send to you from the Father' (Jn 15.26). Jesus' life has to go the Johannine way of glorification – death, resurrection and ascension – before he can send the Spirit to the church (Jn 7.39; 20.22). If we hear Scripture and the sermon as vehicles of God's speaking to us, it is only because it is the Spirit that has first overheard the triune conversation. Jesus hears the Father (Jn 5.30), the Father hears the Son (Jn 11.41), the Spirit communicates what it hears (Jn 16.13) and it is the Spirit's speaking to which we must attend. 'When the Spirit of truth comes, he will guide you into all the truth; for he will not speak on his own, but will speak whatever he *hears*, and he will declare to you the things that are to come' (Jn 16.13). Preaching is attentive to this voice of the Spirit that takes us up into the hearing central to the Fourth Gospel: preaching is a participation in the conversation of the Trinity.[74]

---

72. Balthasar, *Glory of the Lord*, Vol. 1, p. 596.
73. Forsyth, *Faith, Freedom and the Future*, p. 33.
74. Christoph Schwöbel, 'The Preacher's Art: Preaching Theologically' in Colin Gunton, *Theology Through Preaching: Sermons for Brentwood* (Edinburgh: T&T Clark, 2001), pp. 1–20 (2).

Preaching therefore responds to Scripture's claim upon us that as creatures we 'are invited to participate in a conversation that *is already going on* within the Trinity'.[75] For Calvin too the ministry of preaching was nothing less than an incorporation within the triune life, an office made possible by the effectual power of the Spirit: 'by the power of the Spirit He [Jesus] communicates to us His life and all the blessings He has received from the Father'.[76] The Spirit which rested on Jesus and accompanied him throughout his ministry (Jn 3.32) is now 'breathed' out to us in act of new creation (Jn 20.22). Our status as those who have been sent (Jn 17.18; 20.21) is predicated on the basis of the Spirit who is sent to us (Jn 14.26; 15.26). Through this Spirit the church comes to share in the prophetic ministry of Jesus. Preaching is doxological and, as such, it is a Spirit-inspired echo of the praise, love and wonder which Jesus directs towards his Father.

The preacher attentive to the activities of the Spirit of truth – his testifying (Jn 15.26), his speaking (Jn 16.13) and his declaration (Jn 16.13) – knows that preaching is a participant within a distinct economy of communication. In the presence of the Spirit, our time and Jesus' time are brought together as a common time. Preaching removed from attention to the peculiar wisdom of the Spirit will forget that the Spirit helps us plot time around the risen Christ and so is the pledge that Jesus does not abandon us to our own resources but rather draws us into the life of his and now our Father (Jn 14.18; 20.17). The Spirit pulls together much of what we have said therefore about the distinct space in which the preacher finds herself and stands at the centre of this chapter. What Gerhard Sauter calls the 'inner grounding of proclamation' – the prevenient action of God – *is* 'the presence of his Spirit'.[77] The Spirit, sent by the ascended Jesus (Jn 20.22), is the agent of his ascended presence with us. Jesus' promise that 'I will not leave you orphans, I am coming to you' (Jn 14.18) can only mean that 'the Spirit does not replace an *absent* Jesus, but on the contrary renders him present in a new way.'[78] Moreover, it is the Spirit who, over time, trains us to hear sermons as the Word of God. We do not, after all, *want* to hear the difficult words of the gospel. 'This teaching is difficult, who can hear it?' (Jn 6.60), is a fitting summary of the resistance the gospel provokes in us.

In this act of making Jesus present with us, the Spirit comes not to communicate anything novel but to take us deeper into the truth of what has *already been said* (Jn 14.26) and is being said. (Note here the link between what we noted about the ascension and the permanence of Jesus' teaching.) Any eloquence demonstrated in a sermon is a mirror of God's eloquence who wills

75.  Paul S. Fiddes, 'The Canon as Space and Place' in John Barton and Michael Wolter (eds), *Die Einheit der Schrift und die Viefalt des Kanons/The Unity of Scripture and the Diversity of the Canon*, pp. 126–49 (132, emphasis added).

76.  *Comm. Jn. 17.21.*

77.  Gerhard Sauter, *Gateways to Dogmatics: Reasoning Theologically for the Life of the Church* (Grand Rapids: Eerdmans, 2003), p. 129.

78.  Hans Urs von Balthasar, *Theo-Logic*, Vol. III (trans. Graham Harrison; 3 vols; San Francisco: Ignatius Press, 2005), p. 80.

that we are drawn deeper into 'all the truth' (Jn 16.13). As the agent of Jesus' continued speaking and our hearing the Spirit ensures the dynamism of our relationship with the ascended Jesus. This Spirit-led dynamic was articulated by Karl Barth in typically robust style:

> It is in the work of the Holy Spirit that He is present in our sphere of time and history as this speaking Witness, that He strides through it as such, that he acts and operates in it . . . [the Holy Spirit] is the power in which His Word . . . is not only in Him, but where and when He wills goes out also to us men, not returning to Him empty but with the booty or increase of our faith and knowledge and obedience . . . thus establishing communication between Him and us and initiating a history of mutual giving and receiving.[79]

It is important to emphasize that the Spirit is not some extra character drafted in at the conclusion of Jesus' earthly ministry. The *same* Spirit who accompanied Jesus during his earthly ministry (Jn 3.32), who lent his words their power (Jn 6.63), is now present with us in the church's preaching, ensuring that encountering Jesus remains, as depicted in the Fourth Gospel, an aural affair.

If we speak the Word of God it is only because God is already present to us in his risen and ascended son, Jesus. If we hear the Word of God it is only because, through the Holy Spirit, we are first drawn into the triune conversation.

## Preaching is That Which is Heard

Through the Spirit then preaching claims us through our ears. It is Paul, of course, who most influentially articulated the auditory power of preaching when he wrote to the Roman Christians, 'faith comes from what is heard, and what is heard comes through the word of Christ' (Rom. 10.17). Equally prominent has been the claim of Lk. 10.16 that to hear the proclaimed gospel is to be confronted with Jesus himself: 'whoever listens to you listens to me, and whoever rejects you rejects me, and whoever rejects me rejects the one who sent me.' In these striking claims to hear the words of the preacher is to hear Jesus himself for, in the language of the Fourth Gospel, 'anyone who hears my word and believes him who sent me has eternal life, and does not come under judgement . . . and those who hear will live' (Jn 5.24-25).

Our reflection on preaching as that which is heard can be aided by turning to the reflections of the Swiss theologian, Hans Urs von Balthasar. In an essay entitled 'Seeing, Hearing and Reading within the Church', Balthasar illuminates what it is to be a hearer in the church.[80] Seeing remains for Balthasar the queen of the senses, for in the inseparable distance necessarily maintained

---

79.  Barth, *Church Dogmatics* IV/3.1, pp. 420–21.

80.  Hans Urs von Balthasar, 'Seeing, Hearing, and Reading within the Church' in *Explorations in Theology*, Vol. II (trans. Brian McNeil; 3 vols; San Francisco: Ignatius Press, 1991), pp. 473–90. See Raymond Gawronski, *Word and Silence: Hans Urs von Balthasar and the Spiritual Encounter between East and West* (Edinburgh: T&T Clark, 1995), pp. 150–53.

between the beholder and that which is seen reality is allowed to disclose itself 'in the greatest depth'.[81] Hearing, by comparison, is a more direct and immediate form of communication. Whereas in the act of seeing there is the possibility of preparing for the sight by taking up an appropriate stance or distance, Balthasar notes that to hear is to be directly confronted:

> it is not we ourselves who determine on our part what is heard and place it before us as an object in order to turn our attention to it when it pleases us; that which is heard comes upon us, without our being informed in advance, and it lays hold of us without our being asked.[82]

It is a sign of the direct nature of this auditory confrontation that whilst our eyelids can serve to shield our sight, there are no earlids we can close when we hear something we would rather not: that which is heard represents a more intrusive claim upon the senses. At the beginning of the communicative act the one who hears is placed in a position of submissiveness. Hearing the Word is therefore a superior form of communication to reading, for the reading of Scripture has become ubiquitous and evacuated of its sacramental nature.[83] By contrast, in hearing the most appropriate response is humbly to receive and submit to that which speaks to us.[84] Hearing is to be fixed as an act within the obedience of faith, 'the decisive attitude of the Church' which 'aims upwards into an ever more perfect obedience and thus into a creatureliness that distinguishes itself ever more humbly from the Creator'.[85] (For Balthasar, Mary is also the paradigm of the faithful disciple who truly hears and believes.) Within the total context of the liturgy therefore the sermon is an indispensable agent within the economy of hearing, for it 'is not only a moral-ethical exhortation and edification but also a true act of making present the Divine Word itself'.[86] Balthasar's plea is that the church recognizes once more the objective nature of that which is heard:

> both on the part of the preacher and on the part of the listening people, there is seldom the awareness that here the personal word is being made present, the direct continuation of the sending of the Son by the Father.[87]

If Balthasar's emphasis on hearing sounds exotic then it might well be because as the church we simply 'no longer know how to hear',[88] or better, we

---

81.  Balthasar, 'Seeing, Hearing, and Reading', p. 474.
82.  Balthasar, 'Seeing, Hearing, and Reading', p. 475.
83.  Balthasar, 'Seeing, Hearing, and Reading, pp. 489–90.
84.  Balthasar, 'Seeing, Hearing, and Reading', p. 476.
85.  Balthasar, 'Seeing, Hearing, and Reading', p. 480.
86.  Balthasar, 'Seeing, Hearing, and Reading', p. 486.
87.  Balthasar, 'Seeing, Hearing, and Reading', p. 488.
88.  Webb, *Divine Voice*, p. 40.

have paid insufficient attention to Luther's counsel that 'no one listens to Christ except when the Father digs out and opens his ears'.[89] For figures as diverse as Luther, Calvin and Balthasar worship is an intrinsically aural affair.[90] In this setting, preaching is the echo of God's vocal presence with us in Scripture. 'Hear the word of the Lord' is the liturgical imperative because in Calvin's words 'all of Scripture is to be received as if God were speaking'.[91] This is one important way in which we can understand the inseparable bond between preaching and Scripture – not just that both are sanctified auxiliaries of God's salvific outreach, not just that Scripture in a sense 'wills' to be proclaimed,[92] but in an elementary sense because both Scripture and preaching make their claims on us as that which is *heard*. Amidst the din and banality of those sounds with which the world surrounds us the church confesses that in its communal practices of listening to Scripture and preaching God is speaking and it is to *this* sound that we must attend. The church is the 'listening church', and what preachers speak must at all times be a 'consequence and application' of this primary act of *listening*.[93] In his stress on the importance of hearing to the dogmatic task, Karl Barth emphasized that the urgency for the hearing church is less the cultivation of rhetorical speech pleasing to the ear and more the immediate attentiveness to what is set before us in the church's proclamation. Barth's counsel is worth citing here:

> [i]t [the urgency of proclamation] is not a call to piety, to vitality, to sincerity or to depth, but to the realisation of the happening which transcends Church proclamation as such: God has spoken, speaks now and will again speak . . . proclamation itself should be what in virtue of the promise it already is – the Word of God.[94]

As always, Barth's hesitations in relation to the rhetorical mastery of the subject-matter of preaching are couched in the most rhetorical of forms.

89. Martin Luther, *Lectures on Titus, Philemon, and Hebrews* (Jaroslav Pelikan (ed.); trans. Walter A. Hansen; Luther's Works, 29; 55 vols; St Louis: Concordia, 1968), p. 223. Cited in Webb, *Divine Voice*, p. 144.

90. It should be said that for Balthasar the church of Rome represents the purest act of hearing for in its submissive obedience to the Word it does not succumb to the actualism of the pure Word, as Martin Luther and John Calvin do: Balthasar, 'Seeing, Hearing, and Reading', p. 484.

91. Cited in William A. Graham, *Beyond the Written Word: Oral Aspects of Scripture in the History of Religion* (Cambridge: Cambridge University Press, 1987), p. 143. The exact source is not given. For a contemporary reassertion of Scripture as a vocal address see Elizabeth Achtemeier, 'The Canon as the Voice of the Living God' in Braaten and Jenson (eds), *Reclaiming the Bible for the Church*, pp. 119–30.

92. Or, in an equally powerful personification, 'the Word *waits* for us in the words of the prophets and apostles': Karl Barth, 'The Christian Understanding of Revelation' in *Against the Stream: Shorter Post-War Writings* (trans. Stanley Godman; London: SCM, 1954), pp. 203–40 (220, emphasis added).

93. Barth, *Church Dogmatics* I/2, pgs 829, 840.

94. Barth, *Church Dogmatics* I/2, p. 800.

We might also have concerns about a lingering episodic account of God's action. But what we learn from Barth is that the preacher resourced by their hearing will not worry unduly what he or she is to say on Sunday or how he or she is to say it, for in the sure knowledge of God's loquaciousness the secret 'weapon' of sermon preparation is 'continually listening'.[95] Preachers might or might not need to be 'good' speakers, but they unequivocally need to be good hearers. Preaching about Christ, to adapt the famous advice of Bonhoeffer, must begin in silence.[96] The ability to hear is however not just the responsibility of preachers – the whole church needs to be trained to listen well, as Forsyth appreciated,

> [e]very great true sermon is a great true sacrament, the sacrament of the word, in which the people participate as really as the preacher . . . Every true hearer is not a hearer only, but a doer of the word . . . To hear as the Church should hear is really to preach . . . On every such occasion those who hear in faith are not simply present, do not simply listen, they assist in the service.[97]

In this context, it is highly significant that the Fourth Gospel represents a strikingly aural portrayal of Jesus' significance, revealing that for the communities in which this text first circulated Jesus' continuing presence was an intensely oral affair. What more can we learn about the economy of hearing from reading John's Gospel?

The prominence that hearing plays in the Fourth Gospel is indicated by the sheer prevalence of the verb *akouō*; used some 53 times, it can be found in all but three of the Gospel's 21 chapters.[98] Given the prominence and extent of Jesus' speaking in the Fourth Gospel, this should perhaps engender little surprise, for such a fluent speaker clearly needs an audience. The verb first occurs when it is said that two of John the Baptist's disciples (Andrew and the beloved disciple) 'heard' John's proclamation of Jesus as the lamb of God and begin following the one to whom John has witnessed (Jn 1.37, 40). (Interestingly, however, sight and hearing are fused in John's testimony: for that which they hear from John the Baptist is the imperative, 'Behold! The Lamb of God' [Jn 1.29].) Two things are notable here. First, it is not Jesus that calls his first disciples, but his forerunner and witness John the Baptist who hands his

95.  Barth, *Church Dogmatics* I/2, p. 804.

96.  Dietrich Bonhoeffer, *Christ the Center*, p. 27: 'Teaching about Christ begins in silence'.

97.  Forsyth, *Rome, Reform and Reaction*, pp. 217–18.

98.  See Craig Koester, 'Hearing, Seeing, and Believing in the Gospel of John', *Biblica* 70 (1989), pp. 327–48, who argues therefore that hearing plays a pre-eminent role in John's presentation of how people are brought to faith in Jesus. A similar argument is also made by Werner H. Kelber, 'The Authority of The Word in St John's Gospel: Charismatic Speech, Narrative Text, Logocentric Metaphysics', *Oral Tradition* 2 (1987), pp. 108–31. As Kelber notes (115), it is interesting that the Fourth Gospel contains neither a baptismal story nor a transfiguration account. Is this linked to the visual aspects ingredient to both these stories?

own disciples over to Jesus. The first seeds of faith in John are scattered by the voice of the forerunner. Second, John the Baptist's witness is borne from his own attentive hearing of Jesus' voice, for he is the friend of the bridegroom who, 'rejoices greatly at the bridegroom's voice' (Jn 3.29). That which John the Baptist faithfully hears – 'the words of God' in the voice of Jesus (Jn 3.34) – is itself that which Jesus has 'heard' (Jn 3.32; 8.26, 40; 15.25) in the presence of God and now makes available to the world through his teaching. Jesus boldly identifies this teaching with the theophanies of the Old Testament, 'I am, the one who is speaking to you' (Jn 4.26; Deut 32.39; Isa. 41.4; 43.10, 25). Jesus is the Word speaking in flesh, the speaker who is first a hearer and a speaker whose words create faith (Jn 4.41–42).

As the mediator who hears God (and to whom God himself consistently listens – Jn 11.41–42) Jesus makes available to our ears what hitherto has remained inaudible (Jn 5.30, 37), 'the word that you hear is not mine but is from the Father who sent me' (Jn 14.24). To hear Jesus is to be brought to faith in a superior way (Jn 4.42), for the Word which sounds from Jesus' voice is a power of salvation, 'the hour is coming and is now here, when the dead will hear the voice of the Son of God, and those who hear will live' (Jn 5.25). Hearing Jesus the crowd recognize in him the one spoken of in Deuteronomy 18 who would speak the words of God in a definitive, unsurpassable ministry (Jn 7.40; Deut. 18.15–22). However, Jesus' teaching is a stumbling-stone set amidst the smoothness of worldly schemes, such that the question of those who *can* truly hear it is a perplexity. After Jesus' bread of life discourse in John 6 his disciples ask one another, '[t]his teaching is difficult. Who can hear it?' (Jn 6.60). An answer attentive to the way the words go in John must be that those who can 'hear' Jesus and perceive his true status are 'of God' (Jn 8.47) and 'belong to the truth' (Jn 18.37). As is well documented, there is plenty of evidence in the Fourth Gospel of *mis*hearing. It is possible to hear Jesus but not be brought to the truth: such people are struck with fear (Jn 19.8) or even fall to the ground at his revelatory word (Jn 18.6). Likewise, the crowds hear the voice of God from heaven in Jn 12.29 and mistakenly conclude that it was 'thunder'. Appropriately therefore, John's Gospel ends with those who hear Jesus at his beckoning – Mary and Peter especially – and respond with jubilant faith (Jn 20.16; 21.7). In a paragraph that takes on added depths in the light of the Fourth Gospel we can return to more of Calvin's insistence that we prick our ears to the voice of Christ:

> He has, indeed, in few words commended Christ as our teacher when he says 'Hear him' [Matt. 17.5]. But in these words there is more weight and force than is commonly thought. For it is as if, leading us away from all doctrines of men, he should conduct us to his Son alone; bid us seek all teaching of salvation from him alone; depend upon him, cleave to him; in short, hearken . . . to his voice alone.[99]

99.  Calvin, *Institutes*, IV.viii.7, p. 1155.

Alongside this counsel we can place Jesus' statement that 'anyone who hears my word and believes him who sent me has eternal life' (Jn 5.24). Jesus' words in the Fourth Gospel represent the power of salvation and Jesus is the one speaker beyond comparison. 'Never has anyone spoken like this!' (Jn 7.46). Throughout the Fourth Gospel, Jesus' voice is heard to be affective: it does what it says and so we can say that Jesus' words are best viewed 'not as carriers of ideas or records of information, but as manifestations of power'.[100] At his word the disciples 'come and see' (Jn 1.39), the centurion's son lives (Jn 4.50), the cripple walks (Jn 5.8), people are driven to believe in him and his claims (Jn 8.30) and Lazarus is raised from the dead (Jn 11.43). Jesus' word *is* his action. It is entirely appropriate therefore that the risen Jesus should conclude his ministry not by wishing for peace, but by *declaring* it, 'Peace be with you' (Jn 20.19).[101] If Jesus' words enact what they say then this is only because he is the Word of God made flesh, the same word who was with God in the beginning and 'was God' (Jn 1.1–2). As the speech of God in flesh, Jesus gathers up all that God has spoken previously and concentrates it in his person: 'you search the scriptures because you think that in them you have eternal life; and it is they that testify on my behalf' (Jn 5.39).

John's Gospel help us understand the economy of hearing in which preaching 'works' as a salvific power. Preachers must be listened to because like Jesus they too have now been sent: 'he who receives any one who I send receives me, and he who receives me receives him who sent me' (Jn 13.20). To return to our earlier strains, the preacher's commission is rooted in the initial sending of the Son from the Father.[102] So we can say that the eternal fellowship between Father and Son finds its analogue in the relationship between the listening preacher and the listening congregation.

If we speak the Word of God it is only because God is already present to us in his risen and ascended son, Jesus. If we hear the Word of God it is only because, through the Holy Spirit, we are first drawn into the triune conversation. And now we may say as follows: Preaching dares to 'hear' what God makes known to us in his Son.

## The Church and the Peace of Christ

We have emphasized that the preacher is not a freelancer. She is an agent both of the risen Christ and the particular community summoned into being by the risen One – the church. Through time preaching builds up the church as a people who bear witness to the truth of Jesus' Lordship. In this section we therefore move our focus determinedly to fixing preaching in history and time.

---

100. Kelber, 'The Word in St John's Gospel', p. 111.

101. Karl Barth, 'When They Saw the Lord' in *Call for God: New Sermons from Basel Prison* (trans. A. T. Mackay; London: SCM, 1967), pp. 117–25 (121).

102. Torrance, *Theology in Reconstruction*, p. 199.

Such attention is a reminder of an emphasis that has coursed throughout this book: the preacher need not begin with the assumption that there is a gulf between the biblical world and the scriptural world for in the life of the people of God the preacher has already been given a living performance of the script. (This is not of course mutually exclusive with Jesus' Lordly presence.) A further answer to the question of who can hear Jesus' teaching (Jn 6.60) can be found therefore by looking to the church's gospel formation and performance. To be sure, care must be taken not to overload the work of the church and its reading of Scripture, something which my initial emphasis on the agency of Jesus *making himself present* was specifically designed to ensure. So, when Telford Work writes that '[t]he Bible's performance *makes* the absent Lord present in the coalescing assembly of his disciples',[103] I would want to qualify the poetic strains of this assertion in the light of my earlier argument. Overemphasis on the church can lead us to forget that 'the Spirit blows where it wills' (Jn 3.8), a timely warning that 'whether the sermon really is a sermon rests entirely with God'.[104] The primary agent of proclamation is Jesus Christ. The reason why Protestants should adopt a similar attitude towards preaching as Roman Catholics have towards the Mass is that it is the presence of Jesus which protects us from understanding preaching as merely a tool of internal community formation.[105] With appropriate care, we can therefore explore the following claim: *the preacher inscribes the church into the story of the One who is indestructibly present with us.*

After attention to what might be termed (admittedly rather unsatisfactorily) the 'vertical' dimensions of preaching, in this final section I turn now to the 'longitudinal' dimensions of preaching, its embedded and timeful work within a community whose practices seek to extend the biblical narrative. Rendered in the organic language of John, preaching is an aspect of our *abiding* in Jesus (Jn 14.4). This account of how preaching works clearly corresponds to our location of Scripture in the first chapter, and so is necessary if we are to avoid the charge of setting up a blueprint of preaching. If the strains articulated in the sections above sound to some ears like the 'again and again' punctiliar tones familiar to many Protestant vocabularies, in this final section I want to turn to the 'more and more' aspect of preaching – its place in the *ongoing* life of a peaceable church. Preaching has length and we must resist episodic accounts of how it works on the church; not so much an instrument of Christ's presence with his people 'again and again', but rather an instrument of Christ's presence with us 'more and more'. Preaching needs to work *through time* because our natural instinct is to resist the gospel and the church is provided so that we might be trained to hear the gospel faithfully.

---

103. Telford Work, *Living and Active: Scripture in the Economy of Salvation* (Sacra Doctrina; Grand Rapids: Eerdmans, 2002), p. 313.

104. Dehn, *Man and Revelation*, p. 174.

105. See Willimon, *Conversations with Barth*, p. 217.

Knowing that she need not start with the assumption that church and Scripture are at a distance from one another, preachers attentive to the church's participation in Scripture put to work a typological reading which binds the world of Scripture to the world of the church. 'Typology is fundamentally a Christological and ecclesial form of interpretation . . . The movement is from events in the story of Israel through Jesus as the center and "archetype" of the story to the church as the ongoing bearer of the story.'[106] Through typology we learn to coordinate our position in the scripturally rendered world. In asserting the significance of a figural reading of Scripture we are not wandering away from attention to the presence of Jesus as risen and ascended, for *he* is the one in whom all things have been gathered up (Eph. 1.10). As the ongoing bearer of this story, the church makes known the peace which the risen Jesus has achieved and now permanently lodged in this world: 'Peace I leave with you; my peace I give to you' (Jn 14.27). The people of God do not live in fear but in the sure knowledge that Jesus is our peace. 'Take courage; I have overcome the world!' (Jn 16.33). Preaching is embedded within a people embodying through their practices the truth that they need not be afraid for Jesus 'is our peace' (Eph. 2.14).

In a setting which sees the world to be shot through with the grace of figural participation preaching works by discerning those places where Christ's peace is to be made known, extended and participated in. The church *participates* in all that Jesus Christ has singularly achieved by his life, death and resurrection – it does not attempt to *repeat* the life of Jesus, but to follow after him. Accordingly, preaching is not afraid of imagination shaped by the risen Christ – such imagination helps us, to use the terminology of Charles L. Campbell, on the one hand to 'expose' the powers that threaten to rule the world and on the other hand to 'envision' the new world of the gospel.[107] When we attend to the length of preaching, the focus turns to preaching as an exercise of patient formation and less on isolated moments, events and quandaries. The decisive thing is not the latest social issue with which it is presumed the church must preach and act upon.[108] The decisive thing is rather how the people of God are shaped over time to see and understand 'issues' often presented as pre-packaged. Many of these 'issues' begin to look somewhat different when trained by the church's timeful practices. Our response to particular issues are moments 'in a particular history' shaped by preaching.[109] Preachers are charged with giving their hearers tools to interpret the claims made upon us by the world.

---

106.  Campbell, *Preaching Jesus*, p. 253.
107.  Charles L. Campbell, *The Word before the Powers: An Ethic of Preaching* (Louisville: Westminster John Knox, 2002), pp. 105–27. I emphasize that the Christian imagination is shaped by the reality of Christ as risen to counteract any fears that imagination can descend into free-wheeling creativity.
108.  Campbell, *Word before the Powers*, pp. 92–94.
109.  Hovey, *To Share in the Body*, p. 112.

As an exercise in training us to hear and respond, preaching is an irreducibly political act – it points to the people of God as those who dare to re-imagine what is real according to the peace Jesus has left behind in the world. In this task, the preacher looks to the life of the congregation sitting before them – and seeks to draw out and make known *the implications* of the practices of people who visit the sick, name their sins and seek forgiveness from one another. These are the marks of a peaceable community seeking to make visible the peace which the risen Jesus has lodged in this world. 'Peace be with you. As the Father has sent me, so I send you' (Jn 20.21). It is important to note that shortly after declaring the reality of his peace, and sending out the disciples with this peace, the risen Jesus goes on to elucidate a central feature of the peaceable community's life together, 'If you forgive the sins of any, they are forgiven them; if you retain the sins of any, they are retained' (Jn 20.23). The peace-bearing church names sins and forgives one another in the name of the risen Lord. Just as the risen Christ broadcasts salvation and new life so the people of God participate in this reality by naming their sins and offering forgiveness to one another.[110] It is in the context of these kind of gospel actions that preaching 'works'.

If preaching is 'political' – located in the church's visible actions – it is important to clarify what kind of politics the church represents. Help in achieving this can be resourced by looking to the kind of Lordship represented by Jesus' words in Jn 18.36: 'My kingdom is not from this world . . . my kingdom is not from here.' Whilst it may be tempting to read this statement as a validation of the neat division between the 'spiritual' world and the 'political' world Jesus, however, is not speaking in terms of an inner, 'spiritual' kingdom, but is indicating that the kingdom operates within the world, although on radically different lines.[111] An a-temporal view of Jesus' kingship restricted to an airy spirituality would go against what was asserted in the previous chapter: as the one in whom time and eternity decisively meet, Jesus' kingship is both eternal and fixed now in time.[112] Moreover, a Jesus who preached a kingdom of spiritual 'values' and who wanted to rule only our hearts would hardly be a threat to the powers of his day – quite the opposite – and so such interpretations of this verse are left accounting for Jesus' death by appealing to 'some terrible miscommunication between Jesus and Pontius Pilate'.[113] At no point in Jn 18.36 does Jesus deny that he *is* King.[114] Jesus' kingdom does not however

---

110. See McClendon, *Systematic Theology*, Vol. 1, p. 227.

111. Campbell, *Word before the Powers*, p. 61.

112. Stanley Hauerwas with Michael Baxter CSC, 'The Kingship of Christ: Why Freedom of "Belief" Is Not Enough' in Hauerwas, *In Good Company*, pp. 199–216 (211).

113. Stanley Hauerwas, *Disrupting Time: Sermons, Prayers, and Sundries* (Eugene: Cascade Books, 2004), p. 59.

114. Stanley Hauerwas, 'Why Did Jesus Have to Die?: An Attempt to Cross the Barrier of Age', *Princeton Seminary Bulletin* 28 (2007), pp. 181–90 (187).

rest on violence but on patient, non-violent confrontation with those powers that rule (quite literally in Jesus' case). So in the next half of the verse Jesus points to the kind of faithful rather than effective power that he represents: 'If my kingdom were from this world, my followers would be fighting to keep me from being handed over to the Jews.' Jesus' Lordly power over those forces that threaten him is simply rooted in his obedience to the Father (Jn 14.30–31). Preaching is political, fixed in the time of this world, but it is political only in the light of what the gospel reveals as real.

If we speak the Word of God it is only because God is already present to us in his risen and ascended son, Jesus. If we hear the Word of God it is only because, through the Holy Spirit, we are first drawn into the triune conversation. Preaching dares to 'hear' what God makes known to us in his Son. And through time preaching builds up the church as a people who bear witness to the truth of Jesus' Lordship.

## Conclusion

This chapter has presented a theological account of preaching. As an exploration of how Scripture, church and Christ are implicated in one another, I have presumed that a crisis in our understanding of preaching is a sign of our inattention to Christ's indestructible presence, the nature of Scripture and the vocation of the church.[115] But a theological attention to preaching – necessary as it is – is not an attempt to denude preaching of its necessarily human qualities, and nor must it end up confusing the voice of Scripture and the preacher. The preacher is not presiding over an act of transubstantiation in the pulpit but in very human words is simply pointing to Jesus' continued presence and then tracing the implications of this reality.[116] A docetic theology of preaching should be avoided with as much vigour as a docetic Christology: both are flights from God's desire to work in and through our world.

What, in the end, is the distinctive habit of the preacher, say of John's Gospel? The preacher's preoccupation will be with the reality of the strange new world made known in John, not with how this world is to be translated for 'our' age. Moreover, the preacher who is aware that God himself will provide the listeners (Jn 6.44) can afford to be less compulsive about the effectiveness of their sermons. As Luther indicated at the beginning of his own series of preaching on the Fourth Gospel the preacher of John:

> must remain conversant with this evangelist; to this end we must familiarize ourselves
> with his way of speaking. Therefore we propose to consider his Gospel in the name of

---

115.  See Riches, 'After Chalcedon', p. 207, who reminds us that for Joseph Ratzinger 'a crisis of Liturgy is a crisis in Christology'.

116.  See Karl Barth, *Evangelical Theology: An Introduction* (trans. Grover Foley; London: Collins, 1963), p. 178.

the Lord, discuss it, and preach it as long as we are able, to the glory of our Lord Christ and to our own welfare, comfort, and salvation, without worrying whether the world shows much interest in it. Nonetheless, there will always be a few who will hear God's precious word with delight; and for their sakes too, we must preach it. For since God provides people whom He orders to preach, He will surely also supply and send listeners who will take this instruction to heart.[117]

117.   Martin Luther, *Sermons on the Gospel of St. John Chapters 1–4* (Jaroslav Pelikan (ed.); trans. Martin H. Bertram; Luther's Works, 22; 55 vols; Saint Louis: Concordia, 1957), p. 5.

# Chapter 5

## SCRIPTURE, PARTICIPATION AND UNIVERSITIES

*'[K]nowledge is always already political'*[1]

## Introduction

The Bible has secured its position in today's universities variously as a historical source, as a literary narrative or (more recently) as an artefact that has reverberated through art, music, film and literature. In some of these approaches, the Bible is read 'like any other text'. In other approaches, the justification for reading the Bible is articulated in terms of the Bible's long and unique cultural significance. Notwithstanding the academic value of these endeavours, tactically such approaches to the Bible have been extremely shrewd. By building alliances with historians, classicists, literary scholars, art historians and film scholars, it has been possible for theology and the study of the Bible in particular to 'secure for itself a small but honourable place in the throne-room of general science'.[2] Surely then the kind of local attention I have been urging, namely to Scripture as the text of the church and intelligible when set within a series of specific actions, would only make theology's position in the modern university less secure and so represent a retrograde step? Have I not cast aside one of the great discoveries of modernity: in the place of local hermeneutical debates pivoting around dogmatic axes peculiar to the church general hermeneutical approaches allow appeal to resources and categories that are universally accessible?[3] In this closing chapter, it is necessary therefore to ask one final question: can we read Scripture – especially in line with my very theological proposal – in the university? As we needed to explore in what ways the politics of the church sustains the claims it makes about Scripture, so too

---

1. Huebner, *A Precarious Peace*, p. 116.
2. Barth, *Evangelical Theology*, p. 19.
3. Wood, *Barth's Theology of Interpretation*, p. 74–75. Donald Wood cites Odo Marquard, 'The Question, To What Question is Hermeneutics The Answer?' in *Contemporary German Philosophy*, Vol. 4 (Darrel E. Christensen (ed.); 4 vols; trans. Robert M. Wallace; no place cited: Pennsylvania State University Press, 1984), pp. 9–31 where Marquard describes general hermeneutics as 'the search for the context that relativizes the controversy over the absolute understanding of the text in favor of what is uncontroversial, or controversial without consequences' (22–23).

we now need to inquire what kind of university could sustain reading Scripture in the theological vein I have been proposing.

Contained within the question – can we read Scripture in the university? – are three subsidiary questions that successively move out from re-imagining theology to re-imagining the kind of space the university might be. First, how might theology itself need to be reshaped and reconfigured in order that Scripture might be taught theologically? Second, what kind of status should theology have in the modern university? Third, what kind of university could host the kind of theological witness of which I speak? I shall argue not only that the church needs the university, but that understanding of Scripture in the university needs the church. A university responsive to a truth that comes through scriptural participation hosts a witness that overcomes the fragmentation of our lives, a disarray of which our academic disciplines are just one manifestation. The kind of local claims I make in relation to theology are a plea that we stop sheltering behind the pieties of pluralism and start being properly attentive to difference and particularity. For the self-contradictory problems lurking within talk of pluralism can be quickly articulated: such talk cannot accommodate the person who values their difference so greatly that she rejects the assumptions of pluralism. Nor should we forget how tightly policed by secular presumptions academic pluralism is. That there is no such thing as pluralism is therefore an opportunity to enlist a different kind of political imagination and vocabulary. In this setting theology, I argue, should not take refuge in *Christian* universities.[4] Theology departments need to be in the modern university not only because universities need theologians but because universities need to be re-imagined as places of encounter and crisis. Before we get to this argument, we first need to plot theology's current position in the university and then tackle Philip Davies' proposal as to the study of the Bible in the university.

## Universities, Fragmentation and Witness

Much of this book's energy clearly arises from concern at the fragmented, professionalized nature of theology today, a state of affairs which serves students of theology (I include its teachers) as poorly as it does the church. Writing from his American context, Stanley Hauerwas notes that when theology sought respectability in the professional corridors of the modern academy the irony was that theologians became nonpracticioners 'paid to train ministerial practitioners by educating them in matters seen as peripheral to the practice'.[5] (We might add that if theology is seen as largely a technical discipline by the church large parts of the academy are deeply suspicious of it as well, although for somewhat different reasons.) The alienation of theology from the life of the

---

4.  This is contrary to the position of D'Costa, *Theology in the Public Square*, who argues for the establishment of a Christian (specifically Roman Catholic) university in the United Kingdom.

5.  Hauerwas, *Wilderness Wanderings*, p. 175.

church is risky, precisely because it allows us to sequester the investigations of theology away from the kind of knowledge that emerges from the life and witness of the church. A theology marooned in the university is at risk of forgetting that 'knowledge is far too important to be left to the universities' alone.[6]

The boundary that runs between theology and the church (and it is only fair to say that countless theologians are attempting to criss-cross between the two) is reproduced in the numerous frontiers that make their way through theology departments. Pragmatic as these may be in the face of an academic culture which often resembles a publications arms-race, the reality is that such frontiers have had 'the effect of compartmentalizing thought in a way that distorts or obscures key relationships'.[7] Indeed, we know our time to be one of fragmentation because we find ourselves asking a question that would never have occurred to readers throughout the majority of Christian history: what is the relationship between theology (as a discrete series of texts, traditions and thinkers) and Scripture (a text now isolated from this tradition)? Theology's dismembered form in the contemporary university sustains and entrenches the condition which generates the question: what is the relationship between theology and Scripture?[8] And in this fragmented state theology, along with the other disciplines of the university, has merely helped form and then buttress the fragmented and consumer-driven shape of our lives. The arrangement of academic theology itself thus replicates what Alasdair MacIntyre diagnoses as our modern condition – compartmentalization. This condition names our inability to sustain our lives faithfully, our lack of resources to hold together with an 'integrative vision' the different roles we occupy in a variety of spheres.[9] Diagnosing the university's complicity in sustaining our fragmented lives MacIntyre writes that

> recent graduates of the best research universities have tended to become narrowly focused professionals, immensely and even obsessionally hard working, disturbingly competitive and intent on success as it is measured within their own specialized professional sphere, often genuinely excellent at what they do; who read little worthwhile that is not relevant to their work; who, as the idiom insightfully puts it "make time", sometimes with difficulty for their family lives; and whose relaxation tends to consist . . . sometimes of therapeutic indulgence in the kind of religion that is well designed not to disrupt their working lives.[10]

6.   Dallas Willard, 'The Bible, the University and the God Who Hides' in David Lyle Jeffrey and C. Stephen Evans (eds), *The Bible and the University* (Scripture and Hermeneutics Series, 8; Bletchley: Paternoster, 2007), pp. 17–39 (38).

7.   MacIntyre, *After Virtue*, p. 264.

8.   For very similar conclusions see Hauerwas, *Performing the Faith*, p. 154.

9.   Alasdair MacIntyre, 'Catholic Universities: Dangers, Hopes, Choices' in Robert E. Sullivan (ed.), *Higher Learning and Catholic Traditions* (Notre Dame: University of Notre Dame Press, 2001), pp. 1–21 (16).

10.   MacIntyre, 'Catholic Universities', p. 15.

Precisely as a social structure of compartmentalization, the modern university plays its part in the dissolution of that virtue upon which, as MacIntyre contends in *After Virtue*, all moral agency needs to rest – constancy. Constancy both requires and is required by an understanding of a *telos* which transcends our human practices. Just as constancy is that virtue which refers to the 'wholeness of a human life' so a person of constancy is alert to those structures that would threaten the development of such integrity.[11] In this perspective the university, sustained by specialized professionals and in the business of training future professionals, encourages us to flit between roles and spheres,[12] 'each governed by its own specific norms in relative independence of other such spheres'.[13] For character and moral agency to emerge effectively, individuals must be able to do more than drop in and out of roles but rather be able to 'reflect upon their role-playing in ways that are not dictated by those same roles'.[14] In being one more social structure which hinders such development of character, the university loses an opportunity to provide a setting in which the different communities and roles of which people are a part can be integrated. Compartmentalization, in MacIntyre's terms, serves to insulate us from the tensions inherent in the variety of roles or settings of which we are part. The university, as an active player in this fragmentation, is therefore unable to provide the resources which could transcend the moral incoherence of contemporary society that might 'value' constancy but ultimately cannot produce people of constancy.[15] Constancy and integrity are the virtues capable of resisting such fragmentation by directing our attention both to the specific responsibilities of the roles we occupy (as determined by society) and to particular moral systems 'in which that assignment has been put to the question'.[16] Precisely one of those independent, everyday settings where professional roles can be critiqued is, MacIntyre recognizes, the church. (That the church so often fails to provoke

11.   MacIntyre, *After Virtue*, p. 203.

12.   So, as intimated above, the professionalized nature of much university theology sustains this fragmentation by removing theologians from the church and its practices of faith. See Arne Rasmusson, *The Church as Polis: From Political Theology to Theological Politics as Exemplified by Jürgen Moltmann and Stanley Hauerwas* (Notre Dame: University of Notre Dame Press, 1995), p. 41, 'the professionalization of intellectual work also risks to separate and abstract the discipline from the practical activities which are its base. The discipline creates its own community with its own language, creating its own problems and questions, in which requirements of methodological rigour and spurious foundationalist ideas of objectivity play an important role, tend to draw the discipline further and further away from what it supposedly deals with' (*sic*).

13.   Alasdair MacIntyre, 'Social Structures and their Threats to Moral Agency', *Philosophy* 74 (1999), pp. 311–29 (322).

14.   MacIntyre, 'Social Structures', p. 315. Thus MacIntyre writes that 'we need . . . forms of social association in and through which our deliberations and practical judgments are subjected to extended and systematic critical questioning that will teach us how to make judgments in which both we and others may have confidence' (316).

15.   MacIntyre, 'Social Structures', p. 327.

16.   MacIntyre, 'Social Structures', p. 318.

crises of knowledge only prompts Hauerwas' question: are our churches ready to sustain universities?[17]) The New Testament Professor who on Sunday morning finds herself part of a liturgical setting which proclaims the resurrection as history-making and history-defining spends Monday morning teaching undergraduates the 'problem' of the resurrection's historicity (a problem wholly dependent upon an account of history not necessarily informed by theological considerations) is a player within a tension we suppress by talking of different roles. In MacIntyre's terms for this New Testament professor to not recognize the state of tension in which she is living is to be already in the grip of compartmentalization.[18]

Alasdair MacIntyre is characteristically reticent about the role theology could play in addressing this fragmented state. Nevertheless, we can say that in the setting of the modern university theology, in particular the theological reading of Scripture, can witness to a way of knowing that resists the pitfalls of compartmentalization. In this witnessing, theology seeks not to be a hegemonic discourse in the modern university, an inappropriate stance for a subject constantly giving over its language to its object of attention.[19] Far from seeking possession of other discourses theology is a way of speaking that is primarily dispossessed by its fixation. Theological witnesses are rarely in control. The stature of such a witness will be elaborated upon later in this chapter, but for now we need to turn to an argument that uncovers the hegemonic and atomizing impulses within contemporary biblical studies.

### *Philip Davies and the Modern University*

For the purposes of this chapter, Philip Davies' *Whose Bible is it Anyway?* conveniently represents a prominent biblical scholar's view of the Bible's place in the modern university.[20] Davies displays 'the liberal project in its epistemological . . . form',[21] the very kind of imagination that inhibits the particular claims needed to sustain Scripture's theological interpretation. The central chapter of *Whose Bible is it Anyway?*, 'Two Nations, One Womb', aims to show that non-confessional biblical studies and study of Scripture although sometimes confused have different audiences (respectively, the academy and the church) and so should be kept in rigid isolation from one another. Davies

---

17.    Hauerwas, *State of the University*.

18.    We might suppose we could dismiss the conflict within this New Testament Professor as the tension between two different 'theories'. But, MacIntyre reminds us, we are talking of 'a conflict between socially embodied points of view, between modes of practice': 'Social Structures', p. 318.

19.    Williams, *On Christian Theology*, p. 7.

20.    For a very similar manifesto to Davies' see Michael V. Fox, 'Bible Scholarship and Faith Based Study: My View', *Society of Biblical Literature Forum*, February 2006. Available at: http://www.sbl-site.org/publications/article.aspx?articleId=490. Accessed 05/01/09.

21.    Stanley Hauerwas, *After Christendom: How the Church Is to Behave If Freedom, Justice, and a Christian Nation Are Bad Ideas* (Nashville: Abingdon, 1999), p. 35.

understands the biblical texts to be 'cultural phenomena' and wants a discipline exclusively concentrated on reading the Bible naturalistically.[22] In a trenchant statement of conviction, Davies therefore argues that academic study of the Bible should be cleared of all theological commitments: study of the Bible as a secular discipline needs to be kept distinct from study of Scripture with specifically religious commitments. Whereas the former is a legitimate university subject the latter, when it presumes that it has a place within the university, forgets that '[c]hurch and academy . . . operate in separate domains, to different ends'.[23]

There are many points where Davies and I would start off in agreement, although in most cases we would end up in rather different places. I think Davies is right to point out that biblical studies is a largely secular discipline. Writing from his North American context Dale Martin has, for example, recently demonstrated the dominance of the historical-critical method in divinity schools and seminaries.[24] And in a position I am inclined to agree with, Adrian Hastings argues that most *theology* departments already operate along religious studies lines, with little sense of religious commitment.[25] Of course, I draw rather different conclusions from Davies as to the appropriateness to the specific text being studied of such secular reading approaches. Moreover, Davies' observation that academic theology is largely removed from the life of the church corroborates the observations with which this chapter began: for most church-goers theology is regarded as an arcane, professionalized science.[26] But where Davies sees this as an argument for severing altogether the connection between theology and the secular university, I see this as a stimulus to ask how the work of the university (especially its theology departments) and the work of the church might be brought more closely alongside one another. Clearly then the substantial point of disagreement between myself and Davies is his insistence that theological commitments should not be accommodated within the modern university. Vexed by the overlapping commitments that many of his fellow biblical scholars hold, Davies urges that the academy should insist that such exclusive commitments be reserved to Sunday mornings.[27] In a revealing statement, Davies implores that

> We cannot have a *single* discipline in which radically different accounts of how the world works, what human (*sic*) are here for, what knowledge is, how truth is sought,

22.  Philip Davies, *Whose Bible is it Anyway?* (London: T&T Clark International, 2nd edn, 2004), p. 26.
23.  Davies, *Whose Bible is it Anyway?*, p. 24.
24.  Martin, *Pedagogy of the Bible*, pp. 1–28.
25.  Adrian Hastings, 'Pluralism: The Relationship of Theology to Religious Studies' in Ian Hamnett (ed.), *Religious Pluralism and Unbelief: Studies Critical and Comparative* (London: Routledge, 1990), pp. 226–40 (232).
26.  Davies, *Whose Bible is it Anyway?*, p. 19.
27.  Davies, *Whose Bible is it Anyway?*, p. 51.

and so on, can mix together . . . It would seem to me self-evident that a confessional discourse and a non-confessional one cannot possibly combine to form a single discourse.[28]

Upon first reading this talk of a 'single discipline' one wonders what irenic academic circles Davies has been circulating in, for by their very nature all academic disciplines would appear to be fluid entities open to contestation. Upon second reading however the idea encapsulated in this statement is but an aspect of the wider liberal project that looks on our particularities and differences as embarrassing obstructions in the way of creating something more universal. Such a totalizing discourse is curiously impatient, that is anxious to foreclose the conversation and debate inherent to all human projects, in its bid to erect a 'single discipline'. Religion becomes one more choice we have made in a life of choices which we are to put to one side when constructing something less parochial and divisive. Religion taken too seriously becomes a barrier to communication and so rules itself out of the university, so Davies' argument appears to go.[29] And as Davies' statement above hints, the trouble with diversity is not generated by the diversity itself but by the confidence that there is *one* account of rationality, and it is before this account that people should justify themselves.[30] If we fail to measure up to this one account we will find ourselves in trouble. It is no surprise therefore that Davies appends to the secular study of the Bible such virtues of being 'public', 'accessible' and having the capacity to 'work[ing] from *logical* arguments applied to the evidence'.[31] One is left assuming that, in Davies' reckoning, theological study of the Bible is private, inaccessible and illogical and so unfit for the (so-called) public confines of the modern university. Davies' strictures are a reminder of how closely the modern university has been bound to the political imagination of nation-states in modernity and the project of secularism.[32] Yet, as the political philosopher William Connolly writes, whenever such alignments between the

---

28.   Davies, *Whose Bible is it Anyway?*, p. 27 (emphasis original).

29.   Davies, *Whose Bible is it Anyway?*, p. 52.

30.   See Mathewes, 'Faith, Hope, and Agony', p. 130: 'The belief that "the liberal state" is the response to the challenge of pluralism gets things the wrong way round; pluralism is a problem only when you have a monotheism of the state, when the state claims to be the only game in town as regards power and authority. Pluralism is a central problem for modern states not because of pluralism, but because of modern states.' That we can apply Mathewes' statement about nation-states so easily to the university reinforces how closely the university project has been tied to the nation-state project, as I go on to point out in company with Hauerwas.

31.   Davies, *Whose Bible is it Anyway?*, p. 27 (emphasis added).

32.   So Hauerwas, *State of the University*, p. 104: 'Modern universities, whether Christian or secular, have been servants of the emerging nation-state system.' For a searing description of the secularist strategy see Mathewes, *Theology of Public Life*, pp. 112–13.

university and public life have occurred they have not served the complexity of our lives well:

> Many academic secularists, following the lead of Kant, model public life upon an organization of university life they endorse. And vice versa. The field and authority divisions they project in the university among philosophy, theology, arts, and the sciences marshal an idea of thinking and discourse that is insufficient either to the university or to public life. The secular division of labor between 'religious faith' and 'secular argument,' where faith and ritual are to be contained in a protected private reserve and rational argument is said to exhaust public life, suppresses complex registers of persuasion, judgment and discourse operative in public life.[33]

In other words, Davies' kind of biblical studies might not be as public as he might suppose.

That the university has often reflected uncritically the nation-state's management of difference is regrettable because the university could be precisely one of those places which realized an alternative political imagination. Such a political imagination would question any tendency to create a 'single discipline' A single discipline might please Davies by eliminating the discordant contribution of theology as to what counts as 'knowledge', but lost sight of in any quest for a single discipline would be 'a better politics of intellectual exchange'.[34] Herein is an initial indication of the importance of the church to the university – a church that has a sufficient understanding of *itself* as already a public will resist and query those discourses and structures that would seek to place it by claiming to be *more* public.

One problem with approaches that seek to be universal and accessible – features which Davies claims secular biblical studies exemplifies – is that the search for comprehensive and unifying frames of reference always rests upon an exclusion of those who do not wish to be part of such a project, such as those who do not see their 'religion' as a mere choice they have made or those who wish to explore in universities 'what intellectual difference Christian convictions might make for what is considered knowledge'.[35] As Davies' argument proceeds, the extent to which his ire is directed towards theological commitments intruding upon the secular, public space which the university carefully tends becomes clear. In Davies' understanding, far from rationality and faith being mutually informing they are in competition and if we are to have a single rationality then we must exclude anybody who interjects that what they know they know through faith or presume that their reason is sustained by participation in the church's liturgy. For such people, should they wish to be part of

33. William E. Connolly, *Why I Am Not a Secularist* (Minneapolis: University of Minnesota Press, 1999), p. 20.
34. John Webster, 'Conversations: Engaging Difference', *Stimulus* 7 (1999), pp. 2–8 (3).
35. Hauerwas, *Christian Existence Today*, p. 239.

Davies' classes, the university's 'inclusion' has an exacting entry fee. In truth, however, the critical study of the Bible which Davies champions is the logical mode of reading if 'religion', sequestered to Sunday mornings, is assumed to be voluntary, private and a practice that does not inform biblical understanding (at least not any understanding in which the university is interested).[36] Those who think otherwise confuse what is private and accidental with what is essential.[37]

At the heart of Davies' neutrality and inclusion there therefore lies a pervasive logic of exclusion. John Webster identifies this logic with accuracy when he writes that the modern university is a strange combination of pluralism and dogmatism, that is 'a pluralism which suspends all strong claims and traditions and a dogmatism which insists that all such claims and traditions present themselves for inspection before the universal bar of reason'.[38] Davies might castigate Francis Watson for insisting that theology needs to occupy a pre-eminent place in biblical interpretation, but his disagreement is motivated by alarm that such a status would displace the approach he wants to privilege. Far from being neutral and above the fray, Davies' stance is a reminder that all language is content-laden, that 'without an inbuilt sense of what it would be . . . wrong to say, there could be no assertion and no reason for asserting it'.[39] If there is nothing worth saying that does not exclude certain positions and people then this casts a rather different light on Davies' apparent umbrage at his feelings of being 'marginalised or excluded' by Francis Watson's theological arguments.[40] Davies assumes that his principle of separating the Bible's academic study from theological inquiry and his neutral stance treats Christians (or other religious people) as fairly as it does secular people. The truth is that his account privileges *one* dominant account of education.[41] Such an account trades upon a notion of the individual existing prior to the communities of which they are part and correspondingly neglects the formative role of those communities in shaping what we know.[42] (It is interesting to note that, anecdotally, many introductory biblical studies courses will begin with statements from the teacher that students should set to one side what they might have learned about the Bible in the church. Of course the church is not averse to an equivalent suspicion of the academy!) Anybody of Christian conviction can

---

36. Jon D. Levenson, *The Hebrew Bible, the Old Testament, and Historical Criticism: Jews and Christians in Biblical Studies* (Louisville: Westminster John Knox, 1993), p. xiv.

37. See Stanley Fish, *The Trouble with Principle* (Cambridge: Harvard University Press, 1999), p. 57.

38. John Webster, *Theological Theology* (Oxford: Clarendon Press, 1998), p. 20.

39. Fish, *There's No Such Thing As Free Speech*, p. 103.

40. Davies, *Whose Bible is it Anyway?*, p. 45.

41. See Nicholas Wolterstorff, 'Why We Should Reject What Liberalism Tells Us' in Paul J. Weithman (ed.), *Religion and Contemporary Liberalism* (Notre Dame: University of Notre Dame Press, 1997), pp. 162–81 (esp. 176–77).

42. Mathewes, 'Faith, Hope and Agony', p. 129; Connolly, *Why I Am Not a Secularist*, p. 151.

enrol in Philip Davies' class, but they must be willing to accept that their religious convictions have no intellectual leverage in understanding the Bible.[43]

When Davies urges detachment from the subject-matter of the biblical texts by saying that his role is merely to teach *about* religion far from this being a neutral stance it propagates a certain view of learning in which 'the mind remains unaffected by the ideas and doctrines that pass before it, and its job is to weigh and assess those doctrines from a position distanced from and independent of any one of them'.[44] In other words, we are not born detached people but we are made and formed to be detached from the objects we study. As Stanley Fish additionally argues with characteristic vigour, those who would advocate a model of education where religion is taught from a neutral perspective are caught within the contradiction that they

> cannot answer the question "Why be neutral?" without committing themselves to particular goods – social peace, self-expression, self-esteem, ethnic pride or what have you – thereby violating their own desideratum of Neutrality.[45]

To speak of neutrality is not to transport oneself to a content free zone. It may be less of a concern to Davies than it must be to the church, but it is nonetheless important to recognize that 'an education which purports to be neutral between rival controversial religious standpoints always ends up in teaching no religion at all and thereby irreligion'.[46] True enough, in a 'horses for courses' approach *all* religions are treated the same, but this is only to say that the pathological

43.   Fish, *Trouble with Principle*, p. 40, states that in the modern university religion can participate 'so long as it renounces its claim to have a privileged purchase on the truth, which of course is the claim that defines a religion as opposed to a mere opinion'. But as Fish also correctly states (222–23) the 'you are not as neutral as you think' argument is dangerous, insofar as it tempts critics of liberalism onto ground they need not necessarily have any interest in occupying. To score a debating point by accepting the terms of your opponent is not much of a victory. Thus my conception of theology's role in the university is not a bid to be more neutral than so-called neutral liberals or to be more 'inclusive', terms which will only distract us.

44.   Fish, *Trouble with Principle*, p. 197. Davies advocates this model of teaching in *Whose Bible is it Anyway?*, pp. 45–46.

45.   J. Budziszewski, 'The Illusion of Moral Neutrality', *First Things* 35 (August/September 1993), pp. 32–37. Accessed online at www.leaderu.com/ftissues/ft9308/articles/budziszewski.html on 11/08/2008.

46.   Alasdair MacIntyre, *How to Seem Virtuous Without Actually Being So* (Lancaster: Centre for the Study of Cultural Values, 1991), p. 16. So Davies, *Whose Bible is it Anyway?*, p. 28: 'If all theological discourse is an examination of the truth it accepts *a priori*, then the theological discourses of Judaism, Islam and Christianity are unable to mix . . . the search for truth, which is the function of the university, ought not to be short-circuited or foreclosed by the propagation of dogmas that are held as *the* truth, but because academic discourse, being etic, permits various theologies to converse with one another.' Quite apart from the rhetoric, this is an intriguing and revealing set of claims. What would be the purpose of 'mixing' the different claims of Islam, Judaism and Christianity? Whose 'truth' would the university be accessing by this mixing? Certainly not that of the individual religions, for the whole approach of Davies assumes that each religion has a truth

'inability to grasp religions on their own terms' is equally distributed.[47] So although Davies recognizes that 'no discourse is universal' he can afford only to say that his exclusion is *less* than that of theology.[48] What Davies cannot afford to do is trace how deeply his impartiality depends upon a logic of exclusion. If he were to do so he would immediately invalidate his claim to be privileging no one perspective and so would reveal that he remains in the very categories he purports to have overcome. Moreover, such a pursuit would press him to answer the substantive question that the liberal university is precisely unwilling or unequipped to answer – what ends does the university serve?[49] For biblical studies shares the same crisis 'that has engulfed the entire university. At the heart of that crisis lies the loss of a transcendent goal for learning and the weakening of the communities and practices that can sustain the faith and belief upon which all learning – and not only biblical studies – depends.'[50] Unable to answer the question – what transcendent ends does the university serve? – we instead shelter behind the language of 'inclusion', accepting religion as 'mere belief' that can enter the University chapel but not the classroom. We are close here to James Barr's advice that the biblical scholar who is a person of faith should 'to some extent hold his or her faith-commitment in suspense'.[51]

Many theologians would have considerable problems with Davies' insinuation that Christian practices are private and do not have some hold over knowledge of Scripture. For once we accept that Christianity's role is to provide only an overlay of 'values' to knowledge formed independently from the church then we neglect to pay attention to the knowledge that emerges through participation in the church. As Craig Dykstra and Dorothy Bass write, 'practices central to Christian life are conditions under which various kinds and forms of knowledge emerge – knowledge of God, ourselves, and the world; knowledge that is not only personal but public'.[52] In other words, in the face of Davies' very modern concept of free-floating reason it is necessary to

---

inadmissible at his bar of reason. These claims also rest upon the assumption that one can access and understand these religions 'etically', that is, non-participatively.

47. George Dennis O'Brien, *The Idea of a Catholic University* (Chicago: University of Chicago Press, 2002), p. 190.

48. Davies, *Whose Bible is it Anyway?*, p. 48.

49. Davies, *Whose Bible is it Anyway?*, p. 52, where he says of Christian theologians participating in the university, 'Rather than accept that "truth" is a function of discourse, they believe in one objective truth, which is that of Christianity, and accordingly any discourse must in the end address itself to that reality.' In response, I would say that the truth sought by theologians is eschatological – truth is that to which theology is directed. This teleology contrasts with Davies' functional understanding of truth.

50. Levenson, *Hebrew Bible*, p. xiv.

51. James Barr, *The Concept of Biblical Theology: An Old Testament Perspective* (London: SCM, 1999), p. 205.

52. Dykstra and Bass, 'Reconceiving Practice' p. 49. Cited in Treier, *Virtue and the Voice of God*, p. 23.

stress that Christian knowledge is participative knowledge. Asserting a secular interpretation of the Bible, Davies unwittingly confirms Hauerwas' equally trenchant assertion that biblical criticism is an Enlightenment ideology 'in the service of the fictive agent of the Enlightenment – namely, the rational individual – who believes that truth in general (and particularly the truth of the Christian faith) can be known without initiation into a community that requires transformation of the self'.[53] To this charge, Davies would no doubt half-agree: knowledge of the Bible *is* possible apart from the church. In so responding, Davies would confirm the point I made in the opening chapter. When biblical scholars 'abstract what they are interpreting from the relation in which the Bible is what it is',[54] that is by removing Scripture from its relationship with the saving action of the triune God and the practices of the people of God, then we end up with a wholly secular understanding of our task as readers of Scripture.

In my reckoning *Whose Bible is it Anyway?* is best read and critiqued not as a manifesto but as a report and insight into the current state of biblical studies principally but also of theology and the university. Davies' arguments for a secular biblical studies guild are well placed within the modern university, representing as it does the presumption that the church is 'a threat in the quest for truth'.[55] The imaginary we encounter here, those 'precognitive assumptions' that frame our thinking,[56] is that theology is little more than the remnants of a faith system that is subjective, rooted in our interior dispositions and private, in short unfit to enter into the realm of public discussion,[57] or not at least before adjusting what it says to fit the acceptable norms of public discourse. As Stanley Fish (no theologian himself) helps us to see, Davies finds himself in that peculiar place where religion is given as a freedom with one hand and with the other hand touted as an enemy of freedom (in Davies' case, academic freedom). In order to preserve ourselves from the threat religion poses to freedom, whenever believers think their convictions have some intellectual leverage they are to be told their religion is an expression in line with artistic taste or support of

---

53. Hauerwas, *Unleashing the Scripture*, p. 35. On this same page Hauerwas argues that biblical criticism shares this trait in common with fundamentalism – both presume that the truth of Scripture can be known apart from participation within the church. It is unfortunate that Philip Davies does not interact with Hauerwas' book, published a year before Davies' originally was. On the invention of the 'individual' in modernity see MacIntyre, *After Virtue*, p. 61.

54. Bruce L. McCormack, 'The Being of Holy Scripture Is in Becoming: Karl Barth in Conversation with American Evangelical Criticism' in Vincent Bacote, Laura C. Miguélez and Dennis L. Okholm (eds), *Evangelicals and Scripture: Tradition, Authority and Hermeneutics* (Downers Grove: InterVarsity Press, 2004), pp. 55–75 (71).

55. Spinks, *Bible and the Crisis of Meaning*, p. 21.

56. Mathewes, *Theology of Public Life*, p. 148.

57. Cf. Francis Watson, *Text, Church and World: Biblical Interpretation in Theological Perspective* (Edinburgh: T&T Clark, 1994), p. 12.

sports teams.[58] That this has come to make sense is only because we have long imagined it to be so.

The political imagination Davies advocates is that the way to secure peace in modernity is to eliminate our messy particularities and to chase after universal understandings of reason or history. One of the stories we have told ourselves in modernity is that for knowledge to be genuine it 'should lead to convergence and consensus'.[59] For those who seek after something more than our particularities our differences can only be recast as private beliefs which interfere with our participation in public life. In this context, claims that character matters in biblical interpretation, that pacifists enjoy an interpretative advantage over other readers, or that our mode of knowing must be trained to the divine employment of the text will find little hospitable space. The pursuit of a more comprehensive setting free from our situated-ness will however be interminable, insofar as every time we try and substantiate what we mean by 'pluralism' or being 'open-minded' we will always (whether we recognize it or not) have to retreat to particular convictions and practices. Thinking about universities needs to recognize that '[t]here is no "public" that is not just another particular province'.[60] 'Pluralism' and 'open-mindedness' are smokescreens obscuring the reality that any pluralism has its boundaries, any open-mindedness has voices it is not willing to accommodate. Talk of pluralism is therefore implicated in contemporary political arrangements which seek to 'conceal the depth of our conflicts'.[61] Pluralism too often deals with difference and particularity by subsuming them under broader, so-called unifying, categories and values. Yet because there is no substantive shared end to which such efforts can appeal, such categories and values often end up relying upon the imposition of a procedural 'bureaucratized unity'.[62]

The question of the university, and of Scripture's place in the university, is a question relating to our political imaginations. Political theory, an investigation into how humans interact with one another in their particularities, is indeed of little value if it is 'not an exercise of imagination, offering new or different pictures of collective life in the hopes of remoulding, refashioning or altogether altering contemporary political arrangements'.[63] Pointing out the shortcomings of the liberal university is not even half the task. We do need to see how we are shaped by often unseen forces. But we also need to re-imagine universities as places of encounter and engagement.

58. Fish, *Trouble with Principle*, pp. 38–39.
59. C. Stephen Evans, 'The Bible and the Academy' in Jeffrey and Evans (eds), *The Bible and the University*, pp. 303–10.
60. Yoder, *Priestly Kingdom*, p. 40.
61. MacIntyre, *After Virtue*, p. 253.
62. MacIntyre, *After Virtue*, p. 254.
63. Kristen Deede Johnson, *Theology, Political Theory, and Pluralism* (Cambridge Studies in Christian Doctrine, 15; Cambridge: Cambridge University Press, 2007), p. 22.

## Participation, Witness and the Decentred University

Davies' argument is chiefly a problem if we accept one of his key assumptions – that universities, and academic readers of the Bible, have to conform to a single rationality. Contrary to this model, I have suggested that theology will not speak of truth more successfully if we take flight from our particularity and shelter in a supposedly more universal setting. Reading Scripture *as Scripture* is just one such particular stance. Nor need the university succumb to the idea that it must be in the business of hosting a single account of rationality. What I call a decentred university is more radically democratic and more receptive to difference than talk of pluralism allows because it actively resists any panoptical perspectives which would legislate ahead of time how we will engage with difference and particularity.[64] In the spaces made possible by a decentred university, I propose that Christian theologians would take on the role of witnesses. The witness of theology is to resist adopting a universal perspective on truth in abstraction from particular practices, commitments and the narrative of Scripture. Thus John Howard Yoder writes that '[i]nstead of seeking to escape particular identity, what we need, then, is a better way to restate the meaning of a truth claim from within particular identity'.[65]

What is the status of theology's witnessing activity? A few notes on the disruptive vision of witnesses can be sketched here. To witness is to adopt an epistemological tactic. Witnesses are seized by an alternative vision. Witnesses are rarely in control and so operate along noticeably different lines from the coercion latent within talk of impartiality or neutrality.[66] Indeed, the Christian witness to knowledge unmasks the modern projects of disinterested rationality as nothing less than a grasp for power.[67] Witnesses do not seek to *prove* what they point to and so do not appeal 'to some shared criterion beyond the belief in question'.[68] Not only would this represent a strike for power, but it would violate both our creaturely freedom to reject the message as well as the freedom of God to be present when and where he desires. As such, witnesses coax the truth into the world by presenting before the world lives of integrity and constancy, lives that are dispossessed by what permanently distracts them.

---

64. The term 'decentred' I take from Connolly, *Why I Am Not a Secularist*, p. 83, who writes that '[t]he decentering of the nation is pertinent to the refashioning of secularism'.

65. John Howard Yoder, 'On Not Being Ashamed of the Gospel: Particularity, Pluralism, and Validation', *Faith and Philosophy* 9 (1992), pp. 285–300 (290).

66. Yoder, *Priestly Kingdom*, p. 56; Fish, *Trouble with Principle*, p. 223.

67. Craig R. Hovey, *Speak Thus: Christian Language in Church and World* (Eugene: Cascade, 2008), p. 9; David Bentley Hart, *The Beauty of the Infinite: The Aesthetics of Christian Truth* (Grand Rapids: Eerdmans, 2003), pp. 3–4. See George Grant, 'Research in the Humanities' in *Technology and Justice* (Toronto: Anansi, 1986), pp. 97–102, for more on how the dominant account of knowledge in the humanities is one where the investigator remains in control over the objects of inquiry (99).

68. Hovey, *Speak Thus*, p. 8. I have learned much from Hovey's insightful discussion of witnesses.

Witnesses help us see what we otherwise would not see: that accounts of what time and history are might not be necessarily so or that political arrangements are just that, 'arrangements' which we can easily rearrange into alternative shapes that will allow us to engage more receptively with one another. Evidently, if what witnesses witness to is to be seen by others then they must be visible. And, in the context of talking about universities, a witness makes himself most visible neither in Christian universities nor in seminaries, but in the secular university. (Being not in control, theological witnesses are also quite relaxed about working alongside colleagues who adopt non-theological modes of reading the Bible.)

These notes on the disruptive vision of witnesses invite further questions that we will now explore. What more can we say about the substance of theology's pedagogical witness in today's university? What kind of space would the university have to be in order to accommodate such witnesses? And what can we say about theology's place in the university?

Theology witnesses to a truth that is known through participation. This is clearly a rebuff to those ways of thinking which encourage us to think of theoretical *and* practical knowledge. It is this separation between practices and knowledge that helps place us in the fragmented state diagnosed by MacIntyre. The kind of approach to Scripture I have been advocating, aware that 'there are a great number of things our knowledge of which dissolves if we look at them in a thoroughly detached manner',[69] invites us to address this fragmented state by integrating scriptural reading, practices and convictions. Theology, in the setting of a university which has difficulty giving an account of what its freedom is *for*, recognizes that we talk of pursuing knowledge 'for its own sake' only because we are trained to think that the knowledge which theology speaks of does not require our participation. A university which relegates the Christian contribution to the realm of values tempts us to forget that the church is itself a form of knowing the world. It was precisely Yoder's witness to help render visible that 'discipleship is not the deduction of a method properly applied; rather, discipleship *informs* the method appropriate to knowing Jesus Christ'.[70] Such an integrative vision resists seeing practices as the outcome or 'application' of a neutral method. The one who knows that the church '*precedes*' the world epistemologically will be wary of those non-participative accounts which ask how knowledge operates in general *and then* asks what Christianity has to add to this pre-existing structure.[71] A participative account of knowledge

69.  Michael Polanyi, 'Scientific Outlook: Its Sickness and Cure', *Science* 125 (1957), p. 481. Cited in Shuman, *The Body of Compassion*, p. 27.

70.  Harry Huebner, 'The Christian Life as Gift and Patience: Why Yoder Has Trouble with Method' in Ben C. Ollenburger and Gayle Gerber Koontz (eds), *A Mind Patient and Untamed: Assessing John Howard Yoder's Contribution to Theology, Ethics and Peacemaking* (Telford: Cascadia, 2004), pp. 23–38 (23).

71.  Yoder, *Priestly Kingdom*, p. 11 (emphasis added). Harry Huebner, 'Learning Made Strange: Can a University be Christian?' in L. Gregory Jones, Reinhard Hütter and C. Rosalee

deliberately queries the dominant order of knowing at work today, one where the church takes direction from the university in intellectual matters.[72] In this state, the mutual disenchantment between theology departments and churches can only pose a threat to theological scholarship, for separated from the practices of the church theology's pursuit of knowledge is bound to be hampered.[73] This last statement is not a piety – theologians whose knowledge is shaped by the resurrected presence of Jesus Christ are bound to offer a somewhat different account of history than those accounts which are non-theological. That so often theologians and biblical scholars fail even to see the Christian difference in relation to matters such as history is a reminder of why theology needs the lenses provided by the church's liturgy. It is theology's assimilation to dominant voices and accounts in the university that endangers the university's liveliness as a place of engagement and encounter. Theology departments need churches that can sustain them in maintaining distinctive traditions of inquiry. The crisis for knowing contributed by the presence of theology departments is sustainable, to a large extent, by the relationships such departments have with the church.

In a theology department hospitable to such a grasp of theological knowledge, teachers would have a vision alternative to that which encourages them to regard themselves as yet another academic professional, with their own set of self-contained norms appropriate to their disciplinary (sub-) disciplines. Part of the ethics of teaching theology, and of showing how theology is not one more fragmented subject amidst the other fragmented subjects of the modern university which the student must try and put together in their own time, is the responsibility that teachers *themselves* have for making connections across the various loci of theological attention.[74] Practically this could be carried out in a couple of ways. First, every teacher of ethics, church history or theology could, at certain points, be invited to demonstrate to students the connections across to other disciplines within theology and, of course, to Scripture. The rule should be as follows: no teaching on the early church's christological thinking should allow students to think that such debates were separate from biblical interpretation (an integrative vision need not be overly alarmed that the debates were not *just* about the Bible of course). As Dale Martin correctly recognizes an installation of Scripture more nearly at the centre of theological study should *not* be

Velloso Ewell (eds), *God, Truth, and Witness: Engaging Stanley Hauerwas* (Grand Rapids: Brazos, 2005), pp. 280–308 (282).

72. Willard, 'The Bible, the University and the God Who Hides', p. 26.

73. Stephen Fields, 'Catholicism and Academic Freedom: Authorities in Conflict?', *Logos* 4 (2001), pp. 91–111: 'The real tragedy of secularization is not so much that religious denominations lose their affiliated universities. It is that scholarship itself, which benefits from the religiously inspired perspective, is impeded' (101).

74. Bernd Wannenwetsch, 'The Ethics of Doing Theology' in Laurence Paul Hemming and Susan Frank Parsons (eds), *Redeeming Truth: Considering Faith and Reason* (Faith in Reason; London: SCM, 2007), pp. 167–83.

seen as an encroachment of biblical studies upon the disciplines of church history, systematic theology and ethics. Such fears trade upon the unhelpful confusion of attention to Scripture with the professional discipline of biblical studies, a discipline still strongly wedded to the historical critical mode of reading the Bible. Integrating Scripture within and across the theological curriculum would actually dislodge Scripture's false captivity to biblical studies and serve to 'de-emphasize any ownership of the study of the Bible sometimes expected of – or by – biblical scholars'.[75] Put simply, theology teachers would be invited to resist the logic of professionalism that says the sheer quantity of knowledge prohibits crossing boundaries, a stance which 'excludes from *any* discipline the subject-matter of the relevance of the disciplines to each other'.[76] Second, such connections across theology could be eased by team-teaching, with teachers of theology showing by the way the modules are designed that Scripture is indispensable to theological work.[77] It is important to say that repairing the fragmentation of theology is much more than a question of good academic or personnel management. The peculiar, unique claim must be sounded that 'when Christians get their theology wrong, they cannot help but get their lives and their accounts of the world wrong as well'.[78] In other words, how we organize and teach theology cannot afford to be one more manifestation of a world that presumes that God does not matter. How we teach theology, in a manner faithful to the virtue of constancy, is the pedagogical demonstration that faith is the 'telling of a story about ourselves that gives us a comprehensible narrative'.[79]

What then may we say about the kind of space the university would have to be in order to accommodate theology's witnessing activity? The status theology assumes as a witness is a pointer to the kind of decentring that could re-energize the university as a place of disputation. In a 'decentred' university the different subjects and disciplines would not be required to conform to a timeless, ahistorical account of reason that transcends particular traditions of inquiry. Such presumptions would be dethroned. A politics of engagement

75. Martin, *Pedagogy of the Bible*, p. 98. Dale Martin candidly concedes that as a professional biblical scholar he might be seen to have a vested interest in arguing that Scripture should be placed at the centre of the theological curriculum. But John Webster, a systematic theologian, also consistently argues that a renewed theological attention to Scripture has the capacity to bring theology together again as a unified subject.

76. Alasdair MacIntyre, 'The Idea of an Educated Public' in Graham Haydon (ed.), *Education and Values: The Richard Peters Lectures* (London: Institute of Education, 1987), pp. 15–36 (28, emphasis added).

77. Martin, *Pedagogy of the Bible*, p. 95. On this page, Martin also reports the striking idea of Lewis Ayres that students should not be taught Old Testament studies, then New Testament studies and then theology, but this order should be reversed. This would indeed help remove the notion that theology is a violation of the *sola Scriptura* principle.

78. Hauerwas, *With the Grain of the Universe*, p. 215.

79. Mathewes, *Theology of Public Life*, p. 196.

resists resting upon the claim to be 'neutral among differences',[80] and instead looks to our engagements with one another as opportunities to evince the democratic virtues of being 'patient, receptive, forbearing, and attentive to the dangers of imposing on others with different allegiances'.[81] Our differences are not temporary, disposable instances of something more universal, at least not in this world. They are just that – differences.[82] But a Christian contribution to thinking about universities would remind us that such differences will not be resolved through procedural politics, but eschatologically, that future in which we hope for communion.[83] Talk of difference should be careful that it does not become aligned to notions of rootless consumers wandering freely among a variety of perspectives.[84] Difference is not an intrinsic good (hence Christians know difference is not the end of the story) and what matters is the *content* of our particular differences.

A decentred university, committed to what Charles Taylor calls the 'politics of difference',[85] fosters as its first principle particular traditions of inquiry and embraces keenly the disputations that will accompany the visibility of our differences. The presence of what John Webster terms a 'theological theology' will be well placed in just such a decentred university as a disruptive witness to the reality that there is 'no rationality abstract from social practice, no sphere where everything is open for *total* reflection'.[86] To the charge that a decentred university would succumb to relativism, the response must be that this charge is parasitic upon the spectre of foundationalism, the assumption that we can offer an account of rationality independent of our rootedness in traditions of inquiry. In a decentred university, theologians would keep watch at the borders of their rootedness.[87] If we were to presume that in identifying our rootedness we could *then* construct something more universal and less particular, we would be chasing after the panoptical – and elusive – presumption of liberalism 'that the only knowledge worth having is achieved . . . at a remove from one's implication in a particular situation'.[88] One can begin with an emphasis on particularity and assume that some form of consensus will be the result only if

80.  Romand Coles, *Beyond Gated Politics: Reflections for the Possibility of Democracy* (Minneapolis: University of Minnesota Press, 2005), p. 253.

81.  Coles, *Beyond Gated Politics*, p. 257.

82.  If difference is a statement about reality, so too how we negotiate difference is at heart a metaphysical question: see Johnson, *Theology, Political Theory, and Pluralism*, p. 182.

83.  Mathewes, *Theology of Public Life*, writes that a Christian attitude to the public 'asks less of politics immanently, but expects more of it eschatologically' (286).

84.  Webster, 'Conversations', p. 5.

85.  Charles Taylor, *Multiculturalism: Examining the Politics of Recognition* (Amy Gutmann (ed.); Princeton: Princeton University Press, 1994), p. 38.

86.  Webster, *Theological Theology*, p. 24 (emphasis added).

87.  Yoder, *Priestly Kingdom*, p. 42.

88.  Stanley Fish, *Doing What Comes Naturally: Change, Rhetoric, and the Practice of Theory in Literary and Legal Studies* (Oxford: Clarendon Press, 1989), p. 348.

one is willing to contradict the self-proclaimed attention to particularity. While speaking to and debating with one another at the borders of our particular provinces is a more satisfactory way of relating to one another than is the appeal to general categories,[89] it does plainly require of us that we do have specific traditions of inquiry, that we *see* where we stand.

In the setting of a decentred university, theology will have more important work to do than claiming the centre ground. Indeed, the shifting centre of the university in which no one account of rationality takes a ruling presence is a permanent reminder that as Christian theologians we would

> be more relaxed and less compulsive about running the world if we made our peace with our minority situation, seeing this neither as a dirty trick of destiny nor as some great new progress but simply as the unmasking of the myth of Christendom, which wasn't true even when it was believed.[90]

For theology to resist assuming the university's centre and taking charge is, in effect, a claim about the way things are. It is a way of life seen most clearly in the life of Jesus who lived faithfully not always knowing where his trust in God would take him.[91] A theology department wills not to be in control in concert with its grasp of what is true and real. Theology's location and status in the modern university is to conform to its object of study. This should cause no surprise. For if '[t]he life of the community is prior to all possible methodological distillations', then the knowledge that emerges from such participation can only represent a minority stance, not one that is universal.[92]

As a reminder that neither the church nor theology is in control, Scripture's theological interpretation will be carried out more faithfully in decentred universities, rather than Christian universities. This requires us to re-imagine or recommit ourselves to the secular university as a place of debate, encounter and conflict, 'a forum for airing some of our most deep-seated differences and conflicts and learning [how] to live with them'.[93] To this exercise of learning how to live with our differences Christian thinkers will bring the virtue of patience, a virtue lived by observing the life of Christ and participating in the church. As those who live alert to a different time from the world – Charles T. Mathewes suggests Christians are not so much 'other-worldly' but 'other-timely'[94] – Christians need not seek to build Christian universities in a bid to secure theological interpretation of Scripture. Rather, Christians can endure the universities in which they find themselves, knowing that because the end has

---

89.   Yoder, *Priestly Kingdom*, p. 41.
90.   Yoder, *Priestly Kingdom*, p. 158.
91.   See Yoder, 'On Not Being in Charge'.
92.   Yoder, 'Walk and Word', p. 82.
93.   Johnson, *Theology, Political Theory, and Pluralism*, p. 236.
94.   The emphasis throughout Mathewes, *Theology of Public Life*, but see esp. p. 17.

already been announced in Jesus Christ, the disputations of the decentred university will not be interminable.[95] Christians can participate in seemingly endless debates because they know that the story does have an end. And precisely because Christians live energized by the story's end, they need not end the story themselves by imposing any consensus or panoptical categories. Being not in charge, Christians know that the end 'is not achievable by us; its achievement will come like a thief in the night'.[96] It might be tempting to suppose that a Christian university would sustain most faithfully Scripture's theological interpretation, but such a move would represent an impatient strike against the world as it now is.

One final set of questions – seen by many to afflict theology uniquely – needs to be raised before finishing. Does not the reading of Scripture within a community of scholars committed to particular traditions of inquiry represent an assault upon both the student's and the scholar's respective freedoms, to learn and to teach? Has one of the virtues of biblical scholarship not been that it has freed Scripture from its ecclesial captivity? Is not my account of knowledge – one that is to a certain degree constrained by its object of attention – a backwards step in the pursuit of freedom? As we saw when looking to Jesus it is important to clarify what accounts of freedom theology would be wise to invest in heavily and what ones a little less. To do this we must interrogate more precisely what models of freedom are often at work when speaking of academic freedom. Is our dominant model not that of 'negative freedom', a freedom *from* any external impositions, a model that assumes the individual agent to be 'the final authority on his own freedom'?[97]

Hauerwas' seemingly offensive way of starting his classes every year – by declaring that he wants his students not to learn to make up their own minds but to think like him – is an obvious rebuttal of such a freedom. Pedagogically, it rejects the assumption that universities are in the business of catering students with a range of 'positions' from which they may pick with their untrained wills.[98] Echoing our response to Davies' proposal it needs to be said that the choice presented before students is never as open as supporters of liberal education might lead us to think – every education imposes limits. That liberal education restricts its students to study religion at anything less than a healthy distance is a reminder that '[t]he choice is never between indoctrination and free inquiry but between different forms of indoctrination arising from different authorities'.[99] One could of course agree with Stanley Fish that 'autonomous decision making is an unimaginable state' and still opt (with open eyes) for the

95.  Mathewes, *Theology of Public Life*, p. 257.

96.  Mathewes, *Theology of Public Life*, p. 285.

97.  Charles Taylor, 'What's Wrong with Negative Liberty?' in *Philosophy and the Human Sciences – Philosophical Papers 2* (Cambridge: Cambridge University Press, 1985), pp. 211–29 (216).

98.  Hauerwas, *Dispatches from the Front*, p. 5.

99.  Fish, *Trouble with Principle*, p. 158.

subtle coercion of neutrality rather than the indoctrination (a term over-ripe of being retrieved from its liberal detractors) of the church,[100] but too often even this choice is not seen. Just as Hauerwas rightly insists that the story that we have no story other than the one we choose must be exposed as coming from somewhere and not nowhere, so too must encouraging students that they should be prey to their own minds be 'outed' as a form of indoctrination, or what in 1915 the American Association of University Professors spoke of (in *its* description of the dangers of religion to higher education) as 'inculcation'.[101] In the face of accounts of freedom synonymous with self-governance Alasdair MacIntyre offers this pedagogical advice:

> it is a primary responsibility of a university to be unresponsive, to give to its students what they need, not what they want, and to do so in such a way that what they want becomes what they need and what they choose is choice-worthy.[102]

That MacIntyre's advice seems so startling is an indication of how deeply our accounts of freedom trade upon non-participative accounts of human knowing, lending the human subject 'priority in its existence' and assuming that our knowing 'originate[s] spontaneously in us, not as responses to what realities outside the subject do to us and through us'.[103] How we come to understand Scripture and its world(s) – through participation – is linked to our account of freedom. In other words, both how we think of teaching and the accounts of freedom our understanding of theological education depends upon, are not just pedagogical questions but are deeply theological.[104]

Rather than investing in accounts of freedom that see the self as a source which can properly direct its desires only when freed from external impositions, theology is a permanent reminder of the importance of a positive account of what freedom is *for* and *to what* it is directed. Directing our attention to a common object – Jesus Christ – secures freedom more decisively than the creed that only lack of agreement or unbridled choice protects freedom. The former construal – which supposes that freedom is secured by a lack of agreement – leaves us vulnerable to the bureaucratic management of our differences. Such freedom, often buttressed by the language of pluralism, is devoid of any common good and results in 'an individualism which makes its claims in terms of rights and forms of bureaucratic organization which make their claims in

---

100.   Fish, *Trouble with Principle*, p. 160.

101.   Hauerwas, *Dispatches from the Front*, p. 13. See the 1915 Declaration of Principles on Academic Freedom and Academic Tenure, available at http://www.aaupui.org/Documents/Principles/Gen_Dec_Princ.pdf. Accessed 09 October 2008.

102.   MacIntyre, 'Catholic Universities', p. 15.

103.   Mathewes, *Theology of Public Life*, p. 45.

104.   For a theological analysis of freedom, alert to its shifts in modern intellectual history, see Webster, 'Evangelical Freedom'. Webster notes that modern accounts of freedom have a tendency to be deeply conflictual and rooted in negative understandings, that is freedom 'from' (112–13).

terms of utility'.[105] This is the logical result of seeing freedom as a good in itself, something to be jealously guarded, without ever asking for what purpose we are guarding it. When freedom itself is seen as the end, then we end up in interminable procedures to protect our freedoms from being infringed by one another. The latter option – freedom as choice – leaves both our desires and what we want unexamined, resulting in 'an illusory freedom whereby we effectively become prey to wayward desires'.[106] If we are to conceive of education, and theological education in particular, as an introduction to material that we would rather not encounter then such an account of freedom as choice will not suffice.[107] Merely construing freedom as freedom *from* restrictions is too thin an account and, by not protecting us from our untrained desires, fails to secure the very freedom it seeks.

In place of a freedom that is 'urge without direction' theology and the theological reading of Scripture is a reminder of the importance of an ordering teleology.[108] As William Cavanaugh argues, in the context of the modern university, '[t]he loss of teleology in the modern era has not liberated research but merely cast it adrift. If construed positively, freedom is that which allows us to achieve some worthwhile goal.'[109] Rendered in Johannine terms, it is the truth of Jesus Christ, apprehended by discipleship, which accounts for Christian freedom: '"If you continue in my word, you are truly my disciples; and you will know the truth, and the truth will make you free"' (Jn 8.31-32). There can be no account of freedom possible without equal attentiveness to the one who makes our freedom possible.[110] A participative account of Scripture and its understanding is closely bound to such considerations. Just as the fragmentation of the modern university is a symptom of the university's inability to account for what its freedom is *for*, so in this setting theology can take up the role of witnessing to a way of inquiry which relentlessly relates the various facets of its inquiry to one another and explores how Scripture is webbed within a series of practices and doctrines. We might say therefore that a university

105.   MacIntyre, *After Virtue*, p. 71.

106.   David B. Burrell, 'Can We Be Free without a Creator?' in Hütter Jones and Velloso Ewell (eds), *God, Truth, and Witness: Engaging Stanley Hauerwas* (Grand Rapids: Brazos, 2005), pp. 35–52 (51).

107.   Karl Barth, *Ethics* (Dietrich Braun (ed.); trans. Geoffrey W. Bromiley; Edinburgh: T&T Clark, 1981), pp. 364–65. Barth invites us to see that education and salvation are closely linked, for both first meet our flinty resistance.

108.   Fish, *There's No Such Thing as Free Speech*, p. 108. Fish goes on to suggest that 'freedom is a coherent notion only in relation to a goal or good that limits and, by limiting, shapes its exercise' (108).

109.   William T. Cavanaugh, 'Sailing Under True Colors: Academic Freedom and the Ecclesially Based University' in Michael L. Budde and John Wright (eds), *Conflicting Allegiances: The Church-Based University in a Liberal Democratic Society* (Grand Rapids: Brazos, 2002), pp. 31–52 (45).

110.   See David Lyle Jeffrey, 'Biblical Literacy, Academic Freedom and Christian Liberty' in Jeffrey and Evans (eds), *Bible and the University*, pp. 284–302 (298).

need not fear the apparent restrictions upon academic freedom represented by theology, but need fear not having a department exploring what freedom is *for*.

## Conclusion

As we reach the end of this very theological proposal readers may suspect that at various points I have succumbed to the misstep I identified in John Webster's account of Scripture and drafted a set of blueprints, of which this account of Scripture's place in universities might be just one more. I do not think of course that I have produced a blueprint of Scripture but simply tried to make connections across the various loci of theology in order to understand those actions in which Scripture is *already* a participant. To those still sceptical of the value of making such connections I can only end with the hopeful, patient advice of John Howard Yoder: 'The only way to see how this will work will be to see how it will work.'[111]

---

111.  Yoder, *Priestly Kingdom*, p. 45.

## BIBLIOGRAPHY

Achtemeier, Elizabeth, 'The Canon as the Voice of the Living God' in Braaten, Carl E. and Robert W. Jenson (eds), *Reclaiming the Bible for the Church* (Edinburgh: T&T Clark, 1996), pp. 119–30.

Anderson, Benedict, *Imagined Communities: Reflections on the Origin and Spread of Nationalism* (London: Verso, rev. edn, 2006).

Augustine, *Confessions* (trans. Henry Chadwick; Oxford World's Classics; Oxford: Oxford University Press, 1998).

Bader-Saye, Scott, *Following Jesus in a Culture of Fear* (The Christian Practice of Everyday Life Series; Grand Rapids: Brazos, 2007).

—'Figuring Time: Providence and Politics' in Rashkover, Randi and C. C. Pecknold (eds), *Liturgy, Time, and the Politics of Redemption* (Radical Traditions; Grand Rapids: Eerdmans, 2006), pp. 91–111.

Balthasar, Hans Urs von, *Theo-Logic*, Vol. III (trans. Graham Harrison; 5 vols; San Francisco: Ignatius, 2005).

—*You Have Words of Eternal Life: Scripture Meditations* (trans. Dennis Martin; San Francisco: Ignatius, 2004).

—'Seeing, Hearing, and Reading within the Church' in *Explorations in Theology*, Vol. II (trans. Brian McNeil; 3 vols; San Francisco: Ignatius, 1991), pp. 473–90.

—*Mysterium Paschale: The Mystery of Easter* (trans. Aidan Nichols; Edinburgh: T&T Clark, 1990).

—*Theo-Drama: Theological Dramatic Theory*, Vols II and V (trans. Graham Harrison; 5 vols; San Francisco: Ignatius, 1990).

—*The Glory of the Lord: A Theological Aesthetics*, Vol. 1 (trans. Erasmo Leiva-Herikakis; 7 vols; Edinburgh: T&T Clark, 1982).

—*Prayer* (trans. A. V. Littledale; London: SPCK, 1973).

—*A Theology of History* (no translator cited; London: Sheed and Ward, 1964).

Barth, Karl, *Church Dogmatics* I/2, III/1, III/1, IV/1, IV/3.1 (various translators; London: T&T Clark International, 2004).

—*Homiletics* (trans. Geoffrey W. Bromiley and Donald E. Daniels; Louisville: Westminster John Knox, 1991).

—*Witness to the Word: A Commentary on John 1* (trans. Geoffrey W. Bromiley; Grand Rapids: Eerdmans, 1986).

—*Ethics* (Dietrich Braun (ed.); trans. Geoffrey W. Bromiley; Edinburgh: T&T Clark, 1981).

—'When They Saw the Lord' in *Call for God: New Sermons from Basel Prison* (trans. A. T. Mackay; London: SCM, 1967), pp. 117–25.

—*Evangelical Theology: An Introduction* (trans. Grover Foley; London: Collins, 1963).

—*Dogmatics in Outline* (trans. G. T. Thomson; New York: Harper & Row, 1959).

—*The Word of God and the Word of Man* (trans. Douglas Horton; New York: Harper & Row, 1957).

—'The Christian Understanding of Revelation' in *Against the Stream: Shorter Post-War Writings* (trans. Stanley Godman; London: SCM, 1954), pp. 203–40.

—*Come Holy Spirit* (trans. George W. Richards, Elmer G. Homrighausen and Karl J. Ernst; Edinburgh: T&T Clark, 1934).

Bell Jr, Daniel M., 'Deliberating: Justice and Liberation' in Hauerwas, Stanley and Samuel Wells (eds), *The Blackwell Companion to Christian Ethics* (Oxford: Blackwell, 2006), pp. 182–95.

—'Jesus, the Jews, and the Politics of God's Justice', *Ex Auditu* 22 (2006), pp. 87–112.

Benedetto, Robert, *P.T. Forsyth Bibliography and Index* (Westport: Greenwood Press, 1993).

Bonhoeffer, Dietrich, *Worldly Preaching: Lectures on Homiletics* (trans. Clyde E. Fant; New York: Crossroad, 1991).

—*Christ the Center* (trans. Edwin H. Robertson; New York: Harper & Row, 1978).

Bornkamm, Günther, 'Towards the Interpretation of John's Gospel: A Discussion of *The Testament of Jesus*' in Ashton, John (ed.), *The Interpretation of John* (trans. John Ashton; London: SPCK, 1986), pp. 79–98.

Bowald, Mark Alan, *Rendering the Word in Theological Hermeneutics* (Aldershot: Ashgate, 2007).

Bradley, William Lee, *P.T. Forsyth: The Man and His Work* (London: Independent Press, 1952).

Bright, Pamela, 'St Augustine' in Holcomb, Justin S. (ed.), *Christian Theologies of Scripture: A Comparative Introduction* (New York: New York University Press, 2006), pp. 39–59.

Brock, Brian, *Singing the Ethos of God: On the Place of Christian Ethics in Scripture* (Grand Rapids: Eerdmans, 2007).

Brown, Raymond, *The Gospel According to St. John*, Vol. 2 (Anchor Bible; 2 vols; London: Geoffrey Chapman, 1966).

Brown, Robert McAfee, *P.T. Forsyth: Prophet for Today* (Philadelphia: Westminster, 1952).

Budziszewski, J., 'The Illusion of Moral Neutrality', *First Things* 35 (August/September 1993), pp. 32–37. Accessed online at www.leaderu.com/ftissues/ft9308/articles/budziszewski.html on 11 August 2008.

Burgess, Andrew, *The Ascension in Karl Barth* (Barth Studies; Aldershot: Ashgate, 2004).

Burnett, Richard E., *Karl Barth's Theological Exegesis: The Hermeneutical Principles of the Römerbrief Period* (Grand Rapids: Eerdmans, 2004).

Burrell, David B., 'Can We Be Free without a Creator?' in Jones, L. Gregory, Reinhard Hütter and C. Rosalee Velloso Ewell (eds), *God, Truth, and Witness: Engaging Stanley Hauerwas* (Grand Rapids: Brazos, 2005), pp. 35–52.

Burridge, Richard A., *Imitating Jesus: An Inclusive Approach to New Testament Ethics* (Grand Rapids: Eerdmans, 2007).

Butin, Philip W., *Reformed Ecclesiology: Trinitarian Grace According to Calvin* (Studies in Reformed Theology and History; Princeton: Princeton Theological Seminary, 1994).

Calvin, John, *The Gospel According to St John 1-10* (trans. T. H. L. Parker; Calvin's Commentaries Series; Edinburgh: Oliver and Boyd, 1961).

—*The Gospel According to St John 11-21 and the First Epistle of John* (trans. T. H. L. Parker; Calvin's Commentaries Series; Edinburgh: Oliver and Boyd, 1961).

—*Institutes of the Christian Religion* (trans. F. L. Battles; Library of Christian Classics, XX; Philadelphia: Westminster Press, 1960).

Campbell, Charles L., *The Word before the Powers: An Ethic of Preaching* (Louisville: Westminster John Knox, 2002).

—*Preaching Jesus: New Directions for Homiletics in Hans Frei's Postliberal Theology* (Grand Rapids: Eerdmans, 1997).

Candler Jr, Peter M., *Theology, Rhetoric, Manudiction, or Reading Scripture Together on the Path to God* (Radical Traditions; London: SCM, 2006).

Cavanaugh, William T., 'Pilgrim People' in McCarthy, David Matzko and M. Therese Lysaught (eds), *Gathered for the Journey: Moral Theology in Catholic Perspective* (Grand Rapids: Eerdmans, 2007), pp. 88–105.

—'Discerning: Politics and Reconciliation' in Hauerwas, Stanley and Samuel Wells (eds), *The Blackwell Companion to Christian Ethics* (Oxford: Blackwell, 2006), pp. 196–208.

—'Sailing Under True Colors: Academic Freedom and the Ecclesially Based University' in Budde, Michael L. and John Wright (eds), *Conflicting Allegiances: The Church-Based University in a Liberal Democratic Society* (Grand Rapids: Brazos, 2002), pp. 31–52.

Coles, Romand, *Beyond Gated Politics: Reflections for the Possibility of Democracy* (Minneapolis: University of Minnesota Press, 2005).

Coll, Niall, *Christ in Eternity and Time: Modern Anglican Perspectives* (Dublin: Four Courts Press, 2001).

Connolly, William E., *Why I Am Not a Secularist* (Minneapolis: University of Minnesota Press, 1999).

Cyprian, 'Treatise IX: On the Advantage of Patience', in *Ante-Nicene Fathers*, Vol. V (Alexander Roberts and James Donaldson (eds); trans. Ernest Wallis; 10 vols; Peabody: Hendrickson, 1995), pp. 484–91.

Cyril of Alexandria, *On the Unity of Christ* (trans. John Anthony McGuckin; Crestwood: St Vladimir's Seminary Press, 1995).

D'Costa, Gavin, *Theology in the Public Square: Church, Academy and Nation* (Challenges in Contemporary Theology; Oxford: Blackwell, 2005).

—'Revelation, Scripture and Tradition: Some Comments on John Webster's Conception of "Holy Scripture"', *IJST* 6 (2004), pp. 337–50.

Davies, J. G., *He Ascended Into Heaven: A Study in the History of Doctrine* (London: Lutterworth, 1958).

Davies, Oliver, 'Cosmic Speech and the Liturgy of Silence' in Rashkover, Randi and C. C. Pecknold (eds), *Liturgy, Time, and the Politics of Redemption* (Radical Traditions; Grand Rapids: Eerdmans, 2006), pp. 215–26.

Davies, Philip, *Whose Bible is it Anyway?* (London: T&T Clark International, 2nd edn, 2004).

Davis, Ellen F., 'The Soil That Is Scripture' in Brown, William P. (ed.), *Engaging Biblical Authority: Perspectives on the Bible as Scripture* (Louisville: Westminster John Knox, 2007), pp. 36–44.

Davis, Thomas J., 'Preaching and Presence: Constructing Calvin's Homiletical Legacy' in Foxgrover, David (ed.), *The Legacy of John Calvin* (Grand Rapids: Calvin Studies Society, 2000), pp. 84–111.

Dawson, Gerrit Scott, *Jesus Ascended: The Meaning of Christ's Continuing Incarnation* (London: T&T Clark International, 2004).

Dehn, Günther, *Man and Revelation* (London: Hodder and Stoughton, 1936).

Deidun, Tom, 'The Bible and Christian Ethics' in Hoose, Bernard (ed.), *Christian Ethics: An Introduction* (London: Continuum, 1998), pp. 3–47.

DeVries, Dawn, 'Calvin's Preaching' in McKim, Donald K. (ed.), *The Cambridge Companion to John Calvin* (Cambridge: Cambridge University Press, 2004), pp. 106–24.

—*Jesus Christ in the Preaching of Calvin and Schleiermacher* (Louisville: Westminster John Knox, 1996).

Dickens, W. T., 'Hans Urs von Balthasar' in Holcomb, Justin S. (ed.), *Christian Theologies of Scripture: A Comparative Introduction* (New York: New York University Press, 2006), pp. 202–19.

Duke, Robert W., *The Sermon as God's Word: Theologies for Preaching* (Nashville: Abingdon, 1980).

Dykstra, Craig R., 'Reconceiving Practice' in Wheeler, Barbara G. and Edward Farley (eds), *Shifting Boundaries: Contextual Approaches to the Structure of Theological Education* (Louisville: Westminster John Knox, 1991), pp. 35–66.

Dykstra, Craig R. and Dorothy C. Bass, 'A Theological Understanding of Christian Practices' in Volf, Miroslav and Dorothy C. Bass (eds), *Practicing Theology: Beliefs and Practices in Christian Life* (Grand Rapids: Eerdmans, 2002), pp. 13–32.

Edmondson, Stephen, *Calvin's Christology* (Cambridge: Cambridge University Press, 2004).

Evans, C. Stephen, 'The Bible and the Academy' in Jeffrey, David Lyle and C. Stephen Evans (eds), *The Bible and the University* (Scripture and Hermeneutics Series, 8; Milton Keynes: Paternoster, 2007), pp. 303–10.

—'Canonicity, Apostolicity, and Biblical Authority: Some Kierkegaardian Reflections' in Bartholomew, Craig, Scott Hahn, Robin Parry, Christopher Seitz and Al Wolters (eds), *Canon and Biblical Interpretation* (Scripture and Hermeneutics Series, 7; Milton Keynes: Paternoster, 2006), pp. 146–66.

Farrer, Austin, *The Brink of Mystery* (Charles C. Conti (ed.); London: SPCK, 1976).

Farris, Stephen, *Preaching that Matters: The Bible and Our Lives* (Louisville: Westminster John Knox, 1998).

Farrow, Douglas, *Ascension and Ecclesia: On the Significance of the Doctrine of the Ascension for Ecclesiology and Christian Cosmology* (Grand Rapids: Eerdmans, 1999).

Fiddes, Paul S., 'The Canon as Space and Place' in Barton, John and Michael Wolter (eds), *Die Einheit der Schrift und die Vielfalt des Kanons/The Unity of Scripture and the Diversity of the Canon* (Berlin: Walter de Gruyter, 2003), pp. 126–49.

Fields, Stephen, 'Catholicism and Academic Freedom: Authorities in Conflict?', *Logos* 4 (2001), pp. 91–111.

Fish, Stanley, *The Trouble with Principle* (Cambridge: Harvard University Press, 1999).

—*There's No Such Thing as Free Speech, and It's a Good Thing Too* (New York: Oxford University Press, 1994).

—*Doing What Comes Naturally: Change, Rhetoric, and the Practice of Theory in Literary and Legal Studies* (Oxford: Clarendon Press, 1989).

Fodor, James, 'Postliberal Theology' in Ford, David F. (ed.) with Rachel Muers, *The Modern Theologians: An Introduction to Christian Theology since 1918* (Oxford: Blackwell, 3rd edn, 2005), pp. 229–48.

Forrester, Duncan B., 'John Howard Yoder (1927–1997)' in Witte Jr, John and Frank S. Alexander (eds), *The Teachings of Modern Christianity on Law, Politics and Human Nature*, Vol. 2 (2 vols; New York: Columbia University Press, 2006), pp. 481–500.

Forsyth, P. T., *Positive Preaching and the Modern Mind* (Biblical and Theological Classics Library; Carlisle: Paternoster, 1998).

—*The Soul of Prayer* (Biblical and Theological Classics Library; Carlisle: Paternoster, 1998).

—*The Gospel and Authority: A P.T. Forsyth Reader* (Marvin W. Anderson (ed.); Minneapolis: Augsburg, 1971).

—*The Church, The Gospel and Society* (London: Independent Press, 1962).

—*Revelation Old and New: Sermons and Addresses* (John Huxtable (ed.); London: Independent Press, 1962).

—*Faith, Freedom and the Future* (London: Independent Press, 1955).

—*The Principle of Authority in Relation to Certainty, Sanctity and Society: An Essay in the Philosophy of Experimental Religion* (London: Independent Press, 1952).

—*The Cruciality of the Cross* (London: Independent Press, 1948).

—*The Church and the Sacraments* (London: Independent Press, 1947).

—*The Person and Place of Jesus Christ* (London: Independent Press, 1946).

—*The Work of Christ* (London: Independent Press, 1946).

—'The Inner Life of Christ', *The Constructive Quarterly* 7 (1919), pp. 149–62.

—'Unity and Theology: A Liberal Evangelicalism the True Catholicism' in *Towards Reunion: Being Contributions to Mutual Understanding by Church of England and Free Church Writers* (no editor cited; London: Macmillan, 1919), pp. 51–81.

—*The Christian Ethic of War* (London: Longmans, Green, 1916).

—*The Justification of God: Lectures for War-Time on a Christian Theodicy of God* (London: Duckworth, 1916).

—*Theology in Church and State* (London: Hodder & Stoughton, 1915).

—'Regeneration, Creation, and Miracle', *The Methodist Review Quarterly* 63 (1914), pp. 627–43.

—*Christ on Parnassus: Lectures on Art, Ethic and Theology* (London: Hodder and Stoughton, 1911).

—'Orthodoxy, Heterodoxy, Heresy, and Freedom', *Hibbert Journal* 8 (1910), pp. 321–29.

—*Missions in State and Church: Sermons and Addresses* (New York: A. C. Armstrong, 1908).

—'The Need for a Positive Gospel', *London Quarterly Review* 102 (1904), pp. 64–99.

—'Treating the Bible Like Any Other Book', *The British Weekly* (15 August 1901), pp. 401–02.

—*Rome, Reform and Reaction* (London: Hodder & Stoughton, 1899).

—'Mystics and Saints', *The Expository Times* 5 (1894), pp. 401–04.

—'Revelation and the Person of Christ' in *Faith and Criticism: Essays by Congregationalists* (no editor cited; London: Simpson Low Marston, 1893), pp. 95–144.

Fowl, Stephen E., 'The Role of Authorial Intention in the Theological Interpretation of Scripture' in Green, Joel B. and Max Turner (eds), *Between Two Horizons: Spanning*

*Bibliography*

*New Testament Studies and Systematic Theology* (Grand Rapids: Eerdmans, 2000), pp. 71–87.

—'The New Testament, Theology, and Ethics' in Green, Joel B. (ed.), *Hearing the New Testament: Strategies for Interpretation* (Grand Rapids: Eerdmans, 1995), pp. 394–410.

Fowl, Stephen E. and L. Gregory Jones, *Reading in Communion: Scripture and Ethics in Christian Life* (Biblical Foundations in Theology; London: SPCK, 1991).

Fox, Michael V., 'Bible Scholarship and Faith Based Study: My View', *Society of Biblical Literature Forum*, February 2006. Available at http://www.sbl-site.org/publications/article.aspx?articleId=490. Accessed 05 January 2009.

Frei, Hans W., *Types of Christian Theology* (George Hunsinger and William C. Placher (eds); New Haven: Yale University Press, 1992).

—*The Eclipse of Biblical Narrative: A Study in Eighteenth and Nineteenth Century Hermeneutics* (New Haven: Yale University Press, 1974).

Gawronski, Raymond, *Word and Silence: Hans Urs von Balthasar and the Spiritual Encounter between East and West* (Edinburgh: T&T Clark, 1995).

Gibson, David, *Reading the Decree: Exegesis, Election and Christology in Calvin and Barth* (T&T Clark Studies in Systematic Theology; London: T&T Clark International, 2009).

Godsey, John D., *Karl Barth's Table-Talk* (*SJT* Occasional Papers, 10; Edinburgh: Oliver and Boyd, 1963).

Graham, William A., *Beyond the Written Word: Oral Aspects of Scripture in the History of Religion* (Cambridge: Cambridge University Press, 1987).

Grant, George, 'Research in the Humanities' in *Technology and Justice* (Toronto: Anansi, 1986), pp. 97–102.

Gunton, Colin E., *Christ and Creation* (Didsbury Lectures; Carlisle: Paternoster, 1992).

—'Two Dogmas Revisited: Edward Irving's Christology', *SJT* 41 (1988), pp. 359–76.

—*Yesterday and Today: A Study of Continuities in Christology* (London: Darton, Longman and Todd, 1983).

Guroian, Vigen, *Ethics after Christendom: Toward an Ecclesial Christian Ethic* (Eugene: Wipf and Stock, 2004).

Gustafson, James M., 'The Place of Scripture in Christian Ethics: A Methodological Study' in Curran, Charles E. and Richard A. McCormick (eds), *Readings in Moral Theology No. 4: The Use of the Bible in Moral Theology* (New York: Paulist, 1984), pp. 151–77.

Hart, David Bentley, *The Beauty of the Infinite: The Aesthetics of Christian Truth* (Grand Rapids: Eerdmans, 2003).

Hastings, Adrian, 'Pluralism: The Relationship of Theology to Religious Studies' in Hamnett, Ian (ed.), *Religious Pluralism and Unbelief: Studies Critical and Comparative* (London: Routledge, 1990), pp. 226–40.

Hauerwas, Stanley, *The State of the University: Academic Knowledges and the Knowledge of God* (Illuminations: Theory and Religion; Oxford: Blackwell, 2007).

—'Why Did Jesus Have to Die?: An Attempt to Cross the Barrier of Age', *Princeton Seminary Bulletin* 28 (2007), pp. 181–90.

—*Matthew* (Brazos Theological Commentary on the Bible; Grand Rapids: Brazos, 2006).

—*Disrupting Time: Sermons, Prayers, and Sundries* (Eugene: Cascade, 2004).

—*Performing the Faith: Bonhoeffer and the Practice of Nonviolence* (London: SPCK, 2004).

—'Hooks: Random Thoughts By Way of a Response to Griffiths and Ochs', *Modern Theology* 19 (2003), pp. 89–101.

—*The Peaceable Kingdom: A Primer in Christian Ethics* (London: SCM, 2nd edn, 2003).

—*Christian Existence Today: Essays on Church, World, and Living in Between* (Grand Rapids: Brazos, 2001).

—'Foreword' in Craig A. Carter, *The Politics of the Cross: The Theology and Social Ethics of John Howard Yoder* (Grand Rapids: Brazos, 2001), pp. 9–11.

—*Wilderness Wanderings: Probing Twentieth-Century Theology and Philosophy* (Radical Traditions; London: SCM, 2001).

—*With the Grain of the Universe: The Church's Witness and Natural Theology* (Grand Rapids: Brazos, 2001).

—*A Better Hope: Resources for a Church Confronting Capitalism, Democracy and Postmodernity* (Grand Rapids: Brazos, 2000).

—*After Christendom: How the Church Is to Behave If Freedom, Justice, and a Christian Nation Are Bad Ideas* (Nashville: Abingdon, 1999).

—*Sanctify Them in the Truth: Holiness Exemplified* (Edinburgh: T&T Clark, 1998).

—*In Good Company: The Church as Polis* (Notre Dame: University of Notre Dame Press, 1995).

—*Dispatches from the Front: Theological Engagements with the Secular* (Durham: Duke University Press, 1994).

—*Unleashing the Scripture: Freeing the Bible from Captivity to America* (Nashville: Abingdon, 1993).

—*Against the Nations: War and Survival in a Liberal Society* (Notre Dame: University of Notre Dame Press, 1992).

—'The Need for an Ending', *The Modern Churchman* 28 (1986), pp. 3–7.

—'Pacifism: Some Philosophical Considerations', *Faith and Philosophy* 2 (1985), pp. 99–104.

—*A Community of Character: Toward a Constructive Christian Social Ethic* (Notre Dame: University of Notre Dame Press, 1981).

—*Vision and Virtue: Essays in Christian Ethical Reflection* (Notre Dame: Fides Press, 1974).

Hauerwas, Stanley and Samuel Wells, 'How The Church Managed Before There was Ethics' in Hauerwas, Stanley and Samuel Wells (eds), *The Blackwell Companion to Christian Ethics* (Oxford: Blackwell, 2000), pp. 39–50.

Hauerwas, Stanley and William H. Willimon, *The Truth about God: The Ten Commandments in Christian Life* (Nashville: Abingdon, 1999).

Hauerwas, Stanley and James Fodor, 'Remaining in Babylon: Oliver O'Donovan's Defense of Christendom', *SCE* 11 (1998), pp. 30–55.

Hauerwas, Stanley and Charles Pinches, *Christians Among the Virtues: Theological Conversations with Ancient and Modern Ethics* (Notre Dame: University of Notre Dame Press, 1997).

Hauerwas, Stanley and William H. Willimon, *Resident Aliens: A Provocative Christian Assessment of Culture and Ministry for People Who Know that Something Is Wrong* (Nashville: Abingdon, 1989).

Healy, Nicholas M., 'Practices and the New Ecclesiology: Misplaced Concreteness?, *IJST* 5 (2003), pp. 287–308.

—*Church, World and the Christian Life: Practical-Prophetic Ecclesiology* (Cambridge Studies in Christian Doctrine, 7; Cambridge: Cambridge University Press, 2000).

Horrell, David G., *Solidarity and Difference: A Contemporary Reading of Paul's Ethics* (London: T&T Clark International, 2005).

Horton, Michael S., *Lord and Servant: A Covenant Christology* (Louisville: Westminster John Knox, 2005).

—*Covenant and Eschatology: The Divine Drama* (Louisville: Westminster John Knox, 2002).

Hovey, Craig, *Speak Thus: Christian Language in Church and World* (Eugene: Cascade, 2008).

—*To Share in the Body: A Theology of Martyrdom for Today's Church* (Grand Rapids: Brazos, 2008).

Huebner, Chris K., *A Precarious Peace: Yoderian Explorations on Theology, Knowledge, and Identity* (Polyglossia: Radical Reformation Theologies; Waterloo: Herald, 2006).

Huebner, Harry, 'Learning Made Strange: Can a University be Christian?' in Jones, L. Gregory, Reinhard Hütter and C. Rosalee Velloso Ewell (eds), *God, Truth, and Witness: Engaging Stanley Hauerwas* (Grand Rapids: Brazos, 2005), pp. 280–308.

—'The Christian Life as Gift and Patience: Why Yoder Has Trouble with Method' in Ollenburger, Ben C. and Gayle Gerber Koontz (eds), *A Mind Patient and Untamed: Assessing John Howard Yoder's Contribution to Theology, Ethics and Peacemaking* (Telford: Cascadia, 2004), pp. 23–38.

Hunsinger, George, *Disruptive Grace: Studies in the Theology of Karl Barth* (Grand Rapids: Eerdmans, 2000).

Hunter, A. M., *P.T. Forsyth – Per Crucem ad Lucem* (London: SCM, 1974).

Irving, Edward, *The Collected Writings of Edward Irving*, Vol. V (G. Carlyle (ed.); 5 vols; London: Alexander Strahan, 1865).

—*Edward Irving: The Trinitarian Face of God* (Graham W.P. McFarlane (ed.); The Devotional Library; Edinburgh: Saint Andrew's Press, 1996).

Jeffrey, David Lyle, 'Biblical Literacy, Academic Freedom and Christian Liberty' in Jeffrey, David Lyle and Stephen C. Evans (eds), *The Bible and the University* (Scripture and Hermeneutics Series, 8; Milton Keynes: Paternoster, 2007), pp. 284–302.

Jennings, Willie James, 'Undoing our Abandonment: Reading Scripture through the sinlessness of Jesus', *Ex Auditu* 14 (1998), pp. 85–96.

Jenson, Matt, 'Real Presence: Contemporaneity in Bonhoeffer's *Christology*', *SJT* 58 (2005), pp. 143–60.

Jenson, Robert W., 'The Strange New World of the Bible' in Root, Michael and James J. Buckley (eds), *Sharper Than a Two-Edged Sword: Preaching, Teaching and Living the Bible* (Grand Rapids: Eerdmans, 2008), pp. 22–31.

—'For Us. . . . He Was Made Man' in Seitz, Christopher R. (ed.), *Nicene Christianity: The Future for a New Ecumenism* (Grand Rapids: Brazos, 2001), pp. 75–85.

—*Systematic Theology*, Vol. 1 (2 vols; New York: Oxford University Press, 1997).

—'Hermeneutics and the Life of the Church' in Braaten, Carl E. and Robert W. Jenson (eds), *Reclaiming the Bible for the Church* (Edinburgh: T&T Clark, 1996), pp. 89–105.

Johnson, Kristen Deede, *Theology, Political Theory, and Pluralism* (Cambridge Studies in Christian Doctrine, 15; Cambridge: Cambridge University Press, 2007).

Johnson, Luke T. and William S. Kurz, *The Future of Catholic Biblical Scholarship: A Constructive Conversation* (Grand Rapids: Eerdmans, 2002).

Jones, L. Gregory, 'The Psychological Captivity of the Church in the United States' in Braaten, Carl E. and Robert W. Jenson (eds), *Either/Or: The Gospel or Neopaganism* (Grand Rapids: Eerdmans, 1995), pp. 97–112.

—'Alasdair MacIntyre on Narrative, Community, and the Moral Life', *Modern Theology* 4 (1987), pp. 53–69.

Jones, Serene, 'Graced Practices: Excellence and Freedom in the Christian Life' in Volf, Miroslav and Dorothy C. Bass (eds), *Practicing Theology: Beliefs and Practices in Christian Life* (Grand Rapids: Eerdmans, 2002), pp. 51–77.

Kallenberg, Brad J., 'The Master Argument of MacIntyre's *After Virtue*' in Murphy, Nancey, Brad J. Kallenberg and Mark Theissen Nation (eds), *Virtues and Practices in the Christian Tradition: Christian Ethics after MacIntyre* (Harrisburg: Trinity Press International, 1997), pp. 7–29.

Käsemann, Ernst, *The Testament of Jesus: A Study of the Gospel of John in the Light of Chapter 17* (trans. Gerhard Krodel; London: SCM, 1968).

Katangole, Emmanuel, *Beyond Universal Reason: The Relation between Religion and Ethics in the Work of Stanley Hauerwas* (Notre Dame: Notre Dame University Press, 2000).

Kay, James F., *Preaching and Theology* (Preaching and Its Partners; St Louis: Chalice Press, 2007).

—'Reorientation: Homiletics as Theologically Authorized Rhetoric', *Princeton Seminary Bulletin* 24 (2003), pp. 16–35.

Kelber, Werner H., 'The Authority of The Word in St John's Gospel: Charismatic Speech, Narrative Text, Logocentric Metaphysics', *Oral Tradition* 2 (1987), pp. 108–31.

Kenneson, Philip D., *Life on the Vine: Cultivating the Fruit of the Spirit in Christian Community* (Downers Grove: InterVarsity Press, 1999).

Kerr, Nathan, *Christ, History and Apocalyptic: The Politics of Christian Mission* (Theopolitical Visions; Eugene: Cascade, 2009).

Kierkegaard, Søren, 'Of the Difference between a Genius and an Apostle' in *The Present Age* (trans. Alexander Dru; London: Fontana Library, 1962), pp. 101–27.

Koester, Craig, 'Hearing, Seeing, and Believing in the Gospel of John', *Biblica* 70 (1989), pp. 327–48.

Lange, Frits de, *Waiting for the Word: Dietrich Bonhoeffer on Speaking about God* (trans. Martin N. Walton; Grand Rapids: Eerdmans, 2000).

Lash, Nicholas, *Believing Three Ways in One God: A Reading of the Apostle's Creed* (SCM Classics; London: SCM, 2002).

—'Up and Down in Christology' in Sykes, Stephen and Derek Holmes (eds), *New Studies in Theology* 1 (London: Duckworth, 1980), pp. 31–46.

Leith, John H., 'Calvin's Doctrine of the Proclamation of the Word and Its Significance for Today' in George, Timothy (ed.), *John Calvin and the Church: A Prism for Reform* (Louisville: Westminster John Knox, 1990), pp. 206–29.

Levenson, Jon D., *The Hebrew Bible, the Old Testament, and Historical Criticism: Jews and Christians in Biblical Studies* (Louisville: Westminster John Knox, 1993).

Levering, Matthew, *Participatory Biblical Exegesis: A Theology of Biblical Interpretation* (Notre Dame: University of Notre Dame Press, 2008).

Lincoln, Andrew T., "'I Am the Resurrection and the Life": The Resurrection Message of the Fourth Gospel' in Longenecker, Richard N. (ed.), *Life in the Face of Death: The Resurrection Message of the New Testament* (Grand Rapids: Eerdmans, 1998), pp. 122–44.

Lischer, Richard, 'Resurrection and Rhetoric' in Braaten, Carl E. and Robert W. Jenson (eds), *Marks of the Body of Christ* (Grand Rapids: Eerdmans, 1999), pp. 13–24.

Lofthouse, W. F., *The Father and the Son: A Study in Johannine Thought* (London: SCM, 1934).

Long, D. Stephen, 'God is Not Nice' in Laytham, D. Brent (ed.), *God is Not . . .* (Grand Rapids: Brazos, 2004), pp. 39–54.

Long, Thomas G., 'And How Shall They Hear? The Listener in Contemporary Preaching' in O'Day, Gail R. and Thomas G. Long (eds), *Listening to the Word: Studies in Honor of Fred B. Craddock* (Nashville: Abingdon, 1993), pp. 167–88.

Luther, Martin, *Sermons on the Gospel of St. John Chapters 1-4* (Jaroslav Pelikan (ed.); trans. Martin H. Bertram; Luther's Works, 22; 55 vols; Saint Louis: Concordia, 1957).

Marquard, Odo, 'The Question, To What Question is Hermeneutics The Answer?' in *Contemporary German Philosophy*, Vol. 4 (Darrel E. Christensen (ed.); 4 vols; trans. Robert M. Wallace; no place cited: Pennsylvania State University Press, 1984), pp. 9–31.

McClendon, Jr, James Wm., *Systematic Theology*, vols 1 and 2 (3 vols; Nashville: Abingdon, 1994).

McCormack, Bruce L., 'The Being of Holy Scripture Is in Becoming: Karl Barth in Conversation with American Evangelical Criticism' in Bacote, Vincent, Laura C. Miguélez and Dennis L. Okholm (eds), *Evangelicals and Scripture: Tradition, Authority and Hermeneutics* (Downers Grove: InterVarsity Press, 2004), pp. 55–75.

—'The Ontological Presuppositions of Barth's Doctrine of Atonement' in Hill, Charles E. and Frank A. James III (eds), *The Glory of the Atonement: Biblical, Historical and Practical Perspectives* (Downers Grove: InterVarsity Press, 2004), pp. 346–66.

—'For Us and Our Salvation: Incarnation and Atonement in the Reformed Tradition', *The Greek Orthodox Theological Review* 23 (1998), pp. 281–316.

McCurdy, Leslie, *Attributes and Atonement: The Holy Love of God in the Theology of P.T. Forsyth* (Paternoster Biblical and Theological Monographs; Carlisle: Paternoster, 1999).

McGlasson, Paul C., *Invitation to Dogmatic Theology: A Canonical Approach* (Grand Rapids: Brazos, 2006).

McIntosh, Mark A., *Christology from Within: Spirituality and the Incarnation in Hans Urs von Balthasar* (Studies in Spirituality and Theology, 3; Notre Dame: University of Notre Dame Press, 1996).

MacIntyre, Alasdair, *After Virtue: A Study in Moral Theory* (London: Duckworth, 3rd edn, 2007).

—'Catholic Universities: Dangers, Hopes, Choices' in Sullivan, Robert E. (ed.), *Higher Learning and Catholic Traditions* (Notre Dame: University of Notre Dame Press, 2001), pp. 1–21.

—'Social Structures and their Threats to Moral Agency', *Philosophy* 74 (1999), pp. 311–29.

—*How to Seem Virtuous Without Actually Being So* (Lancaster: Centre for the Study of Cultural Values, 1991).

—'The Idea of an Educated Public' in Haydon, Graham (ed.), *Education and Values: The Richard Peters Lectures* (London: Institute of Education, 1987), pp. 15–36.

—'Does Applied Ethics Rest on a Mistake?', *The Monist* 67 (1984), pp. 498–513.

MacKinnnon, Donald M., *Borderlands of Theology and Other Essays* (George W. Roberts and Donovan E. Smucker (eds); London: Lutterworth, 1968).

Macquarrie, John, *Christology Revisited* (London: SCM, 1998).

Martin, Dale, *Pedagogy of the Bible: An Analysis and Proposal* (Louisville: Westminster John Knox, 2008).

Mathewes, Charles T., *A Theology of Public Life* (Cambridge Studies in Christian Doctrine, 17; Cambridge: Cambridge University Press, 2007).

—'Faith, Hope, and Agony: Christian Political Participation Beyond Liberalism', *Annual of the Society of Christian Ethics* 21 (2001), pp. 125–50.

Moberly, R. W. L., *The Bible, Theology, and Faith: A Study of Abraham and Jesus* (Cambridge Studies in Christian Doctrine, 5; Cambridge: Cambridge University Press, 2000).

Morris, Leon, 'The Jesus of Saint John' in Guelich, Robert A. (ed.), *Unity and Diversity in New Testament Theology* (Grand Rapids: Eerdmans, 1978), pp. 37–53.

Muers, Rachel, 'Silence and the Patience of God', *Modern Theology* 17 (2001), pp. 85–98.

Newbigin, Lesslie, *The Household of God: Lectures on the Nature of the Church* (London: SCM, 1953).

O'Brien, George Dennis, *The Idea of a Catholic University* (Chicago: University of Chicago Press, 2002).

O'Donovan, Oliver, *Church in Crisis: The Gay Controversy and the Anglican Communion* (Eugene: Cascade, 2008).

—*Liturgy and Ethics* (Grove Ethical Studies; Bramcote: Grove Books, 1993).

O'Keefe, John J. and R. R. Reno, *Sanctified Vision: An Introduction to Early Christian Interpretation of the Bible* (Baltimore/London: The Johns Hopkins University Press, 2005).

Paddison, Angus, 'Following Jesus with Pope Benedict' in Pabst, Adrian and Angus Paddison (eds), *The Pope and Jesus of Nazareth* (Veritas; London: SCM, forthcoming).

Pasquarello III, Michael, *Christian Preaching: A Trinitarian Theology of Proclamation* (Grand Rapids: Baker Academic, 2006).

Pelikan, Jaroslav, '"Council or Father or Scripture": The Concept of Authority in the Theology of Maximus the Confessor' in Neiman, David and Margaret Schatkin (eds), *The Heritage of the Early Church* (Orientalia Christiana Analecta, 195; Rome: Pont. Institutum Studiorum Orientalum, 1973), pp. 277–88.

Quash, Ben, 'The *Trisagion* and the Liturgical Untilling of Time' in Rashkover, Randi and C. C. Pecknold (eds), *Liturgy, Time, and the Politics of Redemption* (Radical Traditions; Grand Rapids: Eerdmans, 2006), pp. 141–63.

—'Making the Most of the Time: Liturgy, Ethics and Time', *SCE* 15 (2002), pp. 97–114.

Radner, Ephraim, *Leviticus* (SCM Theological Commentary on the Bible; London: SCM, 2008).

—*Hope Among the Fragments: The Broken Church and its Engagement of Scripture* (Grand Rapids: Brazos, 2004).

Rahner, Karl, 'The Word and the Eucharist' in *Theological Investigations*, Vol. IV (trans. Kevin Smyth; 23 vols; London: Darton, Longman and Todd, 1974), pp. 253–86.

—'A Fragmentary Aspect of a Theological Evaluation of the Concept of the Future' in *Theological Investigations*, Vol. X (trans. David Bourke; 23 vols; London: Darton, Longman and Todd, 1973), pp. 235–41.

du Rand, J. A., 'The Characterization of Jesus as Depicted in the Narrative of the Fourth Gospel', *Neotestamentica* 19 (1985), pp. 18–36.

Rasmusson, Arne, 'Historicizing the Historicist: Ernst Troeltsch and Recent Mennonite Theology' in Hauerwas, Stanley, Chris K. Huebner, Harry J. Huebner and Mark Thiessen Nation (eds), *The Wisdom of the Cross: Essays in Honour of John Howard Yoder* (Grand Rapids: Eerdmans, 1999), pp. 213–48.

—*The Church as Polis: From Political Theology to Theological Politics as Exemplified by Jürgen Moltmann and Stanley Hauerwas* (Notre Dame: University of Notre Dame Press, 1995).

Ratzinger, Joseph, *Jesus of Nazareth: From the Baptism in the Jordan to the Transfiguration* (trans. Adrian J. Walker, London: Bloomsbury, 2007).

—'Biblical Interpretation in Crisis: On the Question of the Foundations and Approaches of Exegesis Today' in Neuhaus, Richard John (ed.), *Biblical Interpretation in Crisis: The Ratzinger Conference on Bible and Church* (Grand Rapids: Eerdmans, 1989), pp. 1–23.

Reimer, A. James, 'Theological Orthodoxy and Jewish Christianity: A Personal Tribute to John Howard Yoder' in Hauerwas, Stanley, Chris K. Huebner, Harry J. Huebner and Mark Thiessen Nation (eds), *The Wisdom of the Cross: Essays in Honour of John Howard Yoder* (Grand Rapids: Eerdmans, 1999), pp. 430–49.

Reno, R. R., 'Theology and Biblical Interpretation' in Root, Michael and James J. Buckley (eds), *Sharper Than a Two-Edged Sword: Preaching, Teaching and Living the Bible* (Grand Rapids: Eerdmans, 2008), pp. 1–21.

—'Biblical Theology and Theological Exegesis' in Craig G. Bartholomew, Mary Healy, Karl Möller and Robin Parry (eds), *Out of Egypt: Biblical Theology and Biblical Interpretation* (Scripture and Hermeneutics Series, 5; Bletchley: Paternoster, 2004), pp. 385–408.

Resner, André, *Preacher and Cross: Person and Message in Theology and Rhetoric* (Grand Rapids: Eerdmans, 1999).

Riches, Aaron, 'After Chalcedon: The Oneness of Christ and the Dyothelite Mediation of his Theandric Unity', *Modern Theology* 24 (2008), pp. 199–224.

Ricoeur, Paul, *Interpretation Theory: Discourse and the Surplus of Meaning* (Fort Worth: Texas Christian University Press, 1976).

Ritschl, Dietrich, *A Theology of Proclamation* (Richmond: John Knox, 1963).

Roberts, Richard, 'Karl Barth's Doctrine of Time: Its Nature and Implications' in *A Theology on its Way: Essays on Karl Barth* (Edinburgh: T&T Clark, 1991), pp. 1–58.

Robinson, John A. T., *The Priority of John* (J. F. Coakley (ed.); London: SCM, 1985).

Rodgers, John H., *The Theology of P.T. Forsyth: The Cross of Christ and the Revelation of God* (London: Independent Press, 1965).

Rogerson, J. W., *According to the Scriptures? The Challenge of Using the Bible in Social, Moral, and Political Questions* (London: Equinox, 2007).

Sauter, Gerhard, *Gateways to Dogmatics: Reasoning Theologically for the Life of the Church* (Grand Rapids: Eerdmans, 2003).

Saward, John, *The Mysteries of March: Hans Urs von Balthasar on the Incarnation and Easter* (Washington: Catholic University of America Press, 1990).

Schmemann, Alexander, *The Eucharist: Sacrament of the Kingdom* (trans. Paul Kachur; Crestwood: St Vladimir's Seminary Press, 2003).

Schwöbel, Christoph, 'The Preacher's Art: Preaching Theologically' in Colin Gunton, *Theology Through Preaching: Sermons for Brentwood* (Edinburgh: T&T Clark, 2001), pp. 1–20.

Sherman, Robert, *King, Priest and Prophet: A Trinitarian Theology of Atonement* (Theology for the Twenty-First Century; New York: T&T Clark International, 2004).

Shuman, Joel James, *The Body of Compassion: Ethics, Medicine and the Church* (Radical Traditions; Boulder: Westview Press, 1999).

Song, C. S., *Jesus, the Crucified People* (Minneapolis: Fortress, 1990).

Spinks, D. Christopher, *The Bible and the Crisis of Meaning: Debates on the Theological Interpretation of Scripture* (T&T Clark Theology; London: T&T Clark, 2007).

Spohn, William C., 'Scripture' in Meilaender, Gilbert and William Werpehowski (eds), *The Oxford Handbook of Theological Ethics* (Oxford: Oxford University Press, 2005), pp. 93–111.

Stendahl, Krister, 'Biblical Theology, Contemporary' in Buttrick, G. A. and others (eds), *The Interpreter's Dictionary of the Bible* (New York: Abingdon, 1962), pp. 418–32.

Stibbe, Mark W. G., 'The Elusive Christ: A New Reading of the Fourth Gospel', *JSNT* 44 (1991), pp. 19–37.

Stout, Jeffrey, 'What is the Meaning of a Text?', *New Literary History* 14 (1982), pp. 1–12.

Stroup, George W., *Jesus Christ for Today* (Philadelphia: Westminster, 1982).

Tanner, Kathryn, *Jesus, Humanity and the Trinity: A Brief Systematic Theology* (Current Issues in Theology; Edinburgh: T&T Clark, 2001).

Taylor, Charles, *A Secular Age* (Cambridge, MA: Belknap Press of Harvard University Press, 2007).

—*Philosophical Arguments* (Cambridge, MA: Harvard University Press, 1995).

—*Multiculturalism: Examining the Politics of Recognition* (Amy Gutmann (ed.); Princeton: Princeton University Press, 1994).

—'What's Wrong with Negative Liberty?' in *Philosophy and the Human Sciences – Philosophical Papers 2* (Cambridge: Cambridge University Press, 1985), pp. 211–29.

Tertullian, 'Of Patience', in *Ante-Nicene Fathers*, Vol. III (Alexander Roberts and James Donaldson (eds); trans. S. Thelwall; 10 vols; Peabody: Hendrickson, 1995), pp. 707–17.

Thompson, Marianne M., *The God of the Gospel of John* (Grand Rapids: Eerdmans, 2001).

—*The Humanity of Jesus* (Philadelphia: Fortress, 1988).

Thomson, John B., *The Ecclesiology of Stanley Hauerwas: A Christian Theology of Liberation* (Ashgate New Critical Thinking in Religion, Theology, and Biblical Studies; Aldershot: Ashgate, 2003).

Titus, Eric Lane, 'The Fourth Gospel and the Historical Jesus' in Trotter, F. F. (ed.), *Jesus and the Historian: Written in Honor of Ernest Cadman Colwell* (Philadelphia: Westminster, 1968), pp. 98–113.

Topping, Richard R., *Revelation, Scripture and Church:Theological Hermeneutic Thought of James Barr, Paul Ricoeur and Hans Frei* (Ashgate New Critical Thinking in Religion, Theology and Biblical Studies; Aldershot: Ashgate, 2007).

Torrance, James B., *Worship, Community and the Triune God of Grace* (Didsbury Lectures; Downers Grove: InterVarsity Press, 1996).

—'The Priesthood of Jesus' in Parker, T. H. L. (ed.), *Essays in Christology for Karl Barth* (London: Lutterworth, 1956), pp. 155–73.

Torrance, Thomas F., *Reality and Evangelical Theology: The Realism of Christian Revelation* (Downers Grove: InterVarsity Press, 1999).

—*Space, Time and Resurrection* (Edinburgh: T&T Clark, 1998).

—'Introduction: Biblical Hermeneutics and General Hermeneutics' in *Divine Meaning: Studies in Patristic Hermeneutics* (Edinburgh: T&T Clark, 1995), pp. 5–13.

—*Preaching Christ Today: The Gospel and Scientific Thinking* (Grand Rapids: Eerdmans, 1994).

—*Royal Priesthood: A Theology of Ordained Ministry* (Edinburgh: T&T Clark, 2nd edn, 1993).

—*The Trinitarian Faith: The Evangelical Theology of the Ancient Catholic Church* (Edinburgh: T&T Clark, 1988).

—*The Mediation of Christ* (Didsbury Lectures; Exeter: Paternoster, 1983).

—*God and Rationality* (London: Oxford University Press, 1971).

—*Theology in Reconstruction* (London: SCM, 1965).

—'The Atonement and the Oneness of the Church', *SJT* 7 (1954), pp. 245–69.

Treier, Daniel J., *Virtue and the Voice of God: Toward Theology as Wisdom* (Grand Rapids: Eerdmans, 2006).

Vanhoozer, Kevin J., 'Discourse on Matter: Hermeneutics and the "Miracle" of Understanding', *IJST* 7 (2005), pp. 5–37.

Vanstone, W. H., *The Stature of Waiting* (London: Darton, Longman, and Todd, 1982).

Wannenwetsch, Bernd, 'The Ethics of Doing Theology' in Hemming, Laurence Paul and Susan Frank Parsons (eds), *Redeeming Truth: Considering Faith and Reason* (Faith in Reason; London: SCM, 2007), pp. 167–83.

Ward, Graham, 'A Christian Act: Politics and Liturgical Practice' in Rashkover, Randi and C. C. Pecknold (eds), *Liturgy, Time, and the Politics of Redemption* (Radical Traditions; Grand Rapids: Eerdmans, 2006), pp. 29–49.

Watson, Francis, 'The Scope of Hermeneutics' in Gunton, Colin E. (ed.), *The Cambridge Companion to Christian Doctrine* (Cambridge: Cambridge University Press, 1997), pp. 65–80.

—*Text, Church and World: Biblical Interpretation in Theological Perspective* (Edinburgh: T&T Clark, 1994).

Weaver, Alain Epp, 'Missionary Christology: John Howard Yoder and the Creeds', *The Mennonite Quarterly Review* 74 (2000), pp. 423–39.

Webb, Stephen H., *The Divine Voice: Christian Proclamation and the Theology of Sound* (Grand Rapids: Brazos, 2004).

Webster, John, 'Jesus Christ' in Larsen, Timothy and Daniel J. Treier (eds), *The Cambridge Companion to Evangelical Theology* (Cambridge: Cambridge University Press, 2007), pp. 51–63.

—'Resurrection and Scripture' in Lincoln, Andrew T. and Angus Paddison (eds), *Christology and Scripture: Interdisciplinary Perspectives* (LNTS, 348; London: T&T Clark International, 2007), pp. 138–55.

—*Confessing God: Essays in Christian Dogmatics* II (London: T&T Clark International, 2005).

—'On Evangelical Ecclesiology', *Ecclesiology* 1 (2004), pp. 9–35.

—'Evangelical Freedom' in Sider Hamilton, Catherine (ed.), *The Homosexuality Debate: Faith Seeking Understanding* (Toronto: Anglican Book Centre, 2003), pp. 109–23.

—'"A Great and Meritorious Act of the Church"? The Dogmatic Location of the Canon' in Barton, John and Michael Wolter (eds), *Die Einheit der Schrift und die Viefalt des Kanons/The Unity of Scripture and the Diversity of the Canon* (Berlin: Walter de Gruyter, 2003), pp. 95–126.

—*Holiness* (London: SCM, 2003).

—*Holy Scripture: A Dogmatic Sketch* (Current Issues in Theology; Cambridge: Cambridge University Press, 2003).

—*Word and Church: Essays in Christian Dogmatics* (Edinburgh: T&T Clark, 2001).

—'Conversations: Engaging Difference', *Stimulus* 7 (1999), pp. 2–8.

—'Texts: Scripture, reading, and the rhetoric of theology', *Stimulus* 6 (1998), pp. 10–16.

—*Theological Theology* (Oxford: Clarendon Press, 1998).

—'"Assured and Patient and Cheerful Expectation": Barth on Christian Hope as the Church's Task', *Toronto Journal of Theology* 10 (1994), pp. 35–52.

Wells, Samuel, *God's Companions: Reimagining Christian Ethics* (Challenges in Contemporary Theology; Oxford: Blackwell, 2006).

—*Improvisation: The Drama of Christian Ethics* (London: SPCK, 2004).

—*Transforming Fate into Destiny: The Theological Ethics of Stanley Hauerwas* (Eugene: Cascade, 2004).

—'How Common Worship Forms Local Character', *SCE* 15 (2002), pp. 66–74.

Willard, Dallas, 'The Bible, the University and the God Who Hides' in Jeffrey, David Lyle and C. Stephen Evans (eds), *The Bible and the University* (Scripture and Hermeneutics Series, 8; Milton Keynes: Paternoster, 2007), pp. 17–39.

Williams, Rowan, 'Making Moral Decisions' in Gill, Robin (ed.), *The Cambridge Companion to Christian Ethics* (Cambridge: Cambridge University Press, 2001), pp. 3–15.

—'The Unity of the Church and the Unity of the Bible: An Analogy', *Internationale Kirkliche Zeitschrift* 91 (2001), pp. 5–21.

—*On Christian Theology* (Challenges in Contemporary Theology; Oxford: Blackwell, 2000).

—*Open to Judgement: Sermons and Addresses* (London: Darton, Longman and Todd, 1994).

Willimon, William H., *Conversations with Barth on Preaching* (Nashville: Abingdon, 2006).

Wilson, Jonathan R., *God So Loved the World: A Christology for Disciples* (Grand Rapids: Baker Academic, 2001).

Witten, Marsha G., *All is Forgiven: The Secular Message in American Protestantism* (Princeton: Princeton University Press, 1993).

Wolterstorff, Nicholas, 'Why We Should Reject What Liberalism Tells Us' in Weithman, Paul J. (ed.), *Religion and Contemporary Liberalism* (Notre Dame: University of Notre Dame Press, 1997), pp. 162–81.

—'The Travail of Theology in the Modern Academy' in Volf, Miroslav, Carmen Krieg and Thomas Kucharz (eds), *The Future of Theology: Essays in Honour of Jürgen Moltmann* (Grand Rapids: Eerdmans, 1996), pp. 35–46.

Wood, Donald, *Barth's Theology of Interpretation* (Barth Series; Aldershot: Ashgate, 2007).

—'The Place of Theology in Theological Hermeneutics', *IJST* 4 (2002), pp. 156–71.

Work, Telford, *Living and Active: Scripture in the Economy of Salvation* (Sacra Doctrina; Grand Rapids: Eerdmans, 2002).

Wright, John W., *Telling God's Story: Narrative Preaching for Christian Formation* (Downers Grove: IVP Academic, 2007).

Yeago, David S., 'The Bible' in Buckley, James J. and David S. Yeago (eds), *Knowing the Triune God: The Work of the Spirit in the Practices of the Church* (Grand Rapids: Eerdmans, 2001), pp. 49–93.

—'Crucified Also for Us under Pontius Pilate: Six Propositions on the Preaching of the Cross' in Seitz, Christopher R. (ed.), *Nicene Christianity: The Future for a New Ecumenism* (Grand Rapids: Brazos, 2001), pp. 87–105.

—'The New Testament and the Nicene Dogma: A Contribution to the Recovery of Theological Exegesis', *Pro Ecclesia* 3 (1994), pp. 152–64.

Yoder, John Howard, *Discipleship as Political Responsibility* (trans. Timothy J. Geddert; Scottdale: Herald, 2003).

—'Jesus – A Model of Radical Political Action' in Neville, David and Philip Matthews (eds), *Faith and Freedom: Christian Ethics in a Pluralist Culture* (Hindmarsh: Australian Theological Forum, 2003), pp. 163–69.

—*The Jewish-Christian Schism Revisited* (Radical Traditions; Michael G. Cartwright and Peter Ochs (eds); London: SCM, 2003).

—*Karl Barth and the Problem of War and Other Essays on Barth* (Mark Thiessen Nation (ed.); Eugene: Cascade, 2003).

—*The Original Revolution: Essays on Christian Pacifism* (Scottdale: Herald, 2003).

—*Body Politics: Five Practices of the Christian Community Before the Watching World* (Scottdale: Herald, 2002).

—*Preface to Theology: Christology and Theological Method* (Grand Rapids: Brazos, 2002).

—*To Hear the Word* (Eugene: Wipf and Stock, 2001).

—*The Priestly Kingdom: Social Ethics as Gospel* (Notre Dame: University of Notre Dame Press, 2001).

—'On Christian Unity: The Way from Below', *Pro Ecclesia* 9 (2000), pp. 165–83.

—*The Royal Priesthood: Essays Ecclesiastical and Ecumenical* (Michael G. Cartwright (ed.); Scottdale: Herald, 1998).

—*For the Nations: Essays Public and Evangelical* (Grand Rapids: Eerdmans, 1997).

—'How H. Richard Niebuhr Reasoned: A Critique of *Christ and Culture*' in *Authentic Transformation: A New Vision of Christ and Culture*, with Glen H. Staasen and D. M. Yeager (Nashville: Abingdon, 1996), pp. 31–89.

—'War as a Moral Problem in the Early Church: The Historian's Hermeneutical Assumptions' in Dyck, Harvey L. (ed.), *The Pacifist Impulse in Historical Perspective* (Toronto: University of Toronto Press, 1996), pp. 90–110.

—'Walk and Word: The Alternatives to Methodologism' in Hauerwas, Stanley, Nancey Murphy and Mark Nation (eds), *Theology Without Foundations: Religious Practice and the Future of Theological Truth* (Nashville: Abingdon, 1994), pp. 77–90.

—'On Not Being Ashamed of the Gospel: Particularity, Pluralism, and Validation', *Faith and Philosophy* 9 (1992), pp. 285–300.

—'Against the Death Penalty' in H. Wayne House and John Howard Yoder, *The Death Penalty Debate: Two Opposing Views of Capital Punishment* (Dallas: Word, 1991), pp. 105–79.

—'Ethics and Eschatology', *Ex Auditu* 6 (1990), pp. 119–28.

—'The Anabaptist Shape of Liberation' in Loewen, Harry (ed.), *Why I am a Mennonite: Essays in Mennonite Identity* (Kitchener: Herald, 1988), pp. 338–48.

—'Armaments and Eschatology', *SCE* 1 (1988), pp. 43–61.

—'*The Challenge of Peace*: A Historic Peace Perspective' in Reid Jr., Charles J. (ed.), *Peace in a Nuclear Age: The Bishops' Pastoral Letter in Perspective* (Washington: Catholic University of America Press, 1986), pp. 273–90.

—*He Came Preaching Peace* (Scottdale: Herald, 1985).

—'The Prophetic Task of Pastoral Ministry: The Gospels' in Shelp, Earl E. and Ronald H. Sutherland (eds), *The Pastor as Prophet* (New York: Pilgrim, 1985), pp. 78–98.

—'Exodus and Exile: The Two Faces of Liberation' in Curran, Charles E. and Richard A. McCormick (eds), *Readings in Moral Theology No. 4: The Use of the Bible in Moral Theology* (New York: Paulist, 1984), pp. 337–53.

—*Christian Attitudes to War, Peace, and Revolution: A Companion to Bainton* (Elkhart: Co-Op Bookstore, 1983).

—*The Politics of Jesus: Vicit Agnus Noster* (Grand Rapids: Eerdmans, 1972).

—'The Way of the Peacemaker' in Lapp, John A., (ed.), *Peacemakers in a Broken World* (Scottdale: Herald, 1969), pp. 111–25.

—'The Hermeneutics of the Anabaptists', *The Mennonite Quarterly Review* 41 (1967), pp. 291–308.

# Biblical Index

# Subject Index

# AUTHOR INDEX